DJIBOUTI AND THE HORN
OF AFRICA

DJIBOUTI AND THE HORN
OF AFRICA

Virginia Thompson and Richard Adloff

1968
STANFORD UNIVERSITY PRESS
STANFORD, CALIFORNIA

Other Books by Virginia Thompson and Richard Adloff

The Left Wing in Southeast Asia
Minority Problems in Southeast Asia
French West Africa
The Emerging States of French Equatorial Africa
The Malagasy Republic: Madagascar Today

Photographs 1–8, 10–12, 14–28, 31–35 courtesy of
the Service de l'Information du Territoire Français
des Afars et des Issas. Nos. 13, 29, 30 courtesy
of the Service Intercolonial d'Information et de
Documentation, Paris. No. 9, R. Michaud from
Rapho Guillumette.

Stanford University Press
Stanford, California
© 1968 by Virginia Thompson Adloff and Richard Adloff
Printed in the United States of America
L.C. 68-21289

To Georgiana Stevens

CONTENTS

Introduction   ix

Part I. People and Politics

1   The Historical Background   3

The Coming of the Europeans, 5. The Colony of French Somaliland, 7. The Italians and French Somaliland, 11. World
War II, 15.

2   Nomads and Sedentaries   23

The Nomads, 23. The Sedentaries, 29.

3   The Government Structure   38

Territorial Government, 38. The *Cercles*, 45. The Civil Service, 48. Justice and the Law Courts, 51. Armed Forces, 54.

4   The Political Scene   61

5   External Relations   102

Ethiopia, 104. Somalia, 118. The Arab Countries: Aden and
South Arabia, 130. Egypt, 132.

Part II. The Social and Economic Fields

6   Social Development   139

Religion, 139. Education, 141. Cultural Activities and Communications Media, 156. Health and Social Welfare, 158.

7   The Traditional Economy   166

Water Resources, 166. Agriculture and Forestry, 168. Animal Husbandry, 172. Fishing, 175. Salt and Other Minerals, 176.

8   The Modern Economy   179

Electrical Power, 179. Industries, 180. Finances and Planning, 180. Trade, 190. Transportation, 199. Labor, 212.

Notes   227

Bibliography   235

Index   243

INTRODUCTION

Considering the small dimensions and sparse population of French Somaliland—now officially the Territoire Français des Afars et des Issas—and its
lack of economic resources, a detailed study of that Territory* may seem of
slight scholarly value. Furthermore, the whole Red Sea basin is politically
in such a state of flux that no reliable conclusions can be drawn about the
future of this smallest political entity of the region. In the opinion of all
those directly or indirectly concerned with the evolution of French Somaliland, its present status is a transitional one, the duration of which depends
on many unknown factors. The only certainty that emerges from this
kaleidoscope is that the future of the Territoire Français des Afars et des
Issas will be determined not by the wishes of its inhabitants—although lip
service will undoubtedly be paid to their wishes—but by forces external to it.
So long as France retains control of the country, the relative strength of
those forces probably will not be put to the test of armed conflict. Yet because the eventual elimination of French sovereignty appears to be inevitable, and because Djibouti's strategic situation may conceivably again
give it an international prominence unwarranted by its minuscule proportions, an analysis of developments and forces inside and outside the
Territory against their historical background may be useful in understanding the issues involved. This book will, it is hoped, serve as such a guide for
readers whose knowledge of the Territory has been confined to existing
English-language sources, which are not extensive.

The history of French Somaliland shows that the interest evoked, both
regionally and internationally, by this arid, torrid, underpopulated, and
impoverished Territory has been due basically to its geographical position.
This has remained the Territory's constant asset despite drastic political,
economic, and technological fluctuations in its importance. Specifically, its
role has reflected the development of new means of communication, the con-

* In this book, the word Territory, capitalized, refers to the area formerly called the Côte
Française des Somalis and now called the Territoire Français des Afars et des Issas.

quest and loss of colonial empires in the east and to the south, the discovery and the transportation of oil from the Middle East to Western Europe, and the rise of nationalism, which has led to the formation of unstable, nominally sovereign states throughout the area.

In the Red Sea basin the pendulum has swung back and forth between economic and political interests, although both have always been present in motivating the policies of the regional and imperialist powers involved there. During the years since World War II, regional political forces have gradually gained an ascendancy over international economic interests. For the past century, the international economic stakes in the Horn of Africa not only have changed markedly but, since 1960, have been progressively submerged by regional ideological concepts. In that year, two of the three long-dominant Western powers withdrew from the Horn of Africa, and their place was taken by the economically nonviable Somali Republic, bent on acquiring adjacent territory and related populations at the expense of its neighbors. This turn of events has impelled Egypt, formerly a suzerain in parts of the Horn, as well as the two world superpowers, which are newcomers to the scene, to exert their respective influences there. Although those three nations have thus far remained largely in the wings, their presence indicates the extent to which the cast of characters, as well as the stakes involved, have been modified by recent events in the area.

In ancient times, the attraction of the Somali coast for the south Arabian traders and invaders was almost wholly that of a convenient access route to the Abyssinian highlands, and they did not settle there in large numbers until three Western European nations established colonies in the Horn of Africa during the nineteenth century. Italy was the only one of the three primarily interested in the region itself, and one main consequence of this focus was its conflict with Ethiopia. France and England, on the other hand, initially wanted merely to maintain fueling ports along the coasts, but the opening of the Suez Canal led to the expansion of those ports as trading centers. Inevitably this evolution sharpened the rivalry in the area between the colonial powers, but eventually they settled their respective territorial claims by negotiation. France and England, unlike Italy, did not have recourse to armed force in making the treaties with native chiefs which gave them legal title to their territorial acquisitions in the Horn.

World War II reduced the Italian role in the region to that of temporary administrator of its former colony of Somalia as a trust territory. During the postwar years, because of the progressive shrinkage of the French and British colonial empires and the development of air transportation, the interest taken by the Paris and London governments in their Red Sea dependencies as maritime relay points grew less. This decline was more than offset, however, by a concurrent growth in the area's trade and, above all, by the increasing use of the Suez Canal by ships carrying Middle Eastern petroleum to Western Europe.

In the second postwar decade, the rise of nationalism in South Arabia and in the Horn of Africa itself, as well as the aggravation of Britain's economic stringency, led to the abandonment by London of its territorial possessions in the Red Sea basin between 1960 and 1967. The two prolonged closings of the Suez Canal, in 1956 and 1967, have lessened the importance of that waterway, perhaps permanently. At the same time, the growing activity in the Red Sea basin of the newly independent states of the region has taken on more of a political than an economic coloring. Moreover, this reorientation has contributed to the area's economic decline by transforming what had been politically a relatively quiescent region into an unstable one whose future status is clouded by uncertainty.

Pan-Somalism and Pan-Arabism are ideological concepts, and their partisans in Mogadiscio and Cairo have had little economic motivation for their thrust in the Horn of Africa. Indeed, the upsurge of Somali nationalism and irredentism, if successful, is likely to saddle the government of Mogadiscio with even more difficult economic and political problems than those it now confronts. The economic advantages arising from acquisition of the great port of Djibouti would be more than offset by the difficulties inherent in governing thousands of hostile Afar nomads and by Somalia's being forced, in all likelihood, into a probably disastrous war with Ethiopia. The only country in the region that has a direct and overriding economic stake in the future of the French Territory is Ethiopia, and this is reinforced by political and religious considerations. The government of Addis Ababa would use force not only to prevent the main outlet for its foreign trade from falling into the hands of Somalia but also to preclude realization of its centuries-old fear of being encircled by Muslim powers. Although in political terms neither Ethiopia nor Somalia could afford openly to acquiesce in France's continued sovereignty over its Territory, in reality both are relieved that, at least for the time being, French Somaliland has not become independent and consequently a bone of contention between them.

In view of Djibouti's uncertain economic and political future, the question naturally arises as to why France, alone of the Western colonial powers, has chosen to maintain its foothold on the Somali coast. Certainly a feeling of obligation to the generally loyal Afars has contributed to this attitude, as has the desire to safeguard French vested interests in the Territory's trade and railroad. Then, too, the Territory remains useful in providing posts

for French civil servants and military men no longer employable in Indochina, Madagascar, and West and Equatorial Africa. Furthermore, Djibouti is the only established and convenient relay point still under French
control on the route to France's nuclear-testing area in the South Pacific.
On the debit side of the ledger, the cost of providing subsidies and improvements to the port of Djibouti is heavy for the French taxpayer, who has
never shown any interest in the Territory except at those periods when its
possession has been contested by Italy, England, Ethiopia, and Somalia. In
other than financial ways, too, retention of the Territory is a liability to
France. Opposition to continued French sovereignty exists there on the
part of the most dynamic element of Djibouti's population, as was made
clear at the time of General de Gaulle's visit in August 1966. The outcome
of the referendum of March 1967, which had been designed to prove that
France respected the wishes of the local people in regard to their future,
has not been clear-cut, and the general's image as "the liberator of Africa"
has therefore been somewhat tarnished in the eyes of the Third World.

Inasmuch as French Somaliland is the last of France's dependencies on
the mainland of Africa and has always been the least important of its
African possessions, why should the government of Paris cling to it when
the richer territories of the Dark Continent were granted their independence for the asking? There is apparently no wholly satisfactory answer
to this question. France's continued presence in the Horn of Africa certainly prevented the outbreak of armed conflict between Somalia and Ethiopia, which might conceivably have burgeoned into a war involving the
world superpowers. Not even the most ardent supporters of French policy,
however, seriously consider that it was so disinterestedly motivated. In any
case, the outcome of the referendum has provided a breathing spell during
which the Territory's ultimate independence can be negotiated under
peaceful conditions. In the meantime the Port of Djibouti is being improved
against the day when reopening of the Suez Canal may revive the region's
trade, in which case the Territory's merchants may well benefit from continuing disorders in the rival port of Aden. In addition, Djibouti offers the
advantage of being a well-located center from which General de Gaulle
can further his growing interest in influencing developments in the Middle
East and in disseminating French cultural propaganda throughout the
Horn.

In the preparation of this study, the authors are indebted to many cooperative individuals and institutions. Professor H. Deschamps of the
University of Paris, who was Governor of French Somaliland from 1938
to 1940, generously shared with the writers his reminiscences of the early

World War II period in Djibouti, and they benefited by his criticism of the political chapters. In the United States, invaluable assistance was rendered the authors by the Hoover Institution, where Dr. Peter Duignan and his able assistant, Mrs. Eve Hoffman, spared no effort to obtain relevant documents for their use. In Paris, Monsieur R. Cornevin, director of the Documentation Française center, and MM. J. C. Froelich and G. Malecot of the Centre des Hautes Etudes de l'Afrique et de l'Asie Modernes generously placed the rich resources of their libraries at the authors' disposal. The authors are grateful to the official information services of the French Ministry of Overseas Departments and Territories and of the Djibouti administration, and in particular to Monsieur G. Maurel in Paris and Madame M. Cartier in Djibouti, for providing helpful data and photographs.

January 1968

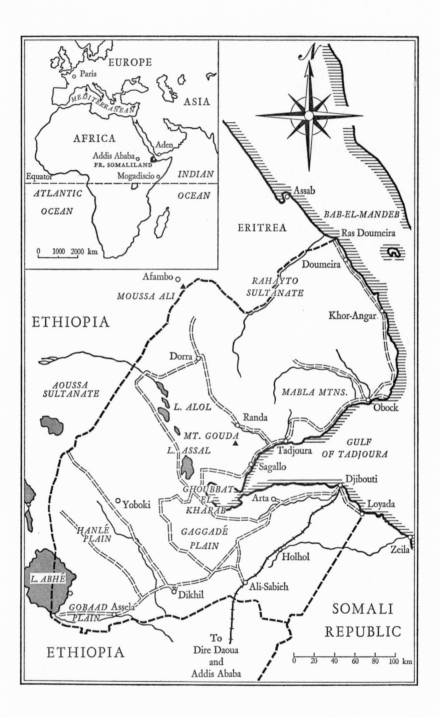

Part I

PEOPLE AND POLITICS

Chapter One

THE HISTORICAL BACKGROUND

The French Territory of the Afars and the Issas, formerly called French Somaliland, is a small country in the Horn of Africa facing the strait of Bab-el-Mandeb, one of the two southern gateways to the Red Sea. Inland, it has frontiers with Eritrea to the north, Somalia to the south, and Ethiopia to the west and south. Its coastline, some 800 kilometers in length, runs from Ras (Cape) Doumeira near the Eritrean frontier, to Loyada, on the northern boundary of what was formerly British Somaliland. This coast is deeply indented by the Gulf of Tadjoura, where there are two harbors, and the gulf is prolonged to the west by a bay, the Ghoubbat-el-Kharab. Most of the hinterland frontier parallels the coast at an average distance of 90 kilometers. The volcanic terrain consists largely of broken plateaus, bordered in many places by huge faults containing vast sunken plains, of which Hanlé is the most important, and lakes, those of Assal and Alol lying well below sea level. The territory has some subterranean rivers but no permanent surface watercourse. Cliffs line the sterile plain between the Ghoubbat-el-Kharab and Djibouti, and basaltic mountain ranges north of the Tadjoura Gulf reach heights of more than 1,500 meters. On the slopes of the two main peaks, Mabla and Gouda, grows the only continuous mass of vegetation to be found throughout French Somaliland, including the unique forest of Daÿ.

Westerners have called the Territory "a valley of hell" and "a country whose landscape is a nightmare." Yet French Somaliland is no more desolate than the other coastal desert regions of the Horn of Africa, and in some places its landscape has a tragic and grandiose quality. It is true that the climate of Djibouti is one of the most continuously hot and humid in the world, and that of the hinterland plains is even less bearable, though much dryer. In Djibouti the temperature averages 85° Fahrenheit and can rise to 107° between May and October, when a sand-laden wind, the *khamsin,* blows from the northwest. Rainfall is scarce and irregular, varying with the altitude. Along the coast, rain falls during about 26 days of the year,

averaging less than five inches annually. In the mountain areas it amounts
to over 20 inches, falling almost exclusively during severe storms. This phenomenon of sudden, excessive rainfall has periodically been disastrous for
that part of Djibouti at sea level.

Invaders and traders alike have used the strait of Bab-el-Mandeb as a
comparatively easy passage between Arabia and the African continent.[1]
Explorations by Aubert de la Rue in the 1930's disclosed evidence of pre-
historic habitation of the coastal region, possibly by the Gallas before they
migrated southward.* The earliest known kingdom was that of Adal,
whose capital was at Zeila. In the third century B.C., this kingdom was cut
in two by Ablé immigrants from Arabia. The northern half, situated between the Bab-el-Mandeb and the port of Thio, then took the name of Ankali or Ankala, while the southern portion retained the name of Adal.†
For several centuries both states paid tribute to the Ablés, during which
time the Ankali prefixed a D to their name. Today the terms Dankali (the
plural of which is Danakil) and Afar, by which they are also known, are
used interchangeably.

Eventually the hegemony of the Ablés was ended by the Abyssinians,
and it is believed that both Ankali and Adal became vassals of Abyssinia.
In A.D. 825, Islam was brought to the area by missionaries, and soon Islamic
states were formed which asserted their independence from Abyssinia. Of
these the most important was the coastal emirate of Adal. Gradually the
emirs of Adal annexed that portion of Ankali which lay along the northern
gulf of Tadjoura. The rest of the Ankali disintegrated into more or less
independent tribes, until, fearing conquest by the Adal, they grouped themselves into the three sultanates of Bidou, Bori, and Térou. Beginning about
A.D. 1200, these Muslim emirates engaged in a series of wars with Christian
Abyssinia, which continued until early in the seventeenth century, when
the Gallas threatened to invade the sultanate of Adal. The Adal gradually
withdrew and in about 1660 settled around Aoussa in Abyssinia, and the
tribes of the northern Tadjoura Gulf seized the chance to revolt and pro-
claim their independence from Adal. They formed sultanates, three of
which—Tadjoura, Rahayto, and Gobaad—have survived to this day.

The Somali Issas arrived much more recently than the Afars in the
southern part of the region. Local legend ascribes their origin to one Cheikh

* In contrast to the views held by other scholars, H. S. Lewis believes that both the Somalis
and the Gallas originated in southern Ethiopia, and that they lived there and in northern
Kenya not later than about 1530, when their migrations began.
† The name Adal first appeared in the thirteenth century; according to E. Chedeville, some
Afars claim an Arabic origin.

Issa, who came from Arabia among perhaps the first wave of Somali invaders of the Horn of Africa. Gradually they drove the Afars out of the southern coastal region. They also fought Abyssinia, not with a view to conquering it for Islam but with the practical aim of acquiring pastureland. By the nineteenth century, the trek areas of the Afars were being whittled away by the Issas, and the hostility between these two ethnic groups has become an increasingly important element in the history of French Somaliland.

The Coming of the Europeans

The Horn of Africa was well known to the seafarers and geographers of the ancient world. The Arabs controlled the trade of that region until the sixteenth century, when the Portuguese briefly competed with them for it. As the Portuguese began making conquests farther east, the Arabs resumed their domination of the Red Sea and the Gulf of Aden. Their two main trading posts along the Somali coast were at Zeila and Tadjoura, which were linked to the Abyssinian plateau by caravan routes. In Afar country, the *caravaniers* had to pay transit taxes to the local chiefs and sultans. On the inbound journey, the camel caravans carried mainly imported cloth and firearms and salt slabs from Lake Assal, and returning to the coast they brought coffee, wax, hides, perfumes, and, above all, slaves.

In the nineteenth century, the pattern of this trade was modified by the coming of the Western imperial powers to the region. England occupied Aden in 1839, and at about the same time France began to show an interest in the mainland coastal area facing it. English policy was dominated by the strategic necessity of assuring imperial communications to India and beyond. During this early period, French interest in the region was partly competitive but France was more concerned with exploration and trade with Abyssinia than was England.

In 1839 the first of two scientific expeditions led by Rochet d'Héricourt explored the semi-independent kingdom of Shoa, and the second (1842–43) culminated in the signing of a Franco-Shoan treaty. Sahlé Salassie, the king of Shoa, gave to the scholar-emissary of Louis-Philippe his friendship and also gifts for the French king. For many years, Rochet d'Héricourt's account of his trip provided the most authoritative information about the kingdom of Shoa. Yet interest in the region lapsed until another French traveler, Dr. Albert Roche, succeeded in 1857 in drawing Napoleon III's attention to a project for developing trade with Shoa. Two years later, Henri Lambert, the French consul at Aden, took the initiative of acquiring for his country the port of Obock on the Tadjoura Gulf. That same year Lambert was murdered in a sailing ship on his way to Tadjoura. France sent an expedition to investigate the circumstances of his death, but nothing further might have come of Lambert's efforts had it not been for French military operations in Cochinchina beginning in 1861. The French began to promote friendly relations with the local Afar chiefs, and in 1862 Dini Ahmed Aboubaker, a cousin of the Sultan of Tadjoura, came to Paris. There he signed a treaty confirming the cession of Obock and of the whole coast from Ras Bir to Ras Doumeira, for which France paid 10,000 thalers.* Furthermore, the Afar chiefs pledged themselves to report to France and to reject any overtures made to them for territorial cessions by other foreign powers. The treaty authorized the raising of the French flag at Obock, but no further steps were taken. A scantily clad Afar was employed to guard the flag, and until 1881 this was the only manifestation of France's presence on the coast, although the next year a French warship paused briefly at Obock. That France's claim was neither confirmed nor challenged seems surprising, for the opening of the Suez Canal in 1869 presaged greater trade with India and the Far East and ushered in an era of imperial expansion in the Red Sea area.

Once again it was an observant French traveler, Denis de Rivoyre, whose writings reawakened his compatriots' interest in the neglected port of Obock. In 1881, Rivoyre founded a trading company there, the Compagnie Franco-Ethiopienne, and in rapid succession three other French firms were formed—the Société Française d'Obock and the Factoreries Françaises in 1882 and the Compagnie Mesnier in 1883. The last-mentioned company installed a coaling station at Obock for French ships, but it was the Société d'Obock that sent out Paul Soleillet with a few settlers to start a French colony there. Among them was the engineer Chefneux, who was later to play a vital role in the construction of the railroad to Addis Ababa. Despite the friendly relations established by the representatives of these companies with the local Afar chiefs and their participation in the trade with Abyssinia, their enterprises were financial failures. It took a succession of international events to induce the French government to relay private initiative and to establish firmly France's foothold on the Somali coast.

In the early 1880's, because of French colonial wars in Tonkin and Madagascar, France increasingly needed a coaling station on the east African coast which would make its ships independent of the port of Aden. Another factor was Italy's expansion from its Eritrean base at Assab, founded in 1869.

---

* The thaler was a silver coin of Austrian origin, worth 71.4 U.S. cents, which was widely used in the Red Sea area.

At about the same time, Great Britain grew concerned about Germany's activities in East Africa and was also becoming more deeply involved in Egyptian affairs. Egypt, which had fallen heir to vague Turkish claims on the region, was forced, because of the Mahdist revolt in 1885, to withdraw its garrisons from the Somali coast and Harar. With the departure of the Egyptians, European imperialism became more active, and the three Western powers already involved in the Horn of Africa strove to fill the vacuum. The British occupied the ports of Zeila and Berbera, the French made treaties with the sultans of Tadjoura and Gobaad for cessions of their territory, and the Italians asserted their claim to the Assab area. In the region around Djibouti, French and British claims overlapped. However, a Franco-British treaty negotiated in 1888 delimited the frontier of their respective possessions to France's advantage and—even more significantly for the future—divided many of the Issas between French and English sovereignty.

France's new and successful aggressiveness was traceable to Léonce Lagarde, who had been named commandant of the territory of Obock in June 1884. Although only 24 years of age at the time, this remarkable administrator and diplomat had already gained experience in international affairs as an official in Paris and Rome. On his arrival at Obock, he found the French companies there on the verge of bankruptcy, a miserable colony of 30 Europeans, and a garrison composed of one sergeant and 26 foot soldiers. To restore the Afars' confidence in France and to extend French frontiers, he negotiated new treaties in 1884 with the sultans of Tadjoura and Gobaad, who thereby placed their emirates under the protection of France. He then proceeded to add to them the Ghoubbat-el-Kharab and the southern coast as far as Ambado. Hearing from his Afar protégés that the British intended to occupy Tadjoura, Lagarde raised the French flag there the night before an English ship arrived to take possession. Similar seriocomic episodes marked the competition between the local French and British authorities to acquire other points on the coast and in the hinterland east of Zeila. In 1885 Lagarde signed treaties with the Issa chiefs of the Ambado and Djibouti regions, in which vows of eternal friendship were exchanged and France promised to protect their peoples against all foreign intervention.

The Colony of French Somaliland

Lagarde's success in wresting from the French government enough funds to develop the settlement of Obock as a military, trading, and administrative center was one of his most remarkable achievements. In recognition of his services, he was named governor of the colony of Obock and dependencies in 1887. It was Obock's lot, however, never to flourish, for the Franco-British treaty negotiated in 1888 opened new and more attractive perspectives. Because Obock was cut off by mountains from the hinterland and was handicapped by an inadequate port, it was abandoned in 1892 in favor of Djibouti,* which had a protected roadstead and easier communications with Harar.

When the French took possession of Djibouti in 1888, it was a group of bare coral islands rising about 40 feet, joined together and with the mainland only at low tide by sandbars. Its "sole inhabitant was a jackal dying of hunger under a thorn tree."[2] By 1896, when Djibouti was made the capital of the newly constituted colony—which was misleadingly named the Côte Française des Somalis—it already had 5,000 inhabitants as compared with Obock's population of 2,000 only eight years before. Already some traders had settled there, a few stone houses had been built, a jetty constructed, streets laid out, and a road built to connect the three plateaus on which stood the village of Djibouti. Its superior location and facilities were increasingly drawing to it the inhabitants of nearby centers, such as Zeila and Tadjoura. By 1899 it had about 10,000 inhabitants, including some 200 Europeans, most of whom had gone there in connection with the project to build a railroad from Djibouti to Addis Ababa.

Lagarde not only was the creator of French Somaliland but was also largely responsible for its good relations with Ethiopia, which made possible the construction of the railroad and which have persisted to this day. As envoy of the French government, Lagarde twice visited the Emperor Menelik, founder of modern Ethiopia, whose friendship he won and who bestowed on him an honorific title. Of more lasting importance were the treaties signed by Menelik and Lagarde on March 20, 1897, in which the frontier between the two countries was defined and Djibouti was designated the official port for Ethiopia's foreign trade.

The peaceful methods by which France acquired its foothold on the Somali coast continued to characterize its relations with the local tribes, which were only occasionally marred by conflict. Such incidents included the imprisonment of the Bey of Djibouti upon the discovery of his alleged plot to remove that settlement from French control. At about the same time, a small French detachment disembarking at Khor Ambado was massacred by Issa tribes. More serious was the subsequent attack on a railroad camp, in which seven Europeans were killed by nomads who feared that con-

---

* Many explanations have been given for the name of Djibouti. According to Père Luc, it is derived from the Afar word *gabouti,* meaning a plate woven of doum-palm fibers and raised on a small pedestal.

struction of the tracks would deprive them of their pasturelands and watering points. The brutality of some of the railroad company's agents in their dealings with native laborers was responsible for other instances of violence in the south. Governor A. Martineau, who succeeded Lagarde in 1899, was able to restore peace by prolonged negotiations and by inducing the railroad company to pay the traditional blood-price of 250 thalers per victim. On the whole, the Issas—like the Afars—accepted European control and respected the treaties made by their chiefs and notables with France. Nevertheless, the nomads successfully frustrated the French administration's many attempts to disarm them and make them pay taxes.

In the years before World War I, the French paid little attention to the hinterland and concentrated most of their efforts on developing Djibouti. For its inhabitants a water-pumping station was built and market gardens developed in the adjacent Ambouli wadi, and a hospital was constructed in the town itself. There, too, the Messageries Maritimes company created an agency and a coaling station for its ships plying between France and and the Far East and the Indian Ocean. Trade between Djibouti and Ethiopia grew with the progress of the railroad, while camel caravans continued to carry merchandise between the port and Harar and Shoa.

Djibouti's astonishingly rapid growth was not due exclusively to the licit Ethiopian trade. Even before the capital was transferred to Djibouti, local merchants and the French administration at Obock had garnered sizable revenues from the traffic in arms and ammunition. The scope of this trade grew considerably at Djibouti, where a syndicate of five merchants, mostly Europeans, succeeded in creating a virtual monopoly. It was they who imported and paid a heavy duty on obsolete firearms, mainly from Belgium, and sold them profitably to Arab middlemen. The latter also made a handsome profit by re-exporting them. For many years such shipments as were sent to Muscat and Ethiopia were legitimate, but most of these arms were contraband and were sold clandestinely the length of the Arabian coast. A participant in the illicit arms traffic was Henri de Monfreid, the adventurer whose tales of pearlfishing and smuggling in the Red Sea area provided the French reading public with almost the only information available to them about their distant colony.[3] At that period, Tadjoura was the center of another lucrative illicit activity—the traffic in slaves taken from Ethiopia for sale in Arabian and Persian markets. Ethiopian chiefs, Afar tribesmen, and Arab merchants all took part in this trade in human beings. After World War I the efforts made by the European powers and by Ethiopia to stamp it out were only partly successful, mainly—according to Monfreid—because the slaves themselves were willing victims of the slavers.

France's humiliation at Fashoda in 1898 seemingly did not undermine French prestige in the eyes of French Somaliland's warrior tribes. When the call came for volunteers during World War I, a battalion of 2,000 mostly native troops was raised, and it fought valiantly on the Western front. These troops reached France in June 1916 after undergoing rapid training at Majunga in Madagascar. When the tribesmen found that they were to be used as manual laborers, they rebelled.[4] They agreed to undertake road building only after being promised that they would soon serve as combat troops. Beginning in October 1916, they fought at Verdun and received collective and individual citations for valor under fire. By the time the war ended, 400 of them had been killed and 1,200 wounded.

In French Somaliland itself, the main wartime event was the completion of the railroad to Addis Ababa in 1917. Transportation by rail soon replaced most of the camel caravans and spelled the decline of all the southern Somali-coast ports except Djibouti. The subsequent growth of that town's trade and prosperity further intensified the preoccupation of the French administration with the capital and the railroad. Elsewhere French control was ineffective, and the anarchic nomads were left free to trek with their herds and engage in intertribal conflicts. Age-old ethnic animosities were kept alive by raiding each other's herds and fighting over pastures and watering points. Some of the raiding parties came from the Ethiopian plateaus, but most of the clashes were between Issas and Afars, the latter tribe usually being worsted. Periodically, and usually when a new governor arrived at Djibouti, the Afars complained to the French that the Issas were violating their traditional rights along trek routes. Finally Governor Chapon-Baissac decided that the government must assert its control over the sultanates of Tadjoura and Gobaad. As his first step, in 1928, he created a post at Dikhil, on the border line between the feuding Issas and Afars. To pacify the region he gave the command of this post to Alphonse Lippmann, the son of a former acting governor of French Somaliland.

Lippmann had come to Djibouti in 1921, entered the local administration, and in due course was appointed president of the native court in the capital. He won the confidence of the population by learning the local customs and languages, and above all by his conversion to Islam.[5] Moreover, his taste for adventure and spirit of enterprise—akin to those of Monfreid, who became his friend—made him a natural choice to head the newly created post at Dikhil. He seems to have succeeded during his four years there in keeping peace between the Issas and Afars of that region, although his own account is obviously self-laudatory.

Most of Lippmann's relations with the local tribesmen were marked by prolonged negotiations, alternating with an occasional show of force. He came to believe that some of the intertribal disputes were inspired by foreign interference. In particular, he was convinced that the British, led by Colonel T. E. Lawrence, were intriguing to oust the French from Dikhil lest their base there lead to the reconstitution of the sultanate of Gobaad and then to France's expansion into Ethiopia.[6] If this was the case, the British found a willing ally in the Sultan of Aoussa, who had long opposed French penetration of the area. In 1898 Lagarde had ignored the claims of Aoussa to Gobaad, because of Aoussa's dependence on Ethiopia, and had bestowed the title of Sultan of Gobaad upon a chief who was willing to sign the treaty of cession to France. (His successor proved uncooperative, and in 1931 the French exiled him to Madagascar.) A deeper grievance of the Sultan of Aoussa was that French control of the region between the coast and the Ethiopian frontier deprived him of the revenues he had formerly derived from the local tribes and the caravan trade.[7] After being ambushed and taken prisoner by Sultan Yayou of Aoussa, Lippmann signed an agreement with him, but the peace that this brought to the region did not long remain undisturbed. In September 1930, Lippmann himself was relieved of his post as a result, he claimed, of the intrigues of an "enemy" who was determined to revive the warfare between Issas and Afars. To the French government's failure to follow his policy and to British machinations Lippmann attributed the murder of a young French administrator, Albert Bernard, and 16 of his Somali troops at Morheito in 1935. (To this day, the anniversary of the disaster is observed in Djibouti.) The massacre finally aroused the French to put an end to raiding in the region, but other troubles soon occurred there as a result of the Italian conquest of Ethiopia and Rome's backing of Aoussa's territorial claims at the expense of France.

The Italians and French Somaliland

The Italian invasion of Ethiopia began in October of the year in which Bernard and his companions were killed. At once the French government proclaimed its neutrality, but its actions soon showed that its sympathies lay with the Ethiopians. Just before the conquest was completed, the French not only allowed the Negus to use the railroad to escape from Addis Ababa but accorded him full military honors on his way through Djibouti to exile, first in Jerusalem and later in London. Also, in conformity with a preexisting agreement with Haile Selassie, a detachment of French troops was sent to Diré Daoua in Ethiopia to protect the railroad workshops and French personnel there. Local French opinion in Somaliland, however, was divided on the issue.

Initially, the Italian conquest had brought increased prosperity to the

French colony. The Italian army, leaving in its wake a war-ravaged country, reached Addis in May 1936, just before the start of the rainy season. They were therefore compelled immediately to use the railroad and port of Djibouti to bring in supplies for their troops and for the Ethiopian population. They found the French managers of the railroad and Djibouti businessmen most willing to cooperate. A private commercial agreement was signed at Rome on July 26, 1936, granting Italy an appreciable reduction in railroad rates, and further rate concessions were made in January 1938. Under growing pressure from the Italians in Addis, the railroad company agreed to spend 70 million francs in increasing the line's carrying capacity by adding to its rolling stock, improving its workshops, and building more housing for its employees.[8] But, according to French sources, the Italian officers abused their position, exhausted the company's food and water supplies, monopolized its telephone services, and were "inflicting vexations" on its personnel, French and native alike. Moreover, the railroad's increased operations were also a direct benefit to Italy's revenues because the Rome government was receiving dividends from the company's shares that it had seized from Ethiopia. The boom period lasted about one and a half years, but came to an abrupt end in October 1937, when the traffic of both Djibouti port and the railroad began to decline sharply. Within a few months it became apparent that this decrease was due not to economic causes but to a deliberate policy adopted by the Italians. At great cost and despite its then straitened finances, Italy was developing the port of Assab in Eritrea and building a road from there to Addis Ababa, which would directly compete with French Somaliland's communications facilities.

The depth and intensity of Italian resentment against France dated back over the preceding 50 years. First the Italians had been frustrated in Tunisia, and then they believed that France was thwarting their expansion in Africa. Djibouti, by its very prosperity, not only contrasted with Italy's Eritrean ports but was preventing their development. "If Tunisia was a pistol pointed at the heart of Italy," wrote one Italian patriot of the Fascist period,[9] "Djibouti is a thorn in the side of the empire." Such reasoning also made France ultimately responsible for the Italian defeat in Aduwa, because the French had refused to permit Italian soldiers to disembark at Djibouti while at the same time they allowed the Ethiopians to use the railroad to import firearms. This was a dog-in-the-manger attitude, in the Italian view, for France had for years ignored its post at Obock and had been moved to activity only by the British acquisition of Aden and by Italian moves in Eritrea. Furthermore, it was because French pride had been humbled at Fashoda that France was expanding along the Somali coast and trying to establish a protectorate over Ethiopia. "France delayed by 40 years our colonial expansion in East Africa. It was France that shoehorned slave-ridden Ethiopia into the League of Nations so as to prevent its conquest by Italy and to keep France's monopolistic grip on Ethiopia's trade."

In this long-simmering resentment, Djibouti had become in Italian eyes both a symbol and a focal point of Italy's East African aspirations. During World War I, the Italians had asserted that the acquisition of Djibouti was a "goal of absolute necessity." In the secret negotiations that led up to Italy's entry into the war on the Allies' side, the Italians wanted Britain and France —which were planning to take over Germany's colonies—to allow them to expand the Italian possessions in Libya and Eritrea. Paris insisted, however, that Djibouti was indispensable to maintain its communications with Indochina and Madagascar. Rome then realized that to persuade Paris to cede Djibouti it must offer compensation in the form of an alternative port, but it was Great Britain, not Italy, that disposed of such potential attractions. Obviously the key to realizing Italy's acquisition of French Somaliland was held by London, for it was inconceivable that the British would allow any power to install itself opposite Aden without their consent. Consequently, Italy tried to work on London's fears of the contraband-arms trade, which was centered in Djibouti, and of French designs on Ethiopia. To counter this, the French attempted to arouse the apprehensions of the British in regard to Italy by instigating the rumor that Rome had offered Tripolitania to Paris in exchange for French Somaliland. London, in turn, tried vainly to convince Rome that French public opinion would never accept cession of Djibouti to Italy but would agree to its acquisition by Britain. None of these maneuvers dislodged the French from Somaliland but instead enhanced its value in the eyes of a heretofore indifferent French public.

In the early 1930's, events took a turn more favorable to Italian aspirations. When Pierre Laval became premier of France, the Paris government proved more amenable to Fascist Italy's overtures. By the terms of the Franco-Italian treaty signed on January 7, 1935, and by the oral assurances reportedly given to Mussolini by Laval, Italy agreed to stop demanding Nice and portions of the colony of Tchad in return for appreciable French concessions. These consisted of 800 square kilometers in the Doumeira region of French Somaliland, some shares in the Franco-Ethiopian railroad company, and above all a free hand for Italy in Ethiopia.[10] This new Franco-Italian entente did not last long, and relations once more grew embittered after the Popular Front government came to power in France in 1936. Nevertheless, the Italians continued trying to persuade the French that Djibouti was of slight importance to France compared with cordial relations with its Latin neighbor, and that French Somaliland was essential to provide Italy with *lebens-raum*. Léon Blum, however, remained deaf to pleas to cede Djibouti, and refused to recognize Victor Emmanuel as emperor of Ethiopia. As a fervent socialist, Blum was adamantly opposed to fascism, whether in Italy or in Africa.

At that period, the French community in Somaliland was divided in its reactions both to Italian covetousness and to the policy of the Paris government. There was considerable resentment of the concessions made by Laval at Somaliland's expense in the 1935 treaty. That same year, some of the local French residents formed a Société de Bienfaisance Somali—an innocuous name which only thinly disguised its basic aims of countering Italian penetration of the Ogaden region of Ethiopia, undermining the loyalty of Italy's Somali subjects, and preventing an apostate son of Menelik from trying to rally Ethiopian Muslims to Italy's side. Yet by no means all of the Djibouti French approved of Blum's foreign or domestic policies. His efforts to extricate the colony's economy from the grip of local big business* and to promote trade unionism in Djibouti naturally annoyed conservative businessmen, who, moreover, were enjoying unprecedented revenues in 1936 as a result of Italy's use of the port and railroad. Other pro-Italian elements were to be found not only among the large Italian community in Djibouti but also among the French civil servants and military officers. Many of them were anti-British, and because they believed that English machinations had lain behind some of the Ethiopian raids into French territory and were the cause of a certain intransigence in regard to the railway's operations, they were not displeased that Italy had beaten Great Britain to the draw in Addis Ababa. Nevertheless, on the eve of World War II, after Italy had become more aggressive and its boycott of Djibouti's communications facilities was beginning to be felt, French opinion in Somaliland became more solidly anti-Italian than before.

In January 1938, Italian soldiers from Ethiopia moved down into the Hanlé plain, where they set up the first of a number of military camps. This move they justified under the terms of the 1897 treaty, which had somewhat vaguely defined the frontier between French Somaliland and Ethiopia. In Paris, Georges Mandel, then Minister of Colonies, reacted vigorously. In cooperation with the officer commanding in Somaliland, General Legentilhomme, he strengthened the colony's defenses. The local garrison was increased to 15,000 men, military posts were set up in the Hanlé plain—as well as at Afambo and Moussa Ali and in some cases behind the Italian line—and the inland defenses of Djibouti were augmented. On

* See p. 195.

November 30, 1938, a belligerent speech by Count Ciano in Rome was followed by Italian demonstrations there and at Addis Ababa, in which the cession of Djibouti was vociferously demanded. In Djibouti itself, a counter-demonstration was organized on December 18, in which virtually all of that town's male population participated. Crowds gathered in front of the governor's palace waving French flags and shouting slogans such as "Djibouti, terre française, doit rester français."[11]

It was because of Italy's aggression against French Somaliland that France was impelled to take an active interest in a colony that theretofore had been known sketchily to French stamp collectors and readers of Monfreid's stories and thoroughly to a mere handful of administrators, soldiers, and missionaries. Many local Frenchmen, doing profitable business as a result of Italy's conquest of Ethiopia and watching Rome there outwit London had been satisfied by their situation, but this did not mean that they would not strongly oppose any move by a foreign power to take Djibouti from France by force. The colony was experiencing the backwash of a minor recession after a period of unprecedented prosperity, its defenses had never been so strong or its defenders so numerous, and its railroad equipment exceeded existing transport needs. Such was the situation of French Somaliland on the eve of the Second World War.

World War II

When the Italians began their conquest of Ethiopia, France's intelligence services at Djibouti started to draw up plans for the future. The principal intelligence agency was the Section d'Etudes, to which was added the Deuxième Bureau of the French Somaliland *état-major* in 1935. The former organization was headed by De Jonquières, a *chef de bataillon,* who operated on the principle that the best defense for French Somaliland was to help the Ethiopian resistance movement with money, arms, clandestine propaganda, and advisers. To this end the intelligence services cultivated contacts with local Ethiopian refugees and with rebel leaders in Eritrea and Ethiopia, whose number increased rapidly during the Italian reign of terror that followed the attempt to assassinate Marshal Graziani in February 1937.

The recruitment of French secret agents to assist Haile Selassie's partisans was entrusted to Colonel P. R. Monnier, a French reserve officer. He and his fellow agents encountered many practical difficulties because of inter-tribal animosities among the partisans and the hostility between native Muslims and Christians, and after 1938 they were further hampered by the presence of Italian troops in the borderland between French Somaliland

and Ethiopia. Monnier died in November 1939 while on a secret mission to Ethiopia, but a testimonial to his effectiveness as an organizer of Ethiopian resistance is still given in an annual ceremony at Addis Ababa. Later, at the request of General de Gaulle, some Free French officers participated in the British offensive of early 1941 against the Axis armies in East Africa. A brigade from Cameroun fought at Kubbub; in March, Lieutenant Pierre Messmer (later governor-general of French Equatorial Africa and of French West Africa and now French Minister of the Armed Forces) participated in the capture of Asmara; and in April, Colonel Monclar carried out a successful raid against Massawa.[12]

Formal Anglo-French cooperation in the defense of their East African areas was slow in getting under way. It was not until June 1939 that the first joint military conference was held at Aden, and seven months passed before a second such meeting was held, at Djibouti. There the decision was reached to base preparations for a revolt in Ethiopia in the Anglo-Egyptian Sudan, where the first steps were taken to organize an Ethiopian Legion from among the Negus's followers who had taken refuge there. This Legion, however, was not to operate openly unless Italy declared war against the Allies. Italy took that step on June 10, 1940, and the next day the French commander at Djibouti, General Legentilhomme, was named supreme commander of the Anglo-French forces in the Somaliland theater.

At that time the Italians had about 40,000 men stationed along the frontier of the Somalilands, whereas the Allies had only some 9,000 troops and a small air force. Consequently General Legentilhomme was ordered to restrict his operations to pinning down the Italians so as to enable the Ethiopians to stage an effective revolt. Although the Italian troops in his area remained surprisingly unaggressive, some fighting did take place along the railroad and around Ali-Sabieh. Then came the Franco-German armistice, followed by General de Gaulle's famous appeal of June 18. These events caused confusion among the French in Somaliland, as they did throughout the French Empire. Wartime developments thereafter, elsewhere in Africa and in the Near and Far East, were to have a profound influence in this very secondary area of conflict.

The appeal of June 18, 1940, launched by an almost unknown officer urging disobedience to the legal head of the French government, the highly honored Marshal Philippe Pétain, went unheeded by many French officers serving in Somaliland. Although none of them voiced any liking for Hitler's Germany and all were humiliated by France's swift defeat, some felt contempt for the politicians of the Third Republic and feared Nazi reprisals against their compatriots and families in France. The latent anglophobia of many Frenchmen in Djibouti was fanned into open hostility by the British attack on Mers-el-Kebir and later by the attempt to capture Dakar. On July 19, the local *conseil d'administration* met and, with the exception of General Legentilhomme, voted unanimously to remain loyal to the Pétain government.

In the meantime, General Legentilhomme had resorted to delaying tactics so as to avoid carrying out the provision of the Franco-Italian armistice of June 25 which called for the demilitarization of Djibouti. In fact, some clashes between French and Italian troops took place between July 1 and 10 in the Hanlé plain, along the railroad, and at Ali-Sabieh. It was not until July 10 that direct communication with France was reestablished and the French government learned that the armistice terms had not yet been carried out in French Somaliland. Pétain therefore sent General Germain to Djibouti with strict orders to see that the terms were enforced. After some difficult negotiations a compromise agreement was reached between Pétain's emissary and the local administration. This involved General Legentilhomme's resignation but also included "explaining" to the Italian Armistice Control Commission (which was to be set up at Djibouti) why it was "practically" impossible and inadvisable to demilitarize French Somaliland. On July 23, General Germain not only replaced General Legentilhomme but also took over the governorship from Hubert Deschamps. That official was recalled to France because he had refused to dismiss the British consul, with whom he had worked out an agreement to provision the colony. Six days later, French Somaliland was declared to be no longer a belligerent in the war. In consequence, British Somaliland was left to fend for itself, and within two weeks, during August 1940, it was overrun by the Italians. On August 2, General Legentilhomme, after refusing to be repatriated on an Italian plane, escaped with two outstanding officers to join the British and Free French forces of the Middle East. One of these officers, Captain Appert, a graduate of St. Cyr and head of the Deuxième Bureau at Djibouti from 1938 to 1940, was later to return to the colony as head of the French troops.

In September 1940 the situation at Djibouti took a turn for the worse. From Aden the British began a sea blockade of the colony, and Pierre Nouailhetas, a former naval officer and administrator in Indochina, succeeded General Germain as governor of the territory. Nouailhetas had been given sweeping powers to root out all opposition to the Vichy regime, and he used them to the full. The bombing of Djibouti from a British plane on September 25, 1940, provided the new governor with the pretext for instituting a draconian regime, in which neither Europeans nor Somalis were spared. Some of the Europeans whom Nouailhetas suspected of having intelligence with the enemy were interned at Obock, but 45 others—most of whom had left the Territory—were condemned either to death or to forced labor. The most pathetic victims of Nouailhetas's regime, however, were six illiterate Africans, who were shot without trial in May 1941 as "examples" to potential defectors.

Nouailhetas's reign of terror was so pointlessly and dangerously cruel even in the eyes of the Vichy authorities that he was recalled in September 1942 and retired by them without a pension. After the Free French came to power in 1944, Nouailhetas fled to Portugal and was condemned to death in absentia by a Paris civil tribunal. Nine years later, to the indignation of many Frenchmen, he was acquitted by a French military court, and this action gave rise to two heated but fruitless debates in the National Assembly in 1953. Nouailhetas's acquittal was due to the lack of hard evidence that he had acted against the law, the cooling of wartime passions in the long interval, and his practical accomplishments. By ruling with an iron hand, he had indeed prevented a civil war from breaking out among the Somaliland French, had kept the Territory going despite a blockade by land and sea, and, above all, had not allowed it to fall into foreign hands, either of the Italian Armistice Commission or of the British army.

The British offensive against the Italian forces in East Africa began in January 1941, and it succeeded rapidly. Mogadiscio fell on February 25, Addis Ababa was taken on April 6, and Haile Selassie returned triumphantly to his capital one month later. The Negus had gone from London to Alexandria in June 1940, and from there soon moved to Khartoum, where his presence gave new impetus to the resistance movement in Ethiopia. By an agreement between him and the British command on January 31, 1942, full sovereignty was restored to Ethiopia, although for the time being the administration of the Ogaden and a Reserved Area would remain under the British military authorities. The Reserved Area included the railroad from Diré Daoua to the French border, and in this way the British felt that they could safeguard the line and also exert pressure on the Djibouti administration.[13] An East Africa brigade was entrusted with the task of guarding the frontier. According to a British historian,[14] "It was quite beyond the grasp of the Askaris, as they kept their monotonous watch around the barren frontier of French Somaliland, to understand why the army that had so rapidly destroyed Italian power in East Africa should hesitate in the face of a handful of Frenchmen, or for what reason there were apparently two kinds of French, one good and one bad." These reasons were many and complicated.

After the British took Addis Ababa in April 1941, they were faced with the problems of provisioning that city and evacuating its Italian residents.[15] Since the use of Djibouti's port and the railroad was the most obvious solution to those problems, the British tried to negotiate with Nouailhetas for permission to use them in return for easing the blockade. In so doing they were influenced by the Free French, who—misjudging the governor's character and overestimating their own powers of persuasion—hoped to rally French Somaliland to the Gaullist cause. The British were willing to help General Legentilhomme and his associates to move close to the frontier, from which they could launch their propaganda, but they would not let their own troops become involved in hostilities against the local pro-Vichy regime. The Free French disseminated tracts in Somaliland, as well as a newspaper called *Djibouti Libre,* in which they urged the local garrison to join them and sought to justify Britain's anti-French military actions at Mers-el-Kebir and Dakar and in Syria. These efforts were largely ineffectual, and Radio Djibouti as well as the official newspaper, *Djibouti Français,* countered them with pro-Vichy propaganda. General Legentilhomme and his British allies concluded that there was little hope of winning over Nouailhetas, who was "so fanatically anti-British and so proud and obstinate that he cannot be expected to act with common sense. The Djibouti traders and the railroad officials are more moderate in their views, but none carries enough weight to stand up to the governor."

Direct negotiations between the British and Nouailhetas were no more successful than was the Free French propaganda. On May 1, 1941, Nouailhetas telegraphed the governor of Aden to the effect that he had received official permission to negotiate with the British authorities. A week later, General Cunningham was ordered to establish contact with Nouailhetas, but only to report his proposals and to make no commitments. Specifically he was to sound out the French governor as to the conditions on which the British would be permitted to use the port and railroad. On June 8, General Wavell in a letter to Nouailhetas laid down the British terms: if the colony would declare its adherence to De Gaulle, the blockade would be lifted and Djibouti would be given provisions for one month; if not, the blockade would be tightened. The Djibouti population was informed of these terms by tracts air-dropped on the town. Nouailhetas replied a week later, dwelling on the increase in Djibouti's infant mortality as a result of malnutrition, but he was adamant in remaining loyal to the Vichy regime. To this communication the British made no reply.

Briefly, the British entertained the idea of taking Djibouti by assault, but the project was abandoned because they did not want to alienate the Somaliland French and in any case needed to use their troops for more important military operations elsewhere in Africa. During the summer of 1941 there was a further exchange of proposals and counterproposals, including a conditional offer by the British to evacuate Djibouti's garrison as well as its European women and children to another French colony. To this, Nouailhetas replied that before he would surrender the colony he would destroy its railroad and port installations. Negotiations had thus reached an impasse.

Djibouti's darkest days came in the last half of 1941. Because of the Italian defeat in Ethiopia, the supplies that had been reaching Djibouti from there were cut off. The town's population had already consumed all the horses, donkeys, and camels available, no more vegetables and fresh fruit were to be had, and beriberi and scurvy were widespread. Many of the native tribesmen returned to the desert rather than starve to death in the town, abandoning many children to be cared for by the Catholic mission, which was unable to provide them with food. According to one firsthand account, some of the Senegalese soldiers went berserk and the hospital became so overcrowded that its exhausted head doctor committed suicide in despair.[16] To be sure, a few Arabs ran the blockade from Djibouti to Obock, and one or two French ships managed to bring in totally inadequate supplies from Madagascar. Early in 1942, however, the situation improved somewhat, for Japan's entry into the war in December 1941 compelled the British to withdraw some of the ships that were blockading Djibouti. Regardless of Nouailhetas's motivation, it was remarkable that a territory that produced nothing but salt, charcoal, and a few undernourished animals managed to survive a desperate situation for two years without a popular uprising.

In the eyes of the Free French and the British, the greatest political crime of Nouailhetas was his having convinced the Djibouti French that it was the English and De Gaulle who were responsible for their misery, thus preventing for two years the 8,000 or so troops stationed in Djibouti from joining the Gaullist forces. There were indeed some individual defections, either from motives of patriotism or merely from the desire to escape from blockaded Djibouti. The handful of officers who had fled from the territory in August 1940 were followed by a few others. Captain Dodelier got together a small air force at Aden with some pilots who had escaped from Djibouti and from Tunisia. French-manned sloops helped to patrol the territorial waters of Somaliland. Captain (later Lieutenant Colonel) Edmond Magendie was able to train some noncommissioned officers from Djibouti, who later formed the backbone of the Somali battalion which fought in Europe during the last year of the war. But there were no large-scale defections from the territory until after the Allied landings in North Africa

in November 1942. Then Colonel Raynal, who commanded the first Senegalese battalion, crossed over into British Somaliland with one-third of Djibouti's garrison.[17] Governor Dupont, who had succeeded Nouailhetas, then
tried to reopen negotiations with the British, but as he offered only an economic agreement and refused to surrender to the Free French, his proposal
was rejected. Late in 1942, however, when the British let it be known that
French rights to the Somaliland colony would be respected if it surrendered
without firing a shot,* the governor capitulated.[18] Colonel Raynal, supported by British armored cars, crossed the frontier on December 26, 1942,
and the colony was taken over by the Free French.

The new administration was headed by Governor Bayardelle, who had
previously served with the Free French in New Caledonia, but late in 1943
he was transferred from Djibouti to Brazzaville. On January 13, 1944, he
was succeeded by another Frenchman from the Antilles, Raphaël Saller,
who was soon to begin a distinguished career in French West Africa.
Within three months, Saller was replaced by Jean Chalvet, a former governor of Mauritania, but Chalvet in turn was replaced a few weeks later by
Governor Beyries. This rapid rotation of governors did not make for stability or consistent policies in the colony. Under the relatively long incumbency of Bayardelle, the French residents of Djibouti had experienced some
sense of security. The recruiting of a Somali battalion to fight in Europe
provided the military with an honorable means of avoiding the consequences of their long acceptance of the Vichy regime, but there was no such
easy escape for the French civil servants and magistrates. Some of them
were transferred to Equatorial and North Africa, but others were dealt with
more severely by the commissions created early in 1944 to study each case.
Although they of course pleaded that they had simply obeyed their supe-
riors' orders, many of them were dismissed and their professional careers
ended in the current wave of strong anti-Vichy feeling. In general, their
wartime record as pro- or anti-Gaullist became the sole criterion by which
they were judged.

By mid-1945, Djibouti had regained much of its prewar aspect. Although
only a few ships had begun using its port, enough of the native population

---

* This move hardly tallies with the view expressed by General de Gaulle in his wartime mem-
oirs. There he contended that the British did not strictly enforce the blockade or take Djibouti
by assault because, if the French remained passive in Somaliland, they could hope to make
the whole Horn of Africa a zone of British influence after the war. "For the few battalions
which Djibouti could supply in a battle that was already won, why should they give up such
a result? This attitude, more or less widespread among the British, explains, in my opinion,
why the Vichy authorities succeeded during two years in provisioning the colony and thereby
keeping it fatally obedient to their orders." De Gaulle, pp. 146–47.

had returned from the hinterland to handle the cargo and also to meet the town's other needs for manual labor. To be sure, Djibouti's electricity functioned only fitfully because a new generating plant was needed, and the trucks and railroad equipment ordered from the United States had not yet been delivered. On the other hand, the colony now had adequate food supplies, being provisioned not only from Ethiopia but also from North Africa and Madagascar.[19] Physically, if not psychologically, French Somaliland was almost ready for the new era that was being ushered in for Overseas France by the reforms of 1945–46.

Chapter Two

NOMADS AND SEDENTARIES

The Nomads

Westerners who have lived long in contact with the Afars and the Issas agree that the similarities between the two tribes are more numerous than the differences. Nevertheless, the differences have become more marked with the passage of time and, above all, as a result of the policy of the French administration.

Their principal points of similarity lie in a common Hamitic language and tribal organization and an overwhelming adherence to tradition and custom, on which their profession of Islam rests lightly. To both Afars and Issas, the tribe is all-important, and frontiers in the Western political sense of the term are irrelevant. They take oaths in the name of their tribe and of Allah, for to them the tribe is sacred and all-embracing. It protects its members, avenging their death or paying the blood-price exacted for it. "It is a small republic, a living and indissoluble cell ... and it is reinforced by Islam and a common language."[1]

The nomadic existence of the Afars and Issas has been conditioned by an extremely harsh physical environment and the lack of natural frontiers against aggressive neighbors. They are an independent people, with strong resistance to external restraint and hardships and a respect for their given word. Quick to learn, violent and cruel, devious and unstable, they are cautious of innovations and only reluctantly take on tasks requiring time and sustained effort.

The tribal organization shared by the Afars and Issas derives largely from their acknowledged descent from a common ancestor. Some heterogeneous peoples living in close proximity to them, however, have been absorbed by both major tribes, a phenomenon more frequent among the Afars than the Issas.[2] Descent from the common ancestor is traced through the male line, and in this respect the Issas have a keener sense of genealogy than do the Afars. Tribes are divided into subtribes and *fractions,* which are made up of a number of related families. Trekking usually is done by families in small groups, which in their search for pasture and water cross political frontiers into countries where related tribes live. Afars and Issas alike are herders of camels, goats, sheep, and rarely cattle, and their basic diet of milk and, on rare occasions, meat is supplied by their animals. They also consume imported cereals, corn, and a type of millet called *dourra*.

Pasturelands and water holes are so scarce in French Somaliland that the Afars and Issas have fought each other fiercely for their possession. Afar power in the region was at its peak in the late eighteenth century, when an Afar chief ruled at Zeila and amassed a large fortune from the slave trade there. From the early nineteenth century on, however, the Issas began to impinge on Afar territory, slowly driving the Afars to the north and west. The frequent battles between these "traditional enemies" in the Dikhil area during the interwar period impelled the French to try to establish peace between them by both force and persuasion. For many years, both Afars and Issas resisted such efforts, but gradually the Afars came to accept French rule as their best guaranty of survival. The Issas, on the other hand, while adapting themselves more readily to the new economic and cultural opportunities created in the Territory by the French, have continued to display a more independent attitude toward the local administration. At first glance it seems curious that the Afars, who outnumber the Issas and have equally bellicose traditions, should have become more docile to an alien authority. The answer seems to lie in the comparative isolation of the Afars as well as in the greater rigidity of their social and political organization.

The Afars. In the Horn of Africa live 250,000 to 300,000 Afars, of whom four-fifths inhabit Eritrea and Ethiopia. Those in French Somaliland are divided into two main groups, the Adoyamara and the Assayamara, which in turn are subdivided into numerous *fractions*. Some scholars have attributed different origins and social strata to these two main groups, whereas others believe that their names merely signify their respective habitats. Since the name Adoyamara means "the white people," it may have been given them because they lived on the cream-colored sands of the Tadjoura gulf. By the same reasoning, the name Assayamara, which means "the red people," may be derived from the color of the soil of the Awash River region, which is the heartland of the group. Possibly at one time these tribes were mutually hostile and were organized into two distinct chieftaincies, but today they have intermingled peacefully in many places. Indeed, both have a strong sense of Afar solidarity, which extends to their more numerous relatives in Ethiopia and Eritrea. It can be ascribed to their sharing a language with only slight dialectical variations and to a common way of life and common traditions.

The Afar sultanate is a feudal-type political and territorial institution superimposed on the tribal hierarchy. Theoretically, the sultan is a despot who can dispose of his people and of the tribal lands at will, but in practice his authority varies with his personality and with the importance of his tribe. Furthermore, he shares his power with a vizir (*banoito*) and the Miglis, a council composed of heads of subtribes and Notables (*okal*), who make many of the major decisions. Of the three surviving Afar sultanates, only that of Tadjoura lies wholly in French territory. The domain covered by the Rahayto sultanate is mainly in Eritrea, but it also includes the northern portion of the Territory, around the Tadjoura gulf. The Afars living in what was formerly the sultanate of Gobaad, in southwestern French Somaliland, are tributary to the sultan of Aoussa, who is a vassal of the Negus of Ethiopia.

By Afar tradition, the supreme tribal authority is vested in certain families, although it is the prerogative of the assembly of Notables to choose which members of those families are to become the sultan and the vizir. The sultan of Tadjoura, who rules over the Adoyamara group, must be chosen alternately from among members of two families of the Adali tribe, the Bourhanto and the Dinetté. For example, when a Bourhanto sultan dies he is succeeded by his Dinetté vizir, and the eldest son of the dead sultan becomes the new sultan's vizir. That this tradition is still observed was demonstrated in May 1963 when the present sultan of Tadjoura was enthroned. His predecessor had died at the end of 1961, and inasmuch as his succession gave rise to "delicate problems," more than the one-year span required by tradition had been allowed to elapse before the new sultan was installed. He was chosen by the customary electoral college composed of representatives of the seven most important subtribes, convened in the mosque traditionally used for this purpose. Ali Aref, the Afar vice-president of the government council at that time, gave political significance to the event by coming to Tadjoura for the coronation.

This respect still shown for Afar tradition, however, cannot disguise the fact that under the French administration the Tadjoura sultanate has lost much of its real power. Like the Notables, although at a higher level, the sultan and his vizir obviously are regarded by the French as super-civil-servants. They collect taxes and maintain order in the tribes under their command as auxiliaries of the administration. It was noteworthy that the governor, in a speech marking the accession of the new sultan, stressed the novel fact that both he and his young vizir had been trained in the Territory's schools and spoke French fluently.[3] Such training has enhanced their usefulness to the French, which suggests that they may not share the fate of the sultan of Gobaad, who was summarily deported by the local administration in 1937. Furthermore, the Tadjoura sultan continues to inspire profound respect among the great majority of his subjects, none of whom owes allegiance to any authority lying outside of French Somaliland.

Reverence for traditional authority within the tribal framework permeates the rigid hierarchy of Afar society. Each of the numerous Afar chieftaincies and *fractions* has its accepted place in the social order—one that is based on seniority and numbers.[4] Yet Afar society is basically egalitarian despite the existence of "noble" tribes who claim descent from a legendary ancestor named Hadalmahis. Perhaps because poverty and the nomadic life are, with few exceptions, the lot of all the Afars, there are no privileged classes or castes among them. Members of subtribes intermarry freely, and young orphans are adopted by their close relatives. The family comprises the paterfamilias, his wives and children, and the wives and children of his sons. A portion of the tribe's traditional trek route is assigned to each family and is inalienable. Only when a family has no male heir does it revert to collective tribal ownership, when it may be reallocated by the chief. Herds belong to the men of the tribe, whereas the daughters receive as dowry from their fathers only a few small animals. In matters of inheritance, marriage, repudiation, and divorce, the Afars have adopted Islamic law, but otherwise they follow tribal traditions. Custom still dictates that girls must, and boys should, marry first cousins. Although in marriage young men have a little more freedom of choice, they must present the gift required by tradition to the bride's family and remain with that family for a long time after marriage. If the husband works in Djibouti, he must leave his wife with her family in Tadjoura for long periods. Such prolonged separations, as well as the custom that sanctions marriage only during two months of the entire year, are responsible in part for the Afars' low birthrate.[5]

In the opinion of E. Chedeville, the outstanding French authority on the Afars, their social and political organization has provided the maximum security to their tribesmen compatible with their adaptation to a very unfavorable physical environment. Afar society has survived as a cohesive, disciplined unit almost untouched by modern economic development, but at the cost of an isolation that has led to virtual economic and cultural stagnation and the stifling of individual initiative. "To outsiders," says Chedeville, "the Afar people give the impression of being old, worn out, and almost refractory to progress and evolution."[6] Their reaction to their dynamic and progressive Somali neighbors is understandably one of resentment and fear.

The Issas. The Issas were the only Somali group encountered by the French as they moved southward from Obock along the coast in the late nineteenth century. That group, which is thought to have numbered from

3,000 to 4,000 at the time, was concentrated in the southern quarter
is now French Somaliland, adjacent to far more numerous related
British territory and, especially, in the Diré Daoua area of Ethiopia. ᴘᴏᴜᴛᴜ
cal frontiers mean little to the Issas, and they spend only the cool season in
French territory, crossing into neighboring countries with their herds in
search of pasturage and water. All of their trek routes lie in areas that are
among the least propitious for habitation in the world. Yet to acquire even
such isolated and desolate regions they have fought long and fierce wars
with the Gallas and the Afars. Although the Issas' sense of tribal solidarity
and ways of life are shared with those nomad enemies, and on occasion
there has even been intermarriage with them, the unremitting struggle of
the Issas for a better life has set them apart from even their fellow Somalis.

In French Somaliland the Issas are divided into three main groups—the
Abgals, the Dalols, and the Wardiqs. The last-mentioned live mainly outside French territory, but it is from among them that the supreme chief of
the Issas, called the Ougaz, is chosen. Of the other two groups, the Abgals
enjoy a certain preeminence over the Dalols, based on genealogical seniority,
but this is only vaguely acknowledged. Issa society, in fact, is not rigidly
hierarchized as it is among the Afars, and the relationship between the Issa
groups is more in the nature of an interfamily pecking order. Yet the Issas
have pariah castes that have no counterpart in Afar society. These are called
by the generic term *sab,* the same that is applied to the negrified Somalis to
the south. They are blacksmiths (*toumal*) and hunters or potters (*midgan*),
whose dialects are different from the pure Somali tongue and whose occupations are considered menial.

From the political standpoint, however, the Issas are more egalitarian
than the Afars. They have no noble tribes, and their Ougaz, although chosen
for life, is a magician-sorcerer rather than a sultan. His religio-judicial influence is largely confined to the Diré Daoua region where he lives.* Elsewhere his role, according to one Issa Notable,[7] is "to make rain so that our
herds can survive but is not to order us about." Issa society is essentially a
patriarchal one, in which authority is based on age and tradition. In the
family group the paterfamilias reigns supreme. Above him the only widely
recognized authority is that of the assembly of Notables, which is composed
exclusively of elders, in contrast to the Afar assemblies, which also include
heads of tribes regardless of their age. On matters of great importance, an

---

* Both the Ougaz and the head of one of the most important Afar tribes live in Ethiopia and
receive stipends from the Ethiopian government. Perhaps for that reason, their influence in
French Somaliland is decidedly limited. See I. M. Lewis, "Recent Developments in the Somali
Dispute."

assembly of 44, whose membership is half Abgal and half Dalol, acts as the tribe's supreme court, and its decisions on policy and on intertribal conflicts are final. Because of their experience and knowledge of custom the Notables wield undisputed authority.

Tradition, as transmitted orally from father to son, has the force of law among the Issas. So all-embracing and minutely detailed are Issa customs that they lay down the procedure to be followed in every conceivable situation, and color the tribesmen's whole attitude toward life. The respect in which custom is held by the Issas is the cohesive force that holds together a society which in other respects is individualistic to the point of being anarchistic. The Issas refuse to acknowledge authority based solely on birth and inheritance, and they recognize as chiefs only those leaders who adhere closely to custom and who have given proof of possessing the personal qualities that they admire.

The stories told to Issa children[8] cast light on this tribe's characteristics, which, to an even greater degree than among the Afar nomads, are the product of their customs and environment. Constantly plagued by hunger and thirst, the Issas, in order to survive, have developed extreme traits of combativeness, boastful pride in tribal traditions, and deviousness and skill in attaining their ends. They feel superior to the Afars, yet they are sensitive to being treated as inferiors by other Somali tribes who are more highly developed than they and who have no mixed blood. Nevertheless, the Issas feel themselves to be members of the Somali world and closely related to the Somalis living outside the Territory, particularly the Issacks of former British Somaliland. This makes them receptive to propaganda for a Greater Somalia, if only for the reason that it would unite them with their blood brothers and also enable them to shake off the control of the Ethiopian and French governments.

All of the Territory's nomads are deeply attached to their migratory existence. Traveling with their herds and armed with their rifles, they feel free and mobile although they are in fact restricted in their movements by the need to find pasture and water. It is difficult for them to adapt to the conditions of modern life, and particularly to contemporary economic conditions, but the Issas have been quicker than the Afars to do so. Although many Issas stay in Djibouti only long enough to earn money to buy more animals, an increasing number have become urbanized. Because of the greater readiness of the Issas to seize the economic and cultural opportunities offered them by the administration, the French government was inclined for many years to favor them above the Afars, comparatively few of whom have become town dwellers.

The Sedentaries

The Afars and, to a lesser extent, the Issas who have come to Djibouti in their search for living conditions less miserable than those in the desert have labored under disadvantages from the beginning. They lacked the skills needed for all but the most menial urban employment, yet were averse to manual labor and regular working hours. In addition, they were seriously handicapped by the habits of their nomadic life and above all by the tribal organization and traditions which they brought with them. The Afars, for example, refused to work together in gangs unless the foreman occupied a higher position in the tribal hierarchy than their own.[9]

Both Afars and Issas, being gullible and unused to a money economy, were easy prey to the more skilled and sophisticated alien immigrants in Djibouti, who exploited their common Islamic faith and especially the nomads' taste for ostentatious expenditure.[10] They encouraged the nomads, as soon as the newcomers had earned enough money, to go on the expensive Mecca pilgrimage or to build up a harem rather than invest their money in a business. Acquiring the title of *hadj* and begetting numerous children gave the Issas and Afars a new sense of dignity and a prestige that promoted them in their own eyes to the rank of a great chief. Furthermore, the nomads resisted the administration's attempt to persuade them to become market gardeners, even when they received substantial aid in money and equipment. As of 1961, only three Issas and two Afars owned plots of arable land in the suburb of Ambouli, from which they earned very little because the former nomads found the work of irrigation too arduous and time-consuming.

An even more serious barrier to their economic advancement was the force of tribal custom, which prevented the Issas and Afars of Djibouti from enjoying the fruits of their labor or, indeed, of having any private life of their own. The Issa and Afar councils of Notables could arbitrarily require one of their tribesmen to contribute financially to tribal expenditures and even to repudiate his wife, and there was no appeal from their decisions. Moreover, he was also expected to keep his door always open to any needy member of his own tribe, who was free to enter and to remain as long as he pleased at his "host's" expense. Such customs greatly discouraged the transplanted nomad's initiative, for whatever a man earned had to be placed at the tribe's disposal. It is little wonder that wage earners in Djibouti spend one-third of their income on buying *khat,** which induces a euphoria that they would never otherwise enjoy.

* See pp. 163–65.

Alien communities. From its earliest years Djibouti attracted foreigners, who initially came to work on its port and the railroad and who found it easy at that time to acquire French nationality without breaking their ties with the countries of their origin. Many aliens took advantage of these facilities and soon began to play an important role in the development of trade unions and later of political parties in Djibouti. They exploited the naiveté of the urbanized nomads and occupied the best posts in the administration and in private employment. On the other hand, they aided the economic and political development of Djibouti through their enterprise and skill. The presence of so many heterogeneous ethnic groups gave Djibouti a cosmopolitan atmosphere not found to the same degree in other Somali coastal towns. The various ethnic groups all lived compartmentalized lives in their own *quartiers,* however, so that Djibouti did not become a melting pot, and tribalism was reinforced there, rather than attenuated.

The Somali immigrants.—Although the Issas have been coming to Djibouti to settle as permanent residents in increasing numbers, they have now been almost submerged there by other Somali tribes. The great majority of Somali immigrants originated in what was British Somaliland until it merged with the Republic of Somalia in 1960. Djibouti was only 20 kilometers from the frontier; moreover, the lack of natural obstacles made it virtually impossible to control the movement of people across the border. As Djibouti prospered and grew, it became an ever-greater pole of attraction for the impoverished Somalis to the south, who formed the largest ethnic group in French Somaliland's capital from the early postwar years until late 1966.

It is very difficult to estimate with any certainty the number of alien Somalis now living in Djibouti. The increase in the Somali community dates from about 1960, but has probably been more than offset by the mass expulsions that occurred for political reasons during late 1966 and early 1967. Moreover, the nationality of the deportees is the subject of heated controversy. The most reliable information on distribution of the city's population is to be found in the 1959 census, although even in that comparatively "normal" year the fluctuations in the number of persons living in Djibouti were so great as to make such statistical data only approximate. In any case, it is clear that for some years Djibouti has contained at least half of the Territory's total population, and that the alien elements living there came to outnumber the indigenous peoples.

In 1959 the largest alien Somali tribe was that of the Issacks, most of whom came from the Hargeisa region of British Somaliland. The census takers in the French territory usually classified them with another alien

Somali group, the Darods, who originated in Italian Somalia. The early Issack-Darod immigrants were enterprising and intelligent, and they soon came to form an important segment of the territorial militia and the clerical staffs of the administration and trading firms. Some set themselves up as small independent merchants, who became strong enough to impose a boycott that forced the Arab shopkeepers to withdraw from the Issack-Darod *quartier*.[11] Like the Issas, the Issack-Darods could always find a relative to live with in Djibouti until they were able to support themselves. Again like the Issas, they were mobile and maintained close contacts with the nomads of their tribe. If they married in Djibouti and established a residence there, they often had another family in the country of their origin to whom they sent regular remittances. The next most important alien Somali group were the Gadaboursis, who, though traditional enemies of the Issas in the desert and their political rivals during the early postwar years, were closer to the Issas in traditions and customs.

In 1959, according to the census, the Issack-Darods formed 23.8 percent of the total population of Djibouti *cercle*; the Issas came next with 17.3 percent; and the Gadaboursis were in fourth place (below the Arabs) with 9.74 percent. The Afars were the smallest ethnic group (under 5 percent of the total population), whereas the Arabs ranked third (16.1 percent).

More recent data were supplied by the registration of voters in the referendum of March 19, 1967, but unfortunately the official registration statistics do not provide a breakdown of the Somali tribes. These figures indicate that there then lived in Djibouti *cercle* 7,800 Issas who were French citizens and 14,900 who were foreigners. Other Somalis classified as French citizens numbered 6,200, and almost twice that number—11,500—were of alien nationality. Of the other principal ethnic groups resident in Djibouti, the Arabs totaled 8,000, of whom 5,000 were foreigners, and the Afars numbered 3,500, all of them French citizens.

The Arabs.—Although Arabs are a numerically substantial element of Djibouti's population, their importance derives largely from the wealth they have amassed and the political influence they are consequently able to wield. The Arabs owe this preeminence to their superior skills, industry, and astuteness, and not to their presenting a united front against other ethnic groups. Indeed, the Arab community in Djibouti is deeply divided by its diverse origins and, even more, by the variations in the economic and social status which its members have attained in French Somaliland.

Most of the Territory's Arabs come from Yemen, some minority groups originating in Aden and Saudi Arabia. They traded profitably in slaves and firearms at Obock and Tadjoura before Europeans installed themselves

along the Red Sea coasts. After the French transferred the capital from
Obock to Djibouti, Arab immigration increased, as did that of other foreigners drawn to that fast-growing city by its economic opportunities. Some
of the Arab immigrants established permanent residence in Djibouti, acquiring French nationality and gaining large fortunes through trading and
investing in urban real estate. Their descendants now constitute the stable
element of local Arab society, in which they occupy the top level because of
their inherited wealth and manner of living. They reside in the European
quarter of Djibouti and imitate the Europeans' way of life, but they remain
apart from the Europeans, who do not accept them socially, and from native
society, which they reject as inferior. The second stratum of Arabs is made
up of Yemenese traders, who have become prosperous by hard work and
self-deprivation. They, too, form a group apart, dispersed throughout the
native quarters, dressing shabbily, living in the back rooms of their stores,
without servants, and hoarding their earnings. Their only luxury is *khat,*
but they spend only half as much on that stimulant as do the Arabs of the
first category. The third main group of Arabs differs even more markedly
from the other two. It is made up exclusively of members of the Hakmi
tribe, whose only activity is market gardening in Ambouli, 4 kilometers
from Djibouti, where they live with their families. The great majority of
them are laborers employed by the few Hakmis who own small plots of
farmland there. The Hakmis perform heavy manual labor, lead austere
lives, and generally suffer from undernourishment, for even the Hakmi
landowners earn little from the sale of their produce. This could be said to
be the only Arab group which the Afars and Issas neither resent nor envy.

In general, the attitude of the native population toward the Arabs—one
of mingled respect and dislike—closely resembles that of the peoples of
Southeast Asia toward the resident Chinese, except that in Somaliland a
religious element further complicates this emotional relationship. In the
French territory, the Arabs inspire respect as the people chosen by Allah
and the one whose language is that of the sacred Koran. This deference
makes it easy for the Arabs to use their common religion, Islam, as the
means of establishing ascendancy over the Afars and Issas. The Arab strategy has been minutely described by a Somali observer, whose account is
enlightening although obviously colored by an anti-Arab bias.[12] According
to this source, the Arabs give rudimentary religious instruction to a few
Djibouti tribesmen whom they call *wadadine.* After they learn a few verses
of the Koran, the *wadadine* are sent to preach to their fellow tribesmen, to
whom they describe the joys of the Muslim paradise from which all white
infidels are excluded. They emphasize that the faithful jeopardize their

chances of salvation if they have contact with Europeans. Thus the
have created a barrier between the Afars and Issas, on the one han..,
Western civilization on the other. They tell the tribal paterfamilias that if
he sends his children to a French school they will be converted to Chris-
tianity. By discouraging the nomad children from attending school, and
thus keeping the cultural level low, the Arabs limit the chances of their
becoming competitors. The Arabs emphasize the virtues of poverty, stressing the Prophet's injunction against amassing riches lest wealth deflect the
attention of the faithful from Allah. This tends to encourage the nomads'
traditional contempt for the merchant. At the same time, the Arabs render
personal services and proffer gifts that eventually place the recipient in a
position of chronic obligation.

By and large, the Somali immigrants in Djibouti are more sophisticated
than the nomads, who may not grasp so readily the inconsistency in the
Arabs' preaching against the spiritual dangers of acquiring wealth and at
the same time their owning 80 percent of the permanent buildings in Djibouti,* as well as controlling 90 percent of the Territory's retail trade. An
admittedly prejudiced source[13] maintains that Arab duplicity in such matters was strikingly demonstrated a few years after the end of World War II,
when many of the Jewish merchants of Djibouti began to emigrate to the
state of Israel, created in 1948. Some well-to-do Issas were interested in acquiring the vacated Jewish shops and apartment houses. However, the
Arabs immediately began an anti-Jewish campaign in the mosques, where
the Issas were told that they would lose their chances of paradise if they
bought Jewish property. A few months later Arabs were installed in the
former Jewish buildings and had even transformed one synagogue into a
shop. The Issacks, on the other hand, seem to have learned a lesson from
the Arabs, and, on occasion, have applied it to the latter's detriment.

In the long run, the Arabs' economic practices aroused the nomads' resistance, yet the tribesmen first showed anti-Arab sentiments in the political
rather than the economic domain. During the late 1940's and early 1950's, it
was the Arabs' open intervention in the territorial elections, in which they
backed candidates pledged to promote Arab interests, that caused serious
clashes in Djibouti. Although the Arabs have continued to be influential
in local politics, their tactics are now more subtle. Furthermore, their political influence has been lessened by the development of an ideological
cleavage between the Arab generations. The older Arabs have been deeply

---

* This percentage was higher before 1950, when the French decided to construct their own
administrative buildings and no longer pay the high rents charged by the Arab proprietors.

impressed by the fate of their compatriots in Zanzibar and consequently favor—albeit very discreetly—the continuance of French rule in Somaliland. The younger generation, on the other hand, is inclined to admire Nasser and to sympathize with the nationalistic aspirations of the Somali youth. There is a widespread uneasiness, however, and for some weeks after the Djibouti riots of August and September 1966, planes flying from Djibouti to Taiz were filled to capacity with Arabs seeking repatriation.[14]

Population centers. With the exception of Tadjoura and Obock, all of the Territory's population centers were created by the French, and aside from Djibouti, they are no more than small villages that have grown up around the administrative and military posts established in French Somaliland's five *cercles.* None has more than a few hundred inhabitants, mainly functionaries and members of the militia and the *gendarmerie,* along with a handful of native and Arab merchants, and their population totals no more than 4,000 to 5,000.

Only Djibouti, which contains more than half of the Territory's total population, can be called a city. Of its heterogeneous population other than Somalis, Afars, and Arabs, no ethnic group is very large and all the groups are unstable. The smallest consist of the Sudanese, mostly shell fishermen, and the Ethiopians, of whom many of the women are prostitutes; together they total only a few hundred persons. The 200-odd Indians are traders and money changers, and they are economically more important than the size of their community suggests, though incomparably less prosperous and numerous than their compatriots in English-speaking East Africa. As for the European component, the number of Italians has fluctuated with the fortunes of their country in Ethiopia, Somalia, and Eritrea, reaching a peak in the years immediately before and during World War II. Greeks are among the longest-established European residents, having come to French Somaliland when Obock was still its chief settlement and having moved with the administration to Djibouti. Today they are a close-knit community with their own club, which is open to all Greek nationals, and a Greek Orthodox Church, whose resident priest ministers to the spiritual needs of 350 members. Together with the Indians, they control those branches of Djibouti's retail trade not monopolized by the Arabs.

Among the Europeans, the French, of course, represent the most important element, occupying all of the top posts in the administration, the two banks, and the railroad company. Most of them are civil servants and members of the armed forces and their families, for only a handful are engaged in private enterprise. The size of the French community varies with that of its military component; it averages from 2,000 to 3,000 individuals, but rises as high as 10,000 during periods of international crisis or local tension. At the time of the March 19, 1967, referendum, there were 10,255 Europeans in the Territory, of whom 7,655 were French citizens, but fewer than 1,000 of these had lived as long as three years in French Somaliland.

Despite such wide variations, the number of persons classed as Europeans and *assimilés* has probably grown over the years, although at any given time the size of this group has been fairly closely related to the status of Djibouti's public-works program. In the late nineteenth and early twentieth centuries, building of the railroad from Djibouti to Addis Ababa brought in as many as 2,000 Europeans of different nationalities, and their coming drastically modified the ethnic composition of the capital. World War I led to an exodus of Europeans, as did completion of the railroad in 1917 and the outbreak of World War II. Since the end of that war, the enlargement of Djibouti's port and other public works financed by government funds have swelled the number of European residents, but only temporarily. Furthermore, during the hot season there is a general scattering of the Europeans, some going to Europe, others to the Ethiopian highlands, to such a degree that Djibouti in summertime has been described as "a city whose population is somewhere else."[15]

Such instability makes unrealistic the number of Europeans described as residents in any of the periodic censuses taken in French Somaliland. Those unreliable figures indicate that the number of Europeans doubled between January 1945 and October 1947, and again doubled between 1951 and 1956. Apparently the proportion of women and children to the total population has risen markedly since World War II, and the number of foreigners has increased far more rapidly than has that of Metropolitan French citizens. What emerges clearly is the recent rapid growth of Djibouti as a town and especially the increase in its Somali element. An official estimate in March 1967 gave the Territory's total population as 125,050, to which it had risen from 74,120 in 1961, and that of Djibouti *cercle* as 62,000, compared with 41,000 six years before.[16] Of the 34,000 persons classified as foreigners, or non-French nationals, 11,500 were Somalis (see table). Because these figures served as the basis for the electorate that voted in the referendum of March 19, 1967, they have been strongly challenged by Somali nationalists, and in any case the massive deportations related to the riots of 1966 and the referendum of 1967 make them no longer valid.

To an increasing extent, political and economic developments in neighboring countries are directly and indirectly affecting the racial composition of Djibouti's population and the relations between its various ethnic groups. Even greater changes can soon be expected, because the future of the Ter-

COMPOSITION OF POPULATION AND ELECTORATE OF FRENCH SOMALILAND
(March 1967)

Ethnic group	Nationality		Number of registered voters
	French	Foreign	
Djibouti *Cercle*			
Europeans and *assimilés*	7,500	2,600	884
Arabs	3,000	5,000	1,334
Issas	7,800	14,900	3,915
Somalis	6,200	11,500	2,946
Afars	3,500	—	1,841
Total	28,000	34,000	10,920
Ali-Sabieh *Cercle*			
Europeans	75	—	9
Arabs	15	20	5
Issa-Somalis	9,100	1,280	4,861
Afars	210	—	101
Total	9,400	1,300	4,976
Dikhil *Cercle*			
Europeans	30	—	7
Arabs	20	50	36
Issa-Somalis	6,500	750	2,876
Afars	13,880	1,000	6,607
Total	20,500	1,800	9,526
Tadjoura *Cercle*			
Europeans	20	—	12
Arabs	20	—	6
Issa-Somalis	160	—	65
Afars	20,100	700	9,038
Total	20,300	700	9,121
Obock *Cercle*			
Europeans	30	—	11
Arabs	44	50	27
Issa-Somalis	59	—	26
Afars	8,867	—	4,417
Total	9,000	50	4,481
Territory as a Whole			
Europeans	7,655	2,600	923
Arabs	3,165	5,120	1,408
Issa-Somalis	29,810	28,430	14,689
Afars	46,570	1,700	22,004
Total	87,200	37,850	39,024

Source: *Le Réveil de Djibouti,* Mar. 11, 1967.

ritory is far from settled. Such uncertainty accentuates the transient character of the European component and of all the other immigrants who have not taken root in the Territory. To what degree Djibouti will remain a pole of economic attraction for the whole region depends on the Suez Canal's availability to international navigation and on how long it will take to find a peaceful solution to the troubled situation in Aden and South Arabia. Djibouti's present economic stagnation automatically causes a decline in the number of immigrants from Somalia, and so long as the French control the Territory, they will try to limit drastically the influx of Somalis because of its effect on the local political scene. Already at least 8,000 Somalis have been expelled from Djibouti, although some of them have probably filtered back into the city.

A few years ago, some observers[17] thought they saw emerging among the city's non-European population a new and authentic "Djiboutian" type of resident. This was attributed to a growth in intermarriage between members of the various ethnic groups and also to a new outlook and way of life which were increasingly differentiating the urbanized Issas and Afars from their fellow tribesmen in the desert. However, the issues of independence and eventual union with Somalia or Ethiopia, which became acute in late 1966 and early 1967, have now deepened the preexisting cleavages between the racial elements that make up Djibouti's population. The traditional hostility between Issas and Afars has been intensified, and the Arabs are regarded with even greater suspicion than before. Since the referendum of March 17, 1967, the victorious Afars have shown an unwillingness to share their new political power with the defeated Issas, although the French government seems to have made some progress in persuading the two groups to reach a *modus vivendi* if not to cooperate more actively. Much depends upon the attitude adopted toward the Territory by the Republic of Somalia. If that country continues, as seems likely, its propaganda for a Greater Somalia, the chances for welding the Issas and Afars into a genuine if tiny nation are slight.

Chapter Three

THE GOVERNMENT STRUCTURE

Territorial Government

In 1884 the Paris government instituted in its new colony of French Somaliland the same charter that it had given to St. Pierre et Miquelon 40 years earlier. To Metropolitan officials of that period, France's foothold on the Somali coast must have seemed of comparable insignificance and size, but in other respects there were few parallels between the damp and chilly islands of the northwestern Atlantic Ocean and the extremely torrid and arid area facing on the Red Sea. Conditions in French Somaliland, with its population of pastoral African nomads and a commercial economy, contrasted sharply with those in St. Pierre et Miquelon, whose isolated inhabitants—all of them white descendants of early emigrants from France—engaged in deep-sea fishing as their sole economic activity. Firmly believing, however, that the basic principles of French civilization and government were universally applicable, France gave to many of its colonies in the late nineteenth century virtually identical administrative structures. Later, adaptations to local conditions had to be made, and those structures were modified many times.

Until after World War II, French Somaliland was administered by a governor, named by the French cabinet, who was directly responsible to the Minister of Colonies, he, in turn, being answerable to the French Parliament. The governor was aided by an Inspector of Administrative Affairs (called secretary-general after World War II), who was usually a high-ranking official of the colonial service. The governor was also assisted by a privy council—later called the *conseil d'administration*—composed of the Procureur de la République (district attorney), the head of the armed forces, the highest-ranking financial official, and a representative of the chamber of commerce. In addition, there was a *conseil du contentieux administratif*.

Extensive changes were made in this structure by the law of November 9, 1945, the most important being the creation of a representative council. That council, with a total membership of 20, was divided into two sections of equal size. One was made up of Metropolitan Frenchmen and the other of natives, and the mandates of both were for a four-year term. In each section the elected members numbered six and the nominees of the government three, the latter being chosen from a list of nine persons drawn up by the chamber of commerce; there was also one labor representative appointed from a list of three candidates presented by the Union des Syndicats. As for the elected councilors, those of the first section were chosen by universal suffrage of all citizens of civil status (almost wholly Metropolitan French), whereas those of the second section were elected by colleges composed of specific categories of citizens of personal status (those Africans and Asians who were born in the Territory). These native colleges included functionaries, holders of diplomas, veterans of the armed forces, commercial employees, recipients of decorations from the French government, property owners, chiefs, and "representatives of indigenous collectivities." This curious mélange seems to have reflected the basic principle of enfranchisement of native citizens whose identity was known to the administration and who had in some way distinguished themselves from the mass of the population.

The representative council was entitled to elect its own officers and a permanent commission of eight members, equally divided between the two sections, which functioned between the two council sessions to be held each year. Behind closed doors, the council was to debate and vote on the budget drawn up by the government, and it could also legislate on such matters as land concessions of appreciable size, leases, and many other affairs in which the interests of the Territory were involved. Council decisions concerning the method of taxation and the collection of direct taxes and duties had to be submitted to the French cabinet for approval, but matters considered to be of lesser importance, such as the raising of loans, required only gubernatorial approbation. On certain subjects the council was obligatorily consulted by the government, and on other matters it could pass resolutions if its members so desired. This council also served as the electorate for French Somaliland's representatives in the Conseil de la République and the French Union Assembly, but the Territory's deputy to the French National Assembly was chosen by the entire electorate voting as a single college.

In many ways French Somaliland's representative council resembled those of the French sub-Saharan territories, which were created at about the same time, but there were important differences, which worked to the disadvantage of Somaliland. The West African and Equatorial African assemblies had a wider range of subjects on which they could legislate, they elected representatives to a federal Grand Council, their meetings were open to the public, and all their members were elected. In French Somaliland, not only was there no Grand Council but only half of the representatives of the native population were elected, and, furthermore, they had to be chosen by the three main ethnic groups—Somalis, Afars, and Arabs—on the basis of two for each. In effect, this arrangement gave French Somaliland not a dual electoral college, as in the sub-Saharan territories, but a four-college system in which—perhaps inevitably—racial lines were sharply drawn. The heterogeneous composition of its population, with its high percentage of nomads, and the natives' lack of political sophistication in comparison with, for example, that of the Senegalese, were the reasons given for the difference in treatment. In any case, this structure was regarded as a temporary one, pending its revision by new decrees that were to become law by July 1, 1947.

The first elections of representative councilors and of a deputy and a senator in 1946 went off smoothly. No decrees were issued by July 1947, or throughout all of 1948, although a project for revising Somaliland's council and electorate had been submitted to the National Assembly early in 1947. On December 19, 1948, French Somaliland's senator was elected to the Conseil de la République, but almost exactly one month later a riot related to his victory took place in Djibouti. This stirred the Paris government to submit the draft proposal to the French Union Assembly, which rejected it on April 13, 1949, and made a counterproposal. There the matter rested, and in August and October of the same year there was more rioting in Djibouti. Although these riots, too, were sparked by local elections, they did not seem to have been motivated by resentment against the restrictions placed on the size of the electorate but to have had other causes.*

In the elections to the representative council in March 1946, the number of registered voters totaled 1,250. Fewer than half of them, however, actually voted, and this indifference to the franchise was as true of the second-section electorate as of the first. Of the 726 citizens of civil status on the rolls, 326 took the trouble to vote; of the 228 Somalis, 150 Arabs, and 146 Afars who were enfranchised, only 118 Somalis, 70 Arabs, and 37 Afars cast their vote.[1] By early 1950 the electorate numbered 1,825 in a total population then estimated at 48,685.[2] This increase in the electorate was not due to any liberalization of the law but to the overall growth in the population, including that of the element which qualified for the franchise. Not only was the number of registered voters an extremely small proportion of the Territory's total population, but the size of the Metropolitan French electorate (768) was about as disproportionately high as before in relation to the native electorate (1,057). Yet the root of the trouble, as indicated by the 1949 riots, did not lie

* See pp. 62–64.

in either of the foregoing inequities but in the racial divisions imposed on the native electorate and on their representation in the council. Each of the three riots was the result of racial conflicts, but in each case the ethnic composition of the warring groups was different.

Obviously the outbreaks of violence at Djibouti arose mainly out of the refusal of its inhabitants to accept any longer the assignment of exactly the same number of seats in the representative council to the Somalis, Arabs, and Afars. Of the three, the Afars were the least involved in these clashes, for they not only were indigenous to French Somaliland but formed the majority group in the Territory even though a minority in the capital city. It was above all the Arabs and the immigrant Somalis who had aroused the ire of the Issas and, to a much lesser extent, that of the Afars, for both ethnic and economic reasons. For many years, the native-born tribesmen had been envious of the economic predominance of the Arabs and Gadaboursi Somalis, who, though largely immigrants, had amassed wealth and occupied the best posts in Djibouti because of their enterprise and superior skills. Only persons born in the Territory were entitled to vote as French citizens, but the registration of vital statistics had been introduced so recently and incompletely there that it was impossible to verify claims to citizenship. Proof of birth in the Territory therefore often had to be supplied by "witnesses," with the result that the wealthy immigrants did not find it difficult to obtain the certificates indispensable for their registration as voters.

Certainly the complexities of this problem of legal identification were one reason why the French Parliament repeatedly postponed the revision of the Territory's electoral system, but there were other cogent reasons for the successive delays. French Somaliland had only three representatives in French Parliamentary bodies, yet they could not agree among themselves on a new formula. The Metropolitan deputies were notoriously indifferent to colonial problems, and on the National Assembly's crowded agenda French Somaliland had a low priority. The Parliament might have continued delaying indefinitely debate on the Territory's problems had it not been for the expiration of the representative council's mandate on March 24, 1950. A week later the National Assembly, without any debate, decided to prolong the council's legal existence until November 1, 1950, and in the meantime to send a mission to conduct an on-the-spot inquiry concerning the wishes of the Somaliland people in the matter of their future governmental system. Initially this was to have been an intraparty mission of three members, headed by J. J. Juglas, president of the Overseas Commission and a member of the Mouvement Républicain Populaire (M.R.P.). As it turned out, Juglas conducted the inquiry alone, as did two other politicians who went to study the Somaliland question at about the same time. Juglas was preceded by Dr. L. Aujoulat of the Indépendants d'Outre-Mer (I.O.M.), secretary of state for Overseas France, and followed by Senator R. Dronne of the Rassemblement du Peuple Français (R.P.F.), emissary of the Conseil de la République. Inevitably these one-man reports were vulnerable to the charge of partisanship, and so the question of Somaliland's political future was dragged into the arena of French party politics. Moreover, the National Assembly debate, which finally opened on July 24, 1950, became involved in the controversy over the dual electoral college, which was then a burning issue for the French Negro African deputies.

The basic proposal examined by the National Assembly was the one originally drafted in 1947 by the Somaliland deputy, Jean Martine, which had already been drastically amended by the French Union Assembly. Further complications were introduced by the three mission leaders, whose reports agreed solely on the urgency of solving French Somaliland's political problems on a new basis. The Martine project, which envisaged universal adult suffrage and a single electoral circumscription for all French Somaliland, was supported only by the Communist Party, the Socialists, and the Rassemblement Démocratique Africain. It was rejected by the Assembly on the ground that it would be unfair to the hinterland tribes because it would give undue influence to the inhabitants of Djibouti. Voted down as well was the proposal made by the Somaliland Arab, Ali Coubèche, which had won the approval of his fellow French Union Assemblymen. His project would have created in the Territory three electoral circumscriptions and a council composed of 16 representatives from Djibouti and only four from the hinterland. Such a system would have perpetuated politically dangerous racial divisions in the population. Juglas argued forcefully that all the chiefs and Notables with whom he had talked, Issa and Afar alike, favored retention for the time being of the separate electoral colleges, although they wanted changes in their composition. The government proposed assigning a specific number of seats to each *quartier* of Djibouti, where the various ethnic groups lived practically segregated lives. By this device, use of the term "separate electoral colleges" was avoided, but in effect it meant voting by tribal entities. The National Assembly as a whole, and the African deputies in particular, strongly disapproved in theory of the multiple-electoral-college system and of an artificially restricted franchise. A majority of its members, nevertheless, yielded to the government's plea that French Somaliland was a unique case and therefore would not serve as a precedent for the other African territories.

The slightly amended government project that became law on August 19, 1950, did indeed provide French Somaliland with a political structure that set it apart from other French African dependencies. The representative council's appointed membership was eliminated and its size and composition were modified, but in most other respects it did not diverge radically from the structure set up in 1946.[8] The name of representative council was retained, as was the principle of multiple electoral colleges; the number and duration of the council sessions, as well as the manner of election of the council's officers and its permanent commission, were not changed. The councilors' mandate was lengthened from four to five years, and although they were not to receive an annual salary, they were entitled to a daily cash allowance for the period when the council was in session. Less than a year after this law was passed, the French Somaliland electorate had grown to 5,208. This rise was the local by-product of the law of May 23, 1951, which enlarged the franchise throughout French tropical Africa but did not materially alter the relative sizes of the Metropolitan and native electorates in the Territory.

Of the reforms introduced by the law of August 19, 1950, the most important were the augmenting of the council's membership from 20 to 25 (a meager majority of one being allotted to its second section) and an increase in the number of tribal candidates who could be elected by native citizens. Metropolitan French citizens continued to form a single electoral circumscription and to choose their 12 representatives by universal adult suffrage, but the second-section electorate was divided into ten circumscriptions, of which half were in Djibouti. Seven of these ten circumscriptions could elect one candidate each, while three of them were each empowered to choose two. The Djibouti electorate was required to vote by ethnic groups, but the number of such groups was increased from three to five. To the Afars, Arabs, and Issa-Gadaboursis were added two other Somali tribes, the Issacks and the Aberoual-Darods.

For the next seven years the governmental structure of French Somaliland remained unchanged but its political parties underwent rapid development. The next step forward was a giant stride, and it came about through application to the Territory of the *loi-cadre* of June 23, 1956, which profoundly altered the status of all of France's tropical African dependencies. Thereafter, French Somaliland was no longer a territory apart, and it shared in the progress made by French West and Equatorial Africa. To align French Somaliland with those territories, however, was not an easy task. It took almost a year for the Parliament to decide just how the general principles laid down in the *loi-cadre* should be applied there. All three Parliamentary bodies debated various proposals, particularly those concerning the number of representatives that the population should elect and the division of seats in the new legislature. Except for the lack of any serious attempt to promote Africanization of the administrative cadres, French Somaliland emerged with a governmental structure closely resembling that of all the other Overseas Territories.

The application of universal suffrage expanded the French Somaliland electorate by about 45 percent. It rose from 7,762 in March 1956 to nearly 11,000 by the summer of 1957, thus enfranchising over 10 percent of a total population—by no means all native-born—estimated then at some 63,000. In particular it boosted Djibouti's electorate, and within a few months after the *loi-cadre* was enacted, nearly 2,700 new voters had been registered on the town's rolls.[4] This inevitably reduced the political importance of the nonindigenous French citizens, especially since members of the armed forces were no longer allowed to vote unless they had lived in the Territory for more than a year. The number of electoral circumscriptions was reduced to three, and they were largely based on the existing administrative divisions. The legislature, now called the territorial assembly, was to be composed of 32 members, of which Djibouti circumscription would elect 16, that of Dikhil–Ali-Sabieh seven, and that of Tadjoura–Obock nine. It is noteworthy that during the parliamentary debates the number of seats allotted to Djibouti was steadily reduced, with the aim of giving the hinterland inhabitants greater representation than before. At the same time, the powers of the new assembly were widened to include control over the territorial civil service, taxation, the granting of concessions, and the organization of education, telecommunications, and the port.

The chief innovation introduced by the *loi-cadre* was a government council, which would share executive power with the governor. Its eight members were to be elected by the assembly, and the candidate who received the largest number of votes was to be named vice-president of the council. His fellow councilors were given the title of minister, and each became responsible for one or more government departments.* Although the government council was an emanation of the assembly, it was not made fully responsible to that body, and was therefore not required to resign following a no-confidence vote by the assembly. This was an inherent weakness that soon had serious political consequences in almost all the French African territories. French Somaliland continued to be represented in the Paris Parliament by one deputy and one senator, and after the French Union Assembly disappeared, the Territory was assigned a seat on the French Economic and Social Council.

* These were the departments of Public Works and the Port; Information and Tourism; Finance, Economic Affairs, and the Plan; Education, Youth, and Sports; the Civil Service; Health and Social Affairs; Labor; and Production (Agriculture and Animal Husbandry).

Almost two years after the *loi-cadre* was passed, General de Gaulle returned to power in France, and three months later the Fifth French Republic was born. The constitution of the new republic, which was accepted by three-fourths of French Somaliland's electorate in September 1958, transformed the relations between the Territory and France far more profoundly than the *loi-cadre* had done. Yet this transformation was less drastic for Somaliland than for France's other tropical African dependencies, because it was the only one on the continent that chose to retain the status of an Overseas Territory. Thus once again French Somaliland's political history and its relations with France followed a divergent course.

If 1960 was the year in which all the French-speaking West African and Equatorial African territories proclaimed their independence, it was no less a crucial one for French Somaliland, although for different reasons. The year 1960 also brought independence to the former Italian colony of Somalia and a merger between it and the newly sovereign British Somaliland, as the Somali Republic. The subsequent resurgence of Somali irredentism has affected the evolution of the French Territory profoundly, both in its internal political and economic development and in its relations with France. Thereafter the evolution of French Somaliland was closely interwoven with that of its neighbors in the Horn of Africa and throughout the Red Sea region.

The Cercles

On March 3, 1949, French Somaliland was divided into four administrative *cercles* of unequal size and importance, whose commandants—all military officers until 1952—were made directly responsible to the governor. These *cercles,* in turn, were subdivided into administrative posts, headed by a lower-ranking civil servant or a noncommissioned officer, both of whom took orders from the *cercle* commandant. Each of these officials, in his own domain, governed with the aid of the traditional chiefs and assemblies of Notables (*okal,* of which the singular is *akel*). Even more than elsewhere in French tropical Africa, the official policy favored direct administration, and tended to transform the customary chiefs and *okal* into minor functionaries of the central government. In theory, the statute given the Territory in July 1967 should lead to greater decentralization.

Of the four *cercles,* that of Djibouti, which included the islands of Waramous, Maskali, and Moucha, was the smallest in area, the most populous, and the only one that could be described as relatively prosperous. It covered 600 square kilometers, and during the first postwar decade its urban population grew to number 43,000, of whom 41,000 lived in the capital city.

The other main settlements were at Ambouli, two kilometers from Djibouti's native quarters, and at Arta, located on a mountain 700 meters high dominating the Gulf of Tadjoura. It was not until after World War II that a hill station was created at Arta, and a road 40 kilometers long was built to connect it with Djibouti. A military post was set up at Wea, and a small palm grove existed at Loyada, which marked the boundary between the British and French Somalilands. Some 2,000 Issa nomads formed the *cercle*'s hinterland population.

Second in importance to Djibouti came Tadjoura *cercle,* which covered the northern part of the Territory and contained the only two settlements in the country that antedated the French occupation. Its area was considerably larger than that of Djibouti *cercle*—13,000 square kilometers—but its population was much smaller, though more homogeneous, since it was inhabited solely by Afars. Its commandant has administrative responsibility for three nearby islands, those of the Ghoubbat-el-Kharab, Djeziret-Seba, and Doumeira, as well as for the nomad sector of Alta and the post at Dorra. Tadjoura's three subdivisions to some degree correspond to the three Afar sultanates, but only that of Tadjoura lies wholly inside French territory. The town of Tadjoura is the residence of French Somaliland's only surviving sultan and is also a pole of attraction for Muslim pilgrims. The town boasts no fewer than seven mosques for a population of less than 2,000, and nearby are the tombs of the legendary Afar saints.

Although Tadjoura has retained tribal and religious significance, it has lost its former economic importance as a terminus for the caravan routes from Harar and Shoa, and its small jetty is accessible only to small boats. Obock, even more than Tadjoura, has been eclipsed by the development of Djibouti as the Territory's administrative as well as economic capital.[5] Although it was raised on September 6, 1963, to the status of headquarters of French Somaliland's fifth *cercle,* Obock is now no more than a minor administrative post, in which Lagarde's fortlike former residence dominates a village lying in ruins on the edge of a desolate plain. Tadjoura *cercle* has a miniature hill station at Randa, 17 kilometers beyond which lies the unusual wooded area called the forest of Daÿ. Tadjoura's economic activity is now restricted to small-scale trading, fishing, herding, and a few indigenous handicrafts. Salt from Lake Assal is bartered there for *dourra* (a kind of millet), tobacco, and butter, and some wood and charcoal are sent to Djibouti in the picturesque sailing boats called *boutres.* There is no agriculture, a little hunting is done, and fishing is engaged in only by some of the inhabitants of the settlements of Tadjoura, Obock, and Khor-Angar. The *cercle*'s main resource is its animal herds, which in winter remain on the

Mabla and Gouda Mountains and upon the arrival of the hot season trek from the coast to the northern plateaus. Tadjoura lives in a closed, tradition-bound economic circuit, which is breached only by the cash remittances sent home from Djibouti by its Afar emigrants.

Ali-Sabieh *cercle,* created as such in 1939, owes its economic existence mainly to the Djibouti–Addis Ababa railroad. All of the line's tracks in French territory pass through Ali-Sabieh, whose only two settlements— Holhol and Daasbiyo—are little more than railroad stations. Ali-Sabieh's 2,400 square kilometers consist of arid plains, and its meager population of 6,280 is made up wholly of Issas and a handful of Europeans. Moreover, the Issa nomads spend only a part of the year in this *cercle,* for they pass the summer on the high plateaus of what was formerly British Somaliland. Agriculture is confined to the few date palms grown in the small oases of Ali-Sabieh, for it is hampered by the sterility and aridity of the soil, not to mention the nomads' mobility and aversion to farming. The administrative post of Ali-Sabieh has a clinic and a school maintained by Catholic nuns, and a brigade of the *gendarmerie* is stationed nearby.

Dikhil *cercle* has a common frontier of 200 kilometers with Ethiopia and a broken coastline 24 kilometers long. Its 7,200 square kilometers cover most of what was formerly the sultanate of Gobaad, to which have been added portions of the Issas' trek routes in the east and those of the Assayamara Afars in the northwest. Early in the nineteenth century this region was peopled wholly by Afars, but they were gradually pushed back by the Issas. To put an end to the warfare between those two groups and to stabilize the Issas along a line running from the Ghoubbat-el-Kharab to Sankal, a fort was built at Dikhil in 1928 as headquarters for the newly created *cercle.* From Dikhil are administered the *cercle*'s three subdivisions of As-Ela (whose population of about 250 are all Afars), Yoboki (200 inhabitants, mostly Afars), and Dikhil itself (with 1,000 inhabitants, more than half Issas). Each of these subdivisions has a primary school, and there is a clinic at Dikhil and first-aid stations in the other two villages.

Dikhil is the most promising economically of all of French Somaliland's hinterland *cercles.* Its climate is relatively healthful, and it has about 2,000 square kilometers of plains, at altitudes ranging between 150 and 500 meters. Its animal herds are fairly numerous (about 5,000 cattle, 4,000 camels, 20,000 sheep, 50,000 goats, and a few hundred donkeys), and they are generally healthy, although they suffer from the aridity and overgrazing of the pasturelands. A deposit of copper exists in the Gaggadé area, some gypsum is to be found on the edges of Lake Assal, and rubies have been discovered in the Chekkeyti wadi. Doum palms grow in some abundance on the Gaggadé plain, and their fibers are woven into mats that are marketed in Djibouti. Date palms have been grown in the Henlé plain, one of the few regions in Somaliland earmarked for experimentation in irrigated cultivation. By drawing on subterranean water sources, it is hoped to grow enough cereals and market-garden crops there to feed the local population, which now depends on the corn and *dourra* brought down by caravan from Ethiopia. Dikhil is also a transit area for some of the Ethiopian coffee and hides that are sold in Djibouti or exported to Aden.

The Civil Service

The situation of Somaliland's civil service during the first postwar years closely resembled that of analogous bureaucracies in French Negro Africa at that period. There was a purge of many of the pro-Vichy officials, which —together with the economies necessitated by the worldwide depression of the early 1930's—resulted in a net decline in the number of European administrators and an increase in that of indigenous functionaries. It was estimated in 1947 that there were fewer Europeans serving in the administration than there had been in 1933 (though their proportion varied considerably from one department to another), and that during that period the natives employed by the government had increased by one-third.[6] Another cause of the shrinkage of the European component was the reluctance of French officials to serve in an isolated territory that had an exceptionally severe climate and offered little promise of economic development.

During the early postwar years, successive devaluations of the French currency and the creation of the CFA franc made inducements such as expatriate bonuses and leave in France every two years seem inadequate. In Somaliland the cost of living rose even more sharply than elsewhere in French tropical Africa because the Territory had to import almost all its food and consumer goods from countries belonging to the sterling and dollar zones. After the first devaluation of the French franc in January 1948, native functionaries received a 20 percent pay raise. European civil servants were not favored with a similar increase until after they had threatened a general strike the following April,[7] the delay probably being due to the fact that their aggregate pay totaled far more than that of their indigenous colleagues. Successive improvements in the material position of Metropolitan civil servants during ensuing years were usually accorded also to their overseas counterparts.

For the next decade such measures kept the European bureaucracy in French Somaliland relatively quiescent, but the same could not be said for its critics. Criticism of the civil service mounted in the mid-1950's with the transfer to Somaliland of many former administrators from Indochina. Another such influx into the Overseas Departments and Territories occurred after the French West African and Equatorial African dependencies became independent in 1960, for only in the former were posts available for administrators who had not yet reached retirement age. Many of the newcomers held high rank and thus further weighed down an already top-heavy administration and an overburdened local budget. In many cases, too, they augmented the politically conservative element among the resident European population.

It would be inaccurate to deduce from the results of the early elections in French Somaliland that the Europeans there were political reactionaries. To be sure, a majority of the French officials voted the R.P.F. ticket. This, however, was the period when the pro-Vichy officials had just been purged, and it would have been disastrous for a French bureaucrat to have shown himself less than a fervent Gaullist. It was also the era of communist ascendency, both in France and in Somaliland, where a deputy of reputedly radical tendencies had just been elected to the National Assembly. Then, as fear of the communist threat receded, the forces of conservatism were strengthened by the arrival of officials embittered by the loss of Indochina. With the development of indigenous political parties and the coming to power of more liberal governments in France, the conservative functionaries came increasingly under nationalist attack. Particularly after the passage of the *loi-cadre* on June 23, 1956, by the Socialist Mollet government, the nationalists began to draw a distinction between the liberalism of the Paris authorities and the conservatism of the local administration. After De Gaulle returned to power in 1958 and began to decolonize French Africa, he became the embodiment of France's liberal spirit, and the local administrators were censured for their failure to carry out fully his reforms. Later this attitude was adopted by the advocates of Pan-Somalism in a manner reminiscent of the wartime distinction drawn by the British between "good" and "bad" Frenchmen.*

Even the partial application to French Somaliland of the *loi-cadre* of 1956, however, brought about some fundamental changes in the Territory's bureaucracy. One of the most important was the separation of territorial from state, or Metropolitan, services,† and the giving of control over the former to the local assembly. Furthermore, a major cause of criticism was

---

* See p. 18.
† The state services included those of finance, economic affairs, *sûreté générale*, justice, labor, radio and telecommunications, transportation, the militia, the *gendarmerie*, and education.

eliminated by France's assuming responsibility for the salaries of state civil servants, though their secretaries, servants, housing, and in some cases transport to and from France remained at the charge of the territorial budget. Even though such top-ranking bureaucrats did not number more than about 30, they were too numerous for so small and underpopulated a territory. It was noted in 1964 that there were no fewer than four *administrateurs de la France Outre-Mer* for the telecommunications and information services in a country that was visited by—on the average—no more than five foreign correspondents a year.[8] When Philippe Decraene tried to learn from official sources the exact size of the bureaucracy, he could obtain no precise information and concluded that the subject was considered a *secret d'état*. Nevertheless, some light was thrown on the matter by Ali Aref, then vice-president of the government council. In a speech to the territorial assembly in December 1964,[9] he said that there were then 565 civil servants, other than those belonging to the local cadres. Members of the latter services, including the *garde indigène,* numbered 1,500. Still more numerous were the employees and contractual agents of the administration, whose pay totaled about the same as that of the local cadres.

Gradually the territorial assembly began using its new powers under the *loi-cadre* to improve the status of territorial civil servants. On May 2, 1960, they were given a new designation, "Cadres des Administrateurs du Territoire de la Côte Française des Somalis," and greater security in regard to status, pay, and promotion. Yet this did not ensure the Africanization of the cadres, one of the cardinal principles on which the *loi-cadre* had been based. In September 1960 there was instituted for the first time in French Somaliland a competitive examination for native aspirants to the higher echelons of the territorial administration. Five of the 15 candidates who passed this examination were accepted for training as *élèves-administrateurs,* and later two of the most promising were sent to the Institut des Hautes Etudes d'Outre-Mer in Paris for more advanced studies. This scarcely affected the existing structure of the administration, however, in which French officials continued to occupy all "posts of command" and to pursue a policy of direct rule. As of November 1959, there were only 13 non-Europeans in the general administrative cadre. Of the 152 non-Europeans in the territorial service, the great majority held manual jobs.[10]

For some years the most vocal critic of this policy was Hassan Gouled, who on three occasions[11] called the attention of his fellow deputies in the Paris National Assembly to the excess of high-ranking Metropolitan bureaucrats in French Somaliland. He went on to say that they performed few indispensable functions, were an unnecessary burden on the territorial budget, and, worse still, by their incumbency prevented native talent from assuming responsibility for the country's vital services. In reply, the French government's spokesman evaded the basic issue, merely saying that "the increase in the number of Metropolitan officials has not been such as to discourage the hopes of the local cadres for promotion." Other defenders of the prevailing policy pointed to the scrupulous care exercised by the Djibouti administration not to show tribal favoritism in its selection of native candidates for the local government service. It was indeed true that exactly the same number of Afars and Issas were recruited for the police, the militia, and the lower echelons of the administration.[12] No mention was made, however, of the easier qualifying examinations given to Afar candidates because they were less well educated than the Issas. This artificially maintained equilibrium was one of the chief causes of Somali frustration, which expressed itself in the independence demonstrations of August 1966. By then, reform of the administration had not even begun to match the Territory's economic and political progress.

The Europeans of Djibouti in general, and its French civil servants in particular, were certainly a socially segregated and economically privileged group. The *administrateurs de la France Outre-Mer* continued to run the country, and they showed little interest in preparing any native candidates to succeed them. How isolated they were even from the native political elite, not to mention the mass of the population, was shown on the occasion of General de Gaulle's visit to the Territory. General Pierre Billotte, then Minister for the Overseas French Territories and Departments, gave an intimation of his shocked surprise at this lack of contact. Specifically, his abrupt dismissal of René Tirant was a clear-cut indication of Billotte's displeasure at the failure of an official who had been governor for four years to warn him of the intensity of the people's pro-independence sentiments.

Justice and the Law Courts

In the eyes of European observers, the Afars and the Issas combine a spirit of independence and courage in enduring suffering and the harshness of nature in French Somaliland with brutality and a propensity for violence. One Frenchman who lived for many years with both tribes, often on terms of personal friendship, has described their history as one of "cruelty, bloodshed, and treachery" and their law that of the jungle.[13]

Intertribal warfare has been the main occupation of the nomads of French Somaliland, and from childhood they hear tales extolling the warrior.[14] Rarely has a man been killed by a member of his own tribe, but the murder of an enemy tribesman is regarded as a glorious deed. In fact, a man must kill at least one of his tribe's traditional enemies before he may marry. Custom dictates the ornamentation, usually ostrich plumes and bracelets, to which each successive murder entitles him.[15] Sometimes a particularly skilled warrior kills so many men that he wins higher prestige than the tribal chief, and after the tenth exploit he acquires a renown that transcends the limits of his own tribe. All nomad boys and girls are circumcised by brutal methods, and it is a widespread practice for the rural tribesmen to file their teeth. An anecdote told to the well-known writer and traveler Jean d'Esme[16] by a missionary who had long lived among the Afars throws a grimly amusing light on Somaliland nomad customs. The missionary found an aged Afar sobbing under a tree, and when he inquired about the cause of the old man's sorrow he received the reply: "It is because I am going to die and I have not yet killed anyone."

As for retaliatory practices, the killing of a member of the aggressor's tribe, if not the aggressor himself, by the relatives of the victim is the most acceptable form of revenge, but it is not the only way of squaring accounts. Compensation, or the blood price (*diya*), can be arranged by intertribal agreement, and usually takes the form of payment, according to a specific scale, of camels and goats. Intrafamily disputes are settled by the paterfamilias whenever possible, and it is his task to see that traditions are respected and transmitted to the next generation. Cases that cannot be settled by conciliation are referred to the tribal chiefs and Notables (*okal*), but here the practices of the Issas and those of the Afars differ.

Among the Issas, cases are disposed of by an assembly of Notables, whose number varies depending on the seriousness of the dispute and can reach a maximum of 44.[17] These Notables are chosen for their knowledge of customary law, and their decisions must be unanimous. Their judgments can be appealed only once and to another similarly constituted assembly. Among the Afars, it is the chiefs of tribes and *fractions* who settle disputes above the level of conciliatory and disciplinary action by the heads of families. In Tadjoura the ultimate legal authority is the sultan, but his subjects rarely appeal the chiefs' judgments to him because his sentences are reputedly very severe and also costly to carry out. The higher the fines exacted by the sultan, the greater his prestige.

Murder, knife wounds, and theft are the crimes that come most frequently to judgment. After the French established more control over the hinterland during the interwar period, they put an end to intertribal vendettas and reduced the number of thefts and mutilations. Theft is now the commonest offense, but it no longer takes the form of reciprocal raiding of herds by the

Issas and Afars. The French stopped this practice by refusing to regard the stolen animals as a legitimate form of war booty and by forcing their restitution. (As with murders, thievery almost never takes place among members of the same tribe, but when it does occur it can be easily handled by the traditional authorities.) French intervention has not been confined to modifying native customs considered incompatible with Western practices. The French have also made changes in the native judicial hierarchy, regulated and expanded the operations of Islamic courts, and increasingly exposed the Afars and Issas to Western legal concepts and practices.

In 1904 France organized its own judicial system in Somaliland. Although it subsequently was expanded, it has never been thoroughly reorganized; now, in the opinion of the highest local legal authorities, it badly needs to be overhauled and modernized.[18] At the head of the system is the *procureur de la République* (district attorney) and his assistant judge, who hold court in Djibouti. Also situated in the capital are the higher court of appeal (which also sits as a criminal court), a court of first instance, and a justice of the peace of ordinary competence. French law handled initially only cases involving Europeans and *assimilés*. After 1946, however, all the inhabitants of French Somaliland were made subject to French penal law as applied by French-trained magistrates, and thus for criminal cases there is now a single, uniform jurisdiction.

In 1947 this major change was followed by the introduction of an *état civil*. Although seemingly less drastic because its organization remains rudimentary and the registration of births and deaths has not yet been made obligatory, this innovation is nevertheless effecting a fundamental transformation. As yet there are only five official centers of the *état civil*, which is clearly inadequate for both a rural people of nomadic habits and also the huge floating population of Djibouti. Another practical difficulty has been the confusion caused by the scarcity of personal names. For the Afars, Issas, and Arabs together there is estimated to be a total of only 500 names, and of these, only 30 are commonly used. A mission sent by the French Union Assembly in 1957 to study this problem found that native opinion was opposed to the introduction of patronymics, but that the indigenous population were increasingly inclined to avail themselves of the *état civil* facilities.[19] The growing registration of vital statistics was caused not only by the increase in the population but also by the requirement of a birth certificate to vote in local elections and to qualify for family allowances. The mission strongly recommended increasing the number of registration centers and of officials authorized to keep the registers.

Courts applying Muslim law have also been reorganized and regulated by the French administration. In each *cercle, shariah* (Islamic law) courts of the first and second degree have been created, and the Cadi of Djibouti has been made head of this system. Traditionally, Muslim marriages and divorces are considered to be valid without official registration, but the law of March 3, 1951, made it obligatory for divorces to be registered by the *shariah* courts. It is expected that in time this obligation will be extended to marriages. For obvious reasons, town dwellers have adapted themselves more readily than the hinterland nomads to these regulations. Indeed, the Cadi of Djibouti has been physically unable to cope with that city's annual average of 1,200 marriages and 500 divorces, and therefore has had to delegate his powers in this respect. Although the number and competence of the *shariah* courts have thus been amplified, and on occasion Issas and Afars take their oaths on the Koran, the influence of Islamic law remains slight as compared with that sanctioned by custom.

To a lesser extent the same could be said in regard to the relative positions of French and customary law. Aside from ending intertribal warfare and mitigating the more savage aspects of the traditional law of retaliation-in-kind, and apart from establishing legally the identity of many indigenous persons, the application of French law and procedures has been hampered by practical difficulties. Among these are the mobility and instability of the population and the scarcity of officials trained to administer French justice. In French Somaliland there are seven magistrates, nine cadis, and 19 court clerks and bailiffs for a territory and population which, though small, are to a great extent inaccessible. Only for reasons of necessity and self-interest have the Issas and Afars accepted French authority, and when French actions have conflicted too sharply with custom, the local population has found ways of evasion. Thus, whenever the French have undermined the existing tribal administrative and judicial structures by appointing *okal* who were not the Notables sanctioned by tradition to administer civil justice, the nomads and to a lesser degree the townspeople have ignored their judgments.

Armed Forces

In theory, the *gendarmerie* and police are the normal law-enforcement agencies for Djibouti and the rural settlements, and the armed forces, including the militia, are responsible for the Territory's defense. In practice, however, all the armed forces help everywhere to maintain order in an emergency; hence there is much overlapping in regard to their functions as well as the geographical area of their operations. From the beginning, it may be noted, the principle of numerically equal recruitment, as between the Issas and the Afars, has been maintained for all branches of the local armed forces.

Because French Somaliland was long considered to be surrounded by friendly nations, with which France had signed treaties, the Territory was initially equipped with only small police forces, which were stationed along the railroad line and in the capital. No *gendarmerie* or *garde indigène* existed until 1919, when three gendarmes were sent to the colony from France. Their number was increased so slowly that by the eve of World War II, only seven newcomers had been added to the original three.[20] Nine more came in 1947, but the majority of these were simply replacements.

It took the intertribal clashes at Djibouti in 1949* to awaken the Paris government to the need for strengthening and reorganizing the Territory's law-enforcement machinery. Because the locally recruited police had refused to intervene against the members of their own tribes who were involved in those clashes,[21] it was obvious that they must be placed under the orders of French gendarmes. Twelve were therefore sent from France to organize a platoon of native police (*askaris*), and three posts were established, at Loyada, Arta, and Ali-Sabieh. The main detachment of 38 men was stationed at Djibouti, and it became a well-organized and disciplined force. One of its main achievements has been to bring under control the thieves and gangs who were preying upon residents and tourists in Djibouti. (In 1964, 2,300 arrests were made, and in 1965, over 1,600.) More remarkable if less spectacular has been the *gendarmerie*'s organization of a filing system, which is said to contain dossiers on 70,000 persons. This covers a very large percentage of the total population,[22] of which about half are nomads and many thousands are foreigners who claim whatever nationality seems advantageous to their interests at the moment.

The *gendarmerie* has its own commanding officer, who is responsible to the mayor of Djibouti. In 1966 this force reached record strength: it then had four French officers and 75 gendarmes, with 200 *askaris* under their orders, in the rural areas; and in Djibouti itself, where the commandant had his headquarters, 12 Metropolitan gendarmes had a force of 120 *askaris* under their orders. (In 1967 the *gendarmerie* was renamed the territorial police.)

Like the *gendarmerie,* the militia is composed of native recruits and has French officers and its own commandant, who is responsible to a civilian authority. The militia differs from the *gendarmerie* in that it was formed

* See pp. 63–64.

before World War I, its officers are temporarily assigned to serve in the Territory from the French infantry, and the responsibility of its commander to the governor passes by way of the head of his military cabinet. The militia—a unique corps, without counterpart in French colonial history—has been used to build strategic roads and military posts, but its officially assigned task is to guard the Territory's land frontiers. It is divided between two camps, situated respectively at Dikhil and Tadjoura, and it includes two *méhariste* (camel-mounted) platoons as well as foot soldiers.

The militia's *esprit de corps* was proved during the 1930's in the campaigns to establish order among the turbulent nomad tribes, and again later during the period of Italian aggression. Because of the loyalty shown by his militiamen to Bernard at Morheito in 1935 and the effectiveness of this force in opposing Italian penetration on the eve of World War II, its value was further enhanced in the eyes of the local administration.* Although the usefulness of the militia has never been questioned, the matter of its financing has given rise to some debate. Initially this expenditure was met from the budget of the French Overseas Ministry, but in the early 1950's, when the militia numbered 360 men, the Territory was made responsible for its upkeep.[23] In 1956, local politicians began complaining that this was too great a burden for the territorial revenues to support,[24] and Hassan Gouled urged that the French government finance it as a part of overseas defense. Finally, in 1957, France agreed to assume the cost of maintaining the militia, which that year amounted to 62 million Metro. francs.

The wide variations in the strength of the armed forces stationed in French Somaliland have accurately mirrored the fluctuating estimates by Paris at different times of its strategic importance to France.

The small garrison of one sergeant and 20 men who accompanied Lagarde to French Somaliland in 1884 was for some years the only military force in the Territory.[25] At the time of the Fashoda incident near the end of the century, French Somaliland's reputation as a military stronghold was fairly high, but after Marchand was forced to withdraw, it fell very low. Obock remained a secondary outlying station for the French navy, but after 1900 it lost even that modest classification.[26] For the ensuing 15 years the only armed forces stationed there were a small native militia and a Somali company that formed part of the first mixed regiment of Madagascar. During World War I, a detachment of Senegalese *tirailleurs*† was sent to French Somaliland to defend Djibouti, which became a minor base for the Allies'

---

* See pp. 11, 14.

† Senegalese is the term loosely applied to all Negro troops from French tropical Africa. In the case of French Somaliland, the "Senegalese" were mainly from Soudan, Guinea, and Tchad.

campaigns in the Middle East. Locally, the *tirailleurs'* sole military achievement was the interception north of Tadjoura of a German military mission en route from Arabia to Ethiopia.

During the interwar period, France decided to form a permanent Somali company composed of native tribesmen. The Paris authorities had been favorably impressed by the enthusiasm of the local inhabitants in responding to the wartime appeal of France for recruits and by the bravery of the Somalis under fire on the Western front.* To be sure, the tribesmen, although courageous, were individual warriors rather than soldiers, and they were both unstable and resistant to discipline. However, the militia was then hard pressed to cope with the turbulence in the frontier area, and the new company proved valuable in helping to maintain order there. Together with the Senegalese company and a tiny French air force, these troops formed the Territory's entire garrison until the mid-1930's.

The outbreak of hostilities between Ethiopia and Italy in 1935 led to a reorganization and strengthening of French Somaliland's defenses. The troops stationed there were detached from the Madagascar command and a French colonel was assigned to command them. Two more Senegalese companies, equipped with artillery and armored cars, were sent in as reinforcements. To protect the railroad headquarters and workshops, a company of French troops was briefly stationed at Diré Daoua in Ethiopia. After the signing of the Laval-Mussolini agreement, however, the Territory's garrison was once more weakened. This respite did not last long, and the growing aggressiveness of the Italians in 1938 determined Paris at long last to create an effective defense of Djibouti's port and airfield. Far stronger and better-equipped reinforcements than ever before were sent, and fortifications were built around the capital. By the time World War II broke out, there were stationed in French Somaliland six Senegalese battalions, one Somali and one Malagasy battalion, and an air squadron, and a naval command post had been set up at Djibouti. Although some of these forces were withdrawn to serve in Europe, most of them remained to sit out the years during which the Territory remained under Vichy's control.† Consequently, when French Somaliland changed sides late in 1942, it brought as a dowry to its new Free French masters three Senegalese battalions, one mixed Somali-Malagasy battalion, and all of its tanks and artillery. Most of these troops and equipment were then assigned to the Free French command in the Middle East theater, and in 1944 a Somali battalion was recruited for the war in North Africa and Europe. It remained in Tunisia

* See p. 10.
† See pp. 16–21.

nearly a year, and by the time it arrived in France in March 1945, it had been integrated with the regiment from French Equatorial Africa. The members of this battalion distinguished themselves in combat, even though belatedly, as their predecessors had done during World War I.

After V-E Day, French Somaliland's garrison was again reduced, as had always been the case when an immediate danger seemed to be past. As of 1949, only two battalions, one Senegalese and the other Somali, were stationed there, along with two French detachments, one of the navy and the other of the air force.[27] A French Union Assembly mission sent to study the Territory's defenses in 1954–55 was shocked at their inadequacy.[28] Its members did not, however, recommend increasing the number of troops beyond their existing strength of 1,400 men, nor did they urge increasing the funds allotted to the Territory's defense, which at the time amounted to 1 billion Metro. francs annually. They insisted, nevertheless, on the need to reorient the local military effort toward a better air defense of the port and city. Although Djibouti was then classified as a naval outlying station (*point d'appui*), it was wholly unprepared for either submarine or air attack.

Subsequently, Djibouti's port and airfield were steadily enlarged, but little was done to improve their defenses until after the early 1960's had brought independence to all of France's tropical African territories and peace to Algeria. Then it was considered advisable to transfer to Somaliland some of the troops that had been stationed in North and West Africa. Early in 1964 a first contingent of 1,000 Foreign Legionnaires arrived, some 800 of whom were Germans. Djibouti greeted them with mixed emotions. Their presence seemed to insure the Territory against Somalia's irredentism, and the tradesmen were pleased because the well-paid Legionnaires were free spenders. On the other hand, many residents of Djibouti were uneasy about the influx of hundreds of Germans and the prospect of their brawling in the streets and bars.[29]

The political repercussions of the presence of a large garrison in Somaliland formed another aspect of the problem that gave concern. During the first postwar political campaigns, the "Senegalese" troops used their recently acquired rights as French citizens to vote in the local elections. To be sure, these alien Negro citizens were not very numerous, but they were transients in the Territory and constituted an appreciable mass of voters compared with the meager native electorate of that period. It was even proposed in the National Assembly[30] that they should vote as members of the first college or form a special electoral circumscription of the second college. No steps were taken to alter the existing situation, however, probably because a better equilibrium was gradually established by the progressive enfranchisement of the native population, beginning in 1951. Yet seven years later, French and foreign critics of the handling of the referendum of September 1958 returned to the charge, complaining that, on such a vital issue as the Territory's future status, alien military forces—both Metropolitan and Negro—should not have been allowed to vote.* The persistence of this imbalance in the electorate gave substance to the Somali nationalists' contention that the military forces in French Somaliland had become arbiters of the political situation there, and that the administration by exerting pressure on them could and did influence the outcome in its favor.

As for the indigenous armed forces, including veterans of the two world wars, they seem to have played no political role as an organized group. Perhaps this was due to their lack of leadership, to indifference, or to the fact that their total number was small. Only once, after the controversial elections of late 1955, did the veterans make a political gesture, albeit a negative one. They prevented the traditional Armistice Day parade from taking place by lying down in the streets through which it was to pass.[31] This incident, however, seems to have merely reflected a widespread malaise among the local population and not to have been a political demonstration by the veterans as such. Rather tardily, as compared with its action in other tropical dependencies, France moved to improve the status of Somaliland's veterans and their families. Late in 1964 the government opened at Djibouti a Centre pour la Promotion Sociale des Anciens Combattants, where veterans and their wives and daughters could receive help and instruction from a trained staff.[32]

When General de Gaulle visited Djibouti in August 1966, its garrison numbered 3,650 men, 3,000 of whom were troops of the land forces, 150 were sailors, and the balance were air force personnel.[33] The explosive demonstrations that occurred then and in September were succeeded by a period of tension, which mounted as the date of the March 19, 1967, referendum approached. To cope with this threatening situation, the local garrison was progressively increased. On this occasion, however, France took care not to lay itself open to the political charge of sending such reinforcements with a view to determining the outcome of the referendum vote. The great majority of the troops stationed in French Somaliland on March 19, 1967, were precluded from voting by the requirement that alien French citizens must have resided continuously in the Territory during the preceding three years.

Among the troops that arrived at Djibouti toward the end of 1966 was

* See pp. 69–71.

the famous 13th Demi-Brigade of the Foreign Legion, which had gained relevant experience in dealing with a native revolt in Algeria. Both its experience and its tactics were demonstrated in the handling of the riots started by the Djibouti Somalis as soon as the official results of the referendum were announced. To supplement its efforts, 300 paratroopers were flown into the Territory, so that by the end of March the armed forces there numbered over 10,000 men. Djibouti became a town in fact, even if not officially, under a state of siege. The barbed-wire enclosure that had been installed months before to keep out foreigners from Somalia, who were infiltrating Djibouti with a view to influencing the outcome of the referendum, was patrolled day and night, and the area around the native quarters was mined. Foreign correspondents who were in Djibouti to witness the referendum were appalled by the brutality with which the native rioters were treated by the soldiers.[34] The troops, aided by the police and militia, rounded up for deportation many thousands of Somalis who could not produce identity cards showing that they were bona fide residents of the Territory. The methods used on this occasion were certainly harsh, but the significant questions remain: were they necessary and were they effective?

In conducting this referendum, France had foresightedly refrained from direct intervention, and the local administration was not charged with fraud or tampering with the ballot boxes. Nevertheless, the presence of so many troops in the Territory weighed down the atmosphere and had an undoubted psychological effect on the populace. Furthermore, by permitting the military to take over responsibility for maintaining order as a result of the riots of March 21, the administration has probably inadvertently created political problems for itself in the future. The troops may have to remain for a long period in Djibouti. As Philippe Decraene, the *Le Monde* correspondent, reported on March 22, 1967, the military presence seemed in any case not only excessive but dangerously inadvisable under the circumstances. A majority of the Territory's inhabitants had just voted in favor of continued association with France; Somalia, although vociferously displeased by the outcome of the vote, was in no position to contest it by force of arms; and Ethiopia, the only neighboring country having a powerful and well-equipped army, declared itself satisfied with the verdict of the referendum.

Chapter Four

THE POLITICAL SCENE

It has often been asserted that before World War II the various tribal groups in French Somaliland lived together in peace and harmony, if largely in mutual ignorance. This was not wholly true, for the Arabs' preeminence during the interwar period had evoked the antagonism of the indigenous tribes to the point of occasional violence, but the basis of the discord was economic competition.* Certainly the extension of French citizenship to all natives of the Territory in 1946, and later the election of territorial representatives to the French Parliament and the local council, exacerbated this hostility and also led to other intertribal conflicts. Early in 1949 it became apparent that racialism would be the dominant force in French Somaliland's internal politics.

To what extent the Europeans in the Territory contributed to this development has been the subject of considerable controversy. It is true that in the early postwar years they formed an electorate whose size was disproportionate to their numerical though not to their economic importance.† Only gradually, however, did the conservative element among them, organized into the R.P.F., gain ascendancy in the local elections through the support of high officials of the administration and the big business enterprises of Djibouti. French Somaliland's first deputy to the National Assembly was Jean Martine, an electrician employed by the railroad company, whose political views were decidedly left of center. His advocacy of universal suffrage and the single electoral college in the National Assembly[1] won him the enmity of the European conservatives in the Territory, who branded him a communist sympathizer. This he warmly denied, and he joined the I.O.M. rather than any of the radical parties in the Parliament. The attempt made to saddle him with responsibility for the cession of Afambo to Ethiopia in 1949,‡ however, was more successful, and he was decisively beaten by the R.P.F. candidate, Colonel Edmond Magendie, in the next legislative election, in June 1951.

* See pp. 31–33.   † See pp. 34–35.   ‡ See pp. 105–7.

From that time until 1956, the political scene in French Somaliland was dominated by the R.P.F., which not only won all the seats in the first section of the representative council in April 1952, but managed to elect as president of that body the European head of the chamber of commerce in 1955. This, however, proved to be the high point locally of both R.P.F. and European influence in local politics, although the votes of the Metropolitan French residents of the Territory were probably decisive in determining the outcome of the referendum of September 1958. In January 1956, the European candidate for election to the National Assembly, Michel Habib-Deloncle, was defeated by the Issa politician, Mahmoud Harbi, and thereafter internal politics in French Somaliland were controlled by native French citizens. Paradoxically, the elimination of European political influence did not diminish but instead reinforced the role played by racial feeling in the politics and economy of the Territory. It is noteworthy that it was Harbi's charge to the effect that Habib-Deloncle was not a white Frenchman but a Jew that reportedly won him the votes of all the Muslim electorate which carried him to victory.[2]

The first overt political manifestation of ethnic loyalties and enmities occurred in January 1949, about a month after the Gadaboursi candidate, Djama Ali, had been elected to the Conseil de la République. His election, as well as that of the Arab, Ali Coubèche, to the French Union Assembly and of Jean Martine to the National Assembly, had passed off calmly. In part this was because the law required the three main ethnic groups in the Territory to vote as separate electorates. It was also in part the result of the absence at the time of any political parties and the inexperience of the electorate, which had not yet learned to associate the holding of political office with both prestige and material advantages.

Because the Somalis as one ethnic group could elect only a single candidate, the two main *fractions* of that tribe in Djibouti, the Issas and Gadaboursis, each strove to win that honor for one of its own members. The Issas, however, who were far less educated and enterprising than the Gadaboursis, could turn up only two men who had some schooling and knowledge of Western ways. After both of them had refused to run, the Issas reluctantly had to vote for the Gadaboursi candidate, Djama Ali. To celebrate his victory, the Gadaboursis brought in singers and poets from their native village in British Somaliland and generally behaved in a manner that the Issas found unbecoming in "outsiders." Reportedly the Gadaboursis even went so far as to say that Djama Ali, now a senator, would help them to evict the Issas from the Territory.[3] The Issas then tried to undermine Djama Ali by denigrating him as only a former sailor whose sole qualification for office was his ability to speak a little French. They also claimed that he was a British subject who had been born in Zeila and had fraudulently obtained a certificate attesting to his birth at Djibouti in 1910.[4] By tactlessly gloating over their electoral victory, the Gadaboursis goaded the Issas to action.

On January 18, 1949, Djama Ali was walking in a street of the native quarter of Djibouti when he received so hard a blow on the head that he fell unconscious, and the policeman who went to his rescue was also attacked by Issa assailants. Djama Ali, upon recovering, hastily departed for France, but he made the mistake of returning to Djibouti the following summer, against the advice of Governor Siriex. By that time, intertribal hostilities had been revived by the debate going on in the French Union Assembly concerning the government's proposal to revise the ethnic division of seats in the representative council. Djama Ali's reappearance in Djibouti on August 18 touched off severe clashes between Issas and Gadaboursis, for which each side blamed the other. Some Issas claimed that the Gadaboursi workers had begun the battle, whereas the Gadaboursis insisted that it was the Issas who started it by throwing stones at their houses. At all events, both sides used not only daggers but guns, which had apparently been taken in large numbers from the stores of firearms left behind by the Italian troops in 1941.[5] The French army intervened and restored order after 300 arrests had been made, but the casualty list included 38 dead and 100 wounded. This episode ended Djama Ali's senatorial career and also the Gadaboursis' political ambitions, but not the Issas' belligerence. Within a few months a conflict broke out within their own ranks over choosing a candidate to fill Djama Ali's place, and even before that the Issas took on a more formidable adversary than the Gadaboursis—the Arab community of Djibouti.

The riches amassed by the Djibouti Arabs had long made them an object of envy on the part of the indigenous tribesmen.* Then, in the early postwar years the Arabs became the objects of further resentment because of their success in the political field. They easily elected Ali Coubèche, the son of Djibouti's richest Arab merchant, to fill the Territory's seat in the French Union Assembly. In Paris, Coubèche put pressure on the French Somaliland deputy, Jean Martine, to sponsor and succeed in having adopted—in a law of July 13, 1948—a proposal enfranchising in the Territory all who could read and write French or Arabic. Some of the volatile Issas decided

* See pp. 31–34.

that the time had come to prevent such a buildup of the Arabs' preponderance. At eight o'clock in the evening of October 19, 1949, four Arabs seated in front of the house of Ali Coubèche's father were shot by four masked men. Ali's brother Mohammed was killed and the three other men were wounded, among them the president of the Young Arabs Club.[6] It is difficult to understand why these men were the targets of the Issas, and, strangely enough, neither the Agence France Presse nor the Paris dailies carried any mention of this event. Probably the Issas chose to attack Ali Coubèche's influential family as a dramatic way of challenging the whole Arab community. A year later, three men believed to have been responsible for the shootings were brought to trial; one was acquitted and the other two were sentenced to two years of forced labor.[7] Although the Arabs were not frightened away from participating in local politics, the Issas' explosive reaction taught them to be more discreet. Since that time they have operated through non-Arab politicians.

Theoretically, the selection of a successor to fill Djama Ali's seat in the senate should not have caused difficulties, because the choice now rested solely with the Issas, but in fact it led to a rift among them which had far-reaching consequences. To select their candidate the elders of the two main Issa *fractions* living in French Somaliland met together to choose between Hassan Gouled, the candidate of the Abgals, and Mahmoud Harbi, sponsored by the Dalols. After a long discussion, the elders agreed on Hassan Gouled because he belonged to the Abgal *fraction* (which, by tradition, held precedence over the Dalols), and they asked Harbi to withdraw his candidacy. Harbi, however, supported by the younger Dalols, refused, saying that ancient customs had no relevance to present-day politics. His obstinacy angered the elders, and they persuaded the native members of the representative council to support their stand that such a flouting of tradition was intolerable. Hassan Gouled's subsequent election to the Conseil de la République in 1952 made Harbi his implacable enemy, and the rivalry between these two men, in Paris and in Djibouti, dominated territorial politics for the next eight years. Hassan Gouled, who had been born in Djibouti in 1916 and had worked there as a contractor until 1952, was better educated and more poised and reasonable than Harbi, but he lacked the latter's flair for oratory and popular leadership. Harbi, who has been described as an "illiterate in both French and Arabic," was even more politically opportunistic and unstable than his rival. Ironically enough, in view of his later history, Harbi was initially a protégé of the R.P.F., which is said to have financed a study trip to France for him early in his career.

After his defeat in the senatorial elections at the hands of tribal authority,

Harbi turned to the leadership of Somali labor as a more promising path to power. To obtain the money needed to launch him in this new career, he cultivated the friendship of wealthy Arabs, but he was prudent enough at the time to seek patrons outside of Djibouti. Harbi hit upon the ingenious scheme of acquiring two lions, which he presented to the Imam of Yemen and the King of Saudi Arabia, and those rulers, in the customary Oriental manner, gave him funds in return for his gifts. He also won financial support from Aden's labor leaders, allegedly by promising to call a strike that would tie up Djibouti's port. In July 1953, soon after his return from Arabia to Djibouti, a minor dispute between the Société des Pétroles and its labor force gave him the opportunity to make good on his promise. He was able to transform the dispute into a general strike that paralyzed the port of Djibouti for four days. All the strikers' demands were met, and this earned great popularity for Harbi.

In January 1956 he ran successfully for election to the National Assembly, defeating eight other candidates, among whom were the two former deputies of the Territory, Martine and Magendie. He thus emerged as far stronger politically than Hassan Gouled, who, although still senator, had failed to be reelected to the representative council on October 30, 1955. Harbi's only other possible competitor at the moment was Mohammed Kamil, the first Afar in the Territory to achieve political prominence. Kamil had been born at Obock in 1917 and was an accountant in the public works administration. He had been appointed by the governor to represent organized labor in the first representative council, and had remained a member of that body until elected to the French Union Assembly in October 1953. After completing his term there he was elected to the Conseil de la République in April 1959. Unlike Hassan Gouled, however, with whom he briefly joined forces, he was also elected to the representative council in 1955 and reelected to it in 1958. Not for some years, nevertheless, did he become a political force in French Somaliland comparable to either Harbi or Hassan Gouled, and the feud between these two men continued to dominate the political stage.

Their rivalry took a new turn in the mid-1950's, as a result of an imprudent statement attributed to Hassan Gouled.[8] Allegedly he expressed the wish that all foreigners should be expelled from Djibouti, beginning with the Arabs, who—he is supposed to have said—were corrupt and were trying to sow discord between the French and the Somalis. Harbi publicly took up the defense of the foreign community, the alien Somalis as well as the Arabs, and asserted that Hassan Gouled was their common enemy. Inasmuch as all who professed Islam were brothers regardless of race, he asserted, Hassan

Gouled was guilty of attacking his fellow Muslims. Harbi's championship of Djibouti's numerous foreign communities was shrewd. He established such close relations with Ali Coubèche in particular and with the Arabs in general that they gave him substantial material support. Hassan Gouled had made a grave mistake in turning against himself not only the Muslims but also those foreigners who formed the only wealthy element in Djibouti's population. As a result, the size of his following shrank steadily, and it was reduced to members of his own tribal *fraction* and persons who wanted his help in getting jobs. To offset Harbi's new alliance with the Arabs, Hassan Gouled turned to the rising young Afar politician, Mohammed Kamil, in the hope of strengthening the forces of opposition to Harbi.

The elections of June 23, 1957, to the territorial assembly had special significance in that they were the first held in French Somaliland under the *loi-cadre*. This meant that all men (but not women) 21 years of age and over could vote, as a single electoral college, and that the composition of the new assembly would determine membership in the government council, the Territory's embryonic cabinet.* Inevitably the adoption of the *loi-cadre* on June 23, 1956, revitalized the rivalry between Harbi and Hassan Gouled, and the struggle was carried on both in Paris and in the Territory. This led to the forming in French Somaliland of the Territory's first genuine political parties. These were Harbi's Union Républicaine, whose support came from Djibouti's alien communities, and Hassan Gouled's Défense des Intérêts Economiques et Sociaux du Territoire (D.I.E.S.T.), whose adherents comprised his own Issa *fraction* and the Afar supporters of Mohammed Kamil. The more important phase of this electoral competition was carried on in the Paris Parliament, where Harbi in the National Assembly, Mohammed Kamil in the French Union Assembly, and Hassan Gouled in the Conseil de la République each strove to formulate decrees applying the *loi-cadre* to the Territory which would favor his own party.

Late in 1956, Harbi drafted a decree that was debated on April 10, 1957, in the National Assembly. He proposed creating a fourth electoral circumscription and enlarging the representative council to 32 members, of which Djibouti would choose 20 and the three other circumscriptions four each. Kamil, in the French Union Assembly session of April 4, 1957, spoke in favor of no change in the number of existing circumscriptions but a revision in the council's size and membership that would allot only 13 seats to Djibouti and give six seats each to Obock–Tadjoura and Ali-Sabieh–Dikhil. His colleagues in that Assembly found a 30-member council too large for

* See p. 44.

so small a Territory and reduced the total to 25. As for the new government council, one European assemblyman said that it was ridiculous for French Somaliland to have a Minister of Agriculture whose only possible task would be to grow lettuce for the governor's table and pick dates from Obock's small palm grove. In the Conseil de la République, Hassan Gouled naturally supported the proposals of his ally Mohammed Kamil, with the additional suggestion that the name of representative council be changed to that of territorial assembly.

The French government and members of the Parliament were bewildered by the contradictory views of the Territory's several representatives, who could not even agree as to the size of their country's population, Harbi maintaining that it numbered 80,000 whereas Kamil claimed that it was only 65,000. Moreover, the French politicians were preoccupied with the larger African tropical dependencies and Madagascar, and their predilection for uniformity inclined them to lump together and find a common electoral solution for "les petits territoires" of the Comoro Islands, New Caledonia, Polynesia, and French Somaliland. The compromise eventually reached gave the Territory a 30-member elected body to be called the territorial assembly, in which Djibouti was assigned 18 seats and Tadjoura–Obock and Ali-Sabieh–Dikhil six each. As to the electorate, only those Europeans who had lived in the Territory for a year would be allowed to vote, with the result that the registered voters there now numbered 11,676. Of these, 7,635 were in Djibouti circumscription, 1,944 in Tadjoura–Obock, and 2,097 in Ali-Sabieh–Dikhil.

Meanwhile, the rivalry in French Somaliland between the two fledgling parties became more acute as election day neared. Each party held meetings several times a week and issued frequent bulletins in which leaders of the opposition were castigated in specific and general charges based on the theme that they were sacrificing the people's interests in their insatiable thirst for personal power. Despite the D.I.E.S.T.'s feverish activity, however, the Union Républicaine won the election by 4,180 votes to its rival's 3,494, in a turnout of 68 percent of the electorate. Under the prevailing system of winner-take-all, Harbi's party filled all 30 seats in the new assembly. Hassan Gouled and Mohammed Kamil at once contested Harbi's victory, alleging irregularities in the counting of votes and partiality on the part of the administration. They asked for a parliamentary mission of investigation and took their case to the courts. The Minister of Overseas France defended the local administration and cited as evidence of its impartiality the circulars that Governor Petitbon had sent to his subordinates instructing them to maintain strict neutrality during the campaign and the election. After some months, the court validated the announced results, the new government council having been set up in the interval.

Harbi, as leader of the winning party, naturally became its vice-president, the office of president being held ex officio by the governor. Appropriately enough, Harbi named Ali Coubèche as Finance Minister in return for his tangible campaign support, and to the sole Frenchman in his cabinet, Pierre Blin, he gave the Education portfolio. Ibrahim Sultan and Osman Ali Bahden, both Issas, became respectively Minister of Health and Minister of the Civil Service, and to an Issack, Hamed Hassan Liban, went the important post of Interior. As Harbi occupied the three top positions of deputy, Minister of the Port and Public Works, and vice-president of the government council, he felt strong enough to dissolve the Union Républicaine party and to move decisively against his political enemies. Not only did he penalize or dismiss from their posts all of Kamil's and Hassan Gouled's followers, including a French teacher who had edited the D.I.E.S.T.'s bulletin, but he also plotted the downfall of his arch-foe, the senator from French Somaliland.

When the elders and okal of the Issa and Afar tribes learned that Harbi was planning to maneuver the election of his friend Ahmed Goumané (then vice-president of the assembly) as Hassan Gouled's successor in the senatorial elections of June 8, 1958, they protested to Harbi as vehemently and as vainly as before. Hassan Gouled himself, fully aware of Harbi's power, did not want to seek reelection, but he was persuaded to do so when the tribal leaders assured him that they could guarantee the support of the territorial assembly. Harbi countered by inviting all the assemblymen, just before the senatorial election, to his home and plying them so copiously with food and drink that when they finally emerged to vote on the morning of June 8, 1958, only six of them voted for Hassan Gouled.[9] Local gossip gives this story an appropriately seriocomic ending. When the new senator left for France, he took with him the wife of a prominent merchant in Diré Daoua. Members of the D.I.E.S.T. party so publicized this affair in their bulletin that the tribal authorities took action. They told Ahmed Goumané that he must either pay compensation to the deprived husband or return his wife. The new senator sent her back to Djibouti and thus settled his tribal account, but the incident harmed his prestige politically. Within a few weeks he and Harbi parted ways, although only temporarily.

A month before the above-mentioned senatorial elections took place, the coup at Algiers occurred that brought General de Gaulle back to power in France. That event, and the profound changes wrought by the General in

France's constitution, introduced a new element into the Territory's politics, which until then had been dominated wholly by local issues. To be sure, the perennial dependence of the Territory's economy on French bounty had given rise to some criticism in regard to the amount of aid and its allocation to the different services and projects. On several occasions in the Senate Hassan Gouled had criticized French subsidies as inadequate and had urged the training of native aspirants to fill the posts held by the over-numerous expatriate officials.* Harbi, too, in the National Assembly had asked that France pay a larger share of the Territory's expenditures and provide a special fund for the training of 30 Somali students in French institutions of higher learning.[10]

These two men, sworn political enemies at home, saw eye to eye on the need for enlargement and reorientation of France's economic policy in Somaliland, but until the summer of 1958 neither ever publicly questioned the existing political relationship between France and French Somaliland. Indeed, Hassan Gouled, writing in a Metropolitan publication in July 1957, stated that "the Territory has only one desire and true interest, that is, to grow alongside France in fidelity and reciprocal confidence and sympathy, and in the climate created ... by the *loi-cadre*."[11] For his part, Harbi, in a "public act of faith" on the occasion of the 1958 anniversary of the famous June 18, 1940, appeal, proclaimed his personal devotion and loyalty to De Gaulle, recalling proudly that he himself had served with the Free French forces.[12] This situation was drastically altered, however, during the following months by the General's decision to hold a referendum in September 1958 on the constitution of the Fifth Republic. The choice to be offered to the overseas populations would be between total independence and joining a new Franco-African Community, in which their territories could become autonomous republics or maintain the status quo.

If the official alternatives outlined above had been the only ones open to the people of French Somaliland on September 28, 1958, a decision would have been comparatively easy to reach. But an extraneous element had come into the picture as the result of developments in neighboring countries. By the summer of 1958 it was already apparent that Somalia would soon become an independent republic and that it would thereafter be joined by British Somaliland. Great Britain had openly encouraged the Greater Somalia movement, whose aim was to bring under the flag of the future republic all the Somalis living in the Horn of Africa. Thus a real if un-

* See pp. 49, 144.

written third choice faced the population of the Territory, especially after Harbi openly espoused the cause of independence and of eventual union with Somalia.

Within five weeks after his declaration of faith in France and General de Gaulle, Harbi had begun to hedge, as was evident from an interview he gave *Le Monde* in Paris on July 24, 1958. In that daily he was quoted as expressing gratitude to France for enabling the Territory to hold a "privileged position" in the Horn of Africa and to resist the encroachments of its neighbors. Then he added significantly: "We want to continue our evolution toward independence and to counter external influences without separating ourselves from France." In a second statement also reported in *Le Monde,* on August 7, it was apparent that he had now taken the plunge: "The independence we ask for is neither divorce nor secession. . . . Our choice has been made: it is with France that we shall form a bloc inside a fraternal alliance whose form will be determined after we have obtained our independence."

The full implications of Harbi's change of front were not immediately seized at Djibouti, where his followers in the former Union Républicaine had already taken a stand in favor of the new constitution. The government council, even though composed wholly of his appointees, was so shocked that it refused to publicize Harbi's statement. Its members even cabled the Paris government that Harbi was expressing only his personal views.[13] Naturally the D.I.E.S.T. party joyfully seized upon this rift between Harbi and his erstwhile supporters. Hassan Gouled at once declared himself a strong advocate of the new constitution and of the referendum as a means of learning the population's wish in regard to its future.[14] More than a year earlier, Hassan Gouled had also expressed in writing his wish for friendly relations with Ethiopia but not absorption of the Territory by that country or by Somalia. He also foresaw the merger of British Somaliland with Somalia, and added that French Somaliland would not be "the dowry brought to such a union."[15]

Early in September 1958, Governor Meker received two declarations, one signed by Senator Goumané and Ibrahim Sultan, and the other by the officers of the territorial assembly, as well as a delegation of 50 Issa Notables. All of them expressed approval of the Territory's joining the new Franco-African Community. On the eve of the referendum, therefore, it seemed that Harbi had been deserted by all of his former followers except his own Issa *fraction* and the Issacks, who enthusiastically endorsed his stand. It was they who swarmed by the hundreds to greet Harbi at the airport upon his return from Paris on the evening of September 18. In overloaded taxis and trucks they noisily escorted him through the streets of Djibouti and applauded vociferously the speech that he made to them at 2 o'clock in the morning, in which he denounced the proposed constitution and extolled the benefits of independence and of union with Somalia.[16] Ten days later, 11,733 of the Territory's 15,914 registered voters went to the polls; 8,882 of them voted in favor of the constitution and 2,851 for independence.

In view of this clear-cut outcome, it is interesting to speculate on the reasons why Harbi came to advocate a negative vote in the referendum. The success of his campaign in favor of independence depended upon two major factors. One was the degree to which the local population desired or feared the merger with Somalia, and the other was what political and economic concessions could be expected from France if a majority voted in favor of the constitution. Those concessions had not been spelled out, and the only certain advantages resulting from perpetuation of French rule were that the Territory would continue to receive financial aid and that it would not be swallowed up by either Ethiopia or Somalia. The report that Ethiopian troops were being massed along the frontier for action, in case the vote should be in favor of independence, undoubtedly influenced the Afars to favor the constitution. Furthermore, they were strongly opposed to any union with Somalia, for the result would be that the numerical superiority of the more enterprising and evolved Somalis would hopelessly submerge them. Under colonial rule the lid had been kept on overt manifestations of the age-old hostility between the two tribes, although occasionally it came to the surface. One highly qualified foreign observer noted that fights between Afars and Somalis still occurred in the Territory, and in January 1957 he himself witnessed a small riot between them at Djibouti.[17] To assuage the Afars' resentment of the Somalis' superior position, as well as to widen the base of his political support, Harbi had named two Afar ministers in his cabinet—but he had only papered over the breach. His stand in favor of independence and of union with Somalia alienated the Afars, who voted massively in favor of continued French rule.

As for the Issas, almost none of their leaders thought that an independent Somaliland would be economically viable without French aid. Moreover, it was not at all certain that a majority of them favored union with Somalia, and the Issas were split by the contradictory views held by the two leading Issa politicians. In the opinion of the foremost English analyst of the Somalis, those in French territory were less affected by external influences than their fellow tribesmen in British Somaliland, and were more strongly devoted to their traditional mode of life. "Generally they think of themselves as Issa rather than Somali, and show little evidence of that wider consciousness of nationhood which is manifest, at least to some extent, in Somalia."[18] The well-to-do Arabs would certainly not approve of the Territory's union with impoverished Somalia, which in any case could not provide the same security and stability of government as the French. Consequently, the only group on which Harbi could count for solid support were the Issack laborers, among whom the number of voters had tripled, thanks to the facilities provided by the Issack Minister of Interior. It is also possible that Harbi was unduly encouraged by the promise of support from the Arab League, with which he maintained close contact by frequent visits to Cairo.[19] Certainly the speech made by Harbi on his return from Paris was given wide publicity by the Cairo radio in its Somali-language broadcasts, but this only served to contribute to the population's fear of foreign intervention rather than to increase Harbi's support.

To Harbi, the rejection of his policy by three-fourths of the voters in the referendum did not necessitate his own dismissal as vice-president of the government council, and indeed there existed no law that required him to resign that post. The degree of confusion caused by this situation can be gauged by the chaotic events that took place within the next few weeks. The day after the referendum, six ministers resigned from the government council in repudiation of Harbi's leadership, but soon four of them reconsidered their decision and withdrew their resignations. On October 2, the governor suspended Harbi, Hassan Liban, and Barkhat Dirieh from their posts, and the next day he called an extraordinary meeting of the territorial assembly. He had expected that body to censure Harbi, but instead they voted continued confidence in his leadership. This vote led three ministers to resign, and then Governor Meker dismissed their remaining colleagues, with the result that the government council ceased to exist. On October 5, Senator Goumané, now reconciled with Harbi, flew to Paris to pull whatever chestnuts he could out of the fire. On the following day, Harbi's supporters, who had been organizing an Istiqlal (Independence) Party, reportedly with the help of Somalia, staged a street demonstration in Djibouti. In the ensuing clash with the police, two former ministers were arrested and Harbi and Hassan Liban were slightly injured. This outbreak seems to have brought the Paris authorities, who had been deluged with contradictory cables, to a decision. On October 21 they dissolved the territorial assembly and set November 23 as the date for new elections. At the same time they increased the number of seats in that body to 32 and reallocated them to the three circumscriptions on a proportional basis.

This gerrymandering tactic indicated a marked shift in the French government's policy in the Territory, and one related directly to the ethnic division of votes in the referendum. Until September 1958 the French authorities had tended to favor the more "progressive" Somalis as against the "backward" Afars, but now they were going to reward the Afars' loyalty by giving them greater participation in the Territory's public life. The success of this new policy was assured by a split in the ranks of Harbi's followers into two parties, of which one (the Union Démocratique des Somalis) he headed himself and the other was formed by Senator Goumané. Since each of these parties presented a complete list of 32 candidates, the forces that had made up the old Union Républicaine were weakened and divided. Hassan Gouled's D.I.E.S.T. party, on the other hand, remained largely intact and commanded the support of most of the Afars, despite the formation of two regional Afar parties by Ibrahim Sultan in Tadjoura and by Barkhat Gourat in Ali-Sabieh–Dikhil.

Surprisingly enough, the elections of November 23, 1958, passed off calmly and the electorate's participation was only slightly smaller than for the referendum. Hassan Gouled's party took 25 seats, Harbi's seven, and Goumané's none. This election caused a marked change in the assembly's ethnic composition. In the previous body, the indigenous tribes, the Issas and Afars, each held the same number of seats, the Issacks had two and the Arabs one. In the new assembly, 13 of the 32 seats went to Afars, eight to Issas, four to Europeans, one to an Arab, and five to Issacks who had shrewdly auctioned off their votes to the highest bidder. This confirmed Harbi's dependence on the Issacks, but even with their support there was no doubt that he and his Issa followers had met with a crushing defeat. Hassan Gouled proceeded to form his government council with one European, four Somali, and three Afar ministers. Like his predecessor, he took over the Public Works and Port portfolio, named his ally Mohammed Kamil to the key post of Interior, and appointed a Frenchman, Raymond Pecoul, Minister of Finance and Economic Affairs. The first important act of the new government council and assembly was to vote for the maintenance of French Somaliland as a French Overseas Territory.

Soon after the elections, Harbi took a plane to Paris, where his mandate as deputy was shortly to expire. After his attempt to present his candidacy for reelection by telegram was rejected, and he was even sentenced in absentia to ten years in prison, he began a series of journeys typical of African revolutionary leaders in voluntary exile. With Cairo as headquarters, he made trips to Communist China and eastern Europe, and used radio facilities wherever possible to broadcast appeals to the people of French Somaliland to revolt and join the Somali Republic. Finally he moved to Mogadiscio, where he became one of the most fervent propagandists for

Pan-Somalism, and it was on a trip back to Somalia from China that he was killed in an airplane crash on September 29, 1960. Mahmoud Harbi was certainly the most colorful personality that French Somaliland has produced, but he could not be called a great leader of his people. One of the first acts of his government council was to vote large salaries for him and his ministers. His record showed neither party loyalty nor ideological consistency, but these same lacks have not prevented other African politicians from being idolized and effective national leaders. One astute observer maintains that Harbi's failure was caused by basic defects in his personality. "He was regarded as clever, but not wise, possessing a dictatorial manner which alienated many supporters."[20]

Harbi's death ended the feud with Hassan Gouled that had overshadowed local politics for nearly a decade. Even before it occurred, however, his withdrawal from the Djibouti scene had eliminated the chief obstacle to his rival's climb to the top of the political ladder. Already by April 1959 Hassan Gouled felt strong enough at home to run—successfully—for election to the National Assembly, and he left the post of vice-president of the government council to be filled by an Afar assemblyman, Ahmed Dini. At about the same time, his old ally, Mohammed Kamil, also resigned from the government council and was duly elected to the Conseil de la République, his post of Minister of the Interior also being taken over by a member of the territorial assembly, Youssouf Aptidon Darar.

The withdrawal from the Djibouti arena of the three politicians who had for years been its star performers and the rise of an obscure Afar to the highest place open to an indigenous politician did not result in any dramatic new political developments locally. Ahmed Dini was a relative of the Sultan of Tadjoura and this gave him prestige among his fellow tribesmen, but he was merely a nurse at the Peltier Hospital in Djibouti at the time of his first election to the territorial assembly in 1957. When he became vice-president of the government council, he was only 27 years old and too inexperienced and also too weak to exert leadership over a turbulent population that was increasingly being subjected to external pressures. During his brief incumbency, which lasted from May 16, 1959, to June 8, 1960, the local situation was calm except for a rise in unemployment, and politics in the Territory lapsed to the level of clan and personal quarrels and alliances. Into this relatively tranquil situation, however, were periodically injected sudden and massive doses of Somali nationalism, which created a latent ferment in Djibouti with which Ahmed Dini was unable to cope. So it was comparatively easy for a more energetic, better educated, and equally well-born Afar, Ali Aref Bourhan, to overthrow the Dini government council and replace him as its vice-president. Except for a brief visit to Djibouti by General de Gaulle in the summer of 1959, the main action during the period of Dini's vice-presidency took place in Paris, Mogadiscio, and Addis Ababa.

In the Paris National Assembly, Hassan Gouled began to take Harbi's place as gadfly to the French government. He urged the French authorities, in increasingly strong terms, to grant his Territory greater political autonomy. Hassan Gouled was doubtless motivated to some extent by the need to find a cause that would increase his popular following at home, but he was also spurred on by developments in neighboring countries. On November 12, 1959, the Franco-Ethiopian treaty was signed,* giving notable advantages to Addis Ababa in the railroad's management; during the long negotiations that preceded this agreement, Hassan Gouled and the territorial assembly had been largely ignored. Still more compelling was the announcement that on June 26 and July 1, 1960, respectively, British Somaliland and Somalia would be granted independence, and this incited Harbi to broadcast ever more fervent appeals to the people of French Somaliland to revolt and join their southern neighbors. Moreover, his former party, the Union Démocratique des Somalis, was represented at the meeting that organized the Pan-Somali movement at Mogadiscio on August 30, 1959. General de Gaulle's declaration on July 3, 1959, at Djibouti that "France, no matter what happens elsewhere, will never shirk its humanistic duty here" provided Hassan Gouled with the leverage he needed to exert more pressure on the French government. If the General's hands-off warning to Somali nationalists was to be more than empty words, he argued, France must give more satisfaction to the Territory's aspiration to manage its own affairs and to become a full-fledged member of the Community.

In the year 1960 all of France's tropical dependencies in West and Equatorial Africa became sovereign states, and their example made the political stagnation of French Somaliland seem even more conspicuous than before. Nearer home, British Somaliland and Somalia merged to become the independent Somali Republic on July 1, and this event promised to modify profoundly the future of the Horn of Africa. Less than three weeks later, Hassan Gouled placed before the National Assembly a proposal to revise article 76 of the constitution of the Fifth Republic so as to enable an Overseas Territory to change the statute for which it had earlier opted. As he argued this cause:[21]

* See pp. 107–8.

Before the referendum, formal assurances were given that those territories could change their statute. Now for some of them, including French Somaliland, that time has come. Urgent and imperious political necessities of both an internal and external order absolutely require this territory to evolve if French influence is to be maintained there. To delay this evolution would favor the pernicious activity of a large and growing opposition, which, since 1958, has been working both locally and in foreign countries against the continuation of French protection.

On October 25, Hassan Gouled returned to the charge more vehemently that before. All the power in French Somaliland, he claimed, still lay in the hands of the governor, and the territorial assembly was no more than a sounding board. If the Territory were not granted internal autonomy in the near future, said he, "it may well move in the opposite direction. I am not for one moment dreaming of total secession from France ... and we reject all 'solicitations' whether they come from Moscow, Cairo, or elsewhere. ... But if France insists on maintaining the status quo, time is running out for her.... I have always been a faithful supporter of General de Gaulle and I remain unshakably Gaullist. I repeat that I have confidence in General de Gaulle's policy."

Despite this declaration, Hassan Gouled's warnings apparently went unheeded. Their only perceptible echo was a speech by Governor Compain (who had replaced Governor Meker after the referendum) in which he repeated the General's assurance that France would remain in the Territory. "The departure of such an arbitrator [as France] would lead to certain disaster while tribal rivalries are still acute."[22] There were, however, several unpublicized explanations for France's immobilism in regard to the Territory. A minor one was the creation of an embryonic Issa separatist movement at Zeila in September 1960. There was a slight chance that, if the movement developed, it might hinder the spread of Pan-Somali organizations, although it was equally possible that it might move toward a merger with the Greater Somalia movement.[23] Far more influential with the French authorities were the attitudes assumed by French Somaliland's senator, Mohammed Kamil, and by the vice-president of the government council, Ali Aref. Both men were Afars and therefore were subject to tribal pressures different from those felt by the Issa, Hassan Gouled, and yet they disagreed with each other. Kamil wanted simply to maintain the Territory's status quo, whereas Ali Aref's more sensitive political position required him to keep an open mind. He headed a government council of which all the members were territorial assemblymen and in which the Afars were in a minority, and he had overthrown Dini with the help of Somali assemblymen.* He had to take into consideration Somali nationalism for both political and personal reasons, for he was related by marriage to Mahmoud Harbi. His opposition to the Pan-Somali movement, however, had been made clear in 1958 when he campaigned in favor of the constitution and voted in the Assembly for the status of Overseas Territory.

Not unnaturally, the acquisition of power began to change Ali Aref's views. In his first speech to the territorial assembly after becoming vice-president of the government council, he said that he "counted upon France to lead our country in the direction in which all Africa is traveling."[24] He seemed content, nevertheless, with Premier Debré's cabled assurance that "if in the years to come an evolution is recognized as being desirable and profitable, France would not oppose changes and modifications in the law resulting from the freely expressed wishes of the population." In July 1960 he went to Paris, where, in an interview published in *Le Monde* the following August 5, he is quoted as having said: "I believe we still have a long road to go with France before changing our statute." Yet in a broadcast he made after talking with the Paris authorities, he indicated that the tempo of change would be accelerated, adding, "I shall try to make modifications in it (the *loi-cadre*) so that we may move forward to complete sovereignty."

At that time Ali Aref began to be more concerned by the possible expansionism of Ethiopia than by that of Somalia. As an Afar he wanted good relations with Ethiopia for economic reasons, "but in other domains we have reservations, mainly because of the lot of the important Afar minority in Ethiopia, who are our ethnic brothers and who are not treated there as we would like them to be."[25] The abortive coup d'état against the Ethiopian ruler in December 1960 apparently added to Ali Aref's concern over events in that country. Rumors spread in Djibouti to the effect that Nasser had inspired the coup as part of an overall program of extending his control throughout the Horn of Africa.[26] Perhaps in consequence of the rumors, Ali Aref's government council formally asked the French government for a revision of the Territory's statute, and the territorial assembly voted to send a mission to Paris to discuss the subject.

Ali Aref having thus gravitated much closer to the position taken by Hassan Gouled, leaving Kamil as the only one of the Territory's three main political leaders in favor of maintaining the status quo, the Paris authorities at long last made a cautious move. In February 1961 they sent a Minister of State, Robert Lecourt, to study the situation at first hand, but the only clear conclusion that could be reached after his visit was that the gulf that sep-

* His council was composed of three Afars (including himself), a European, and four Somalis.

arated the Somalis from the Afars had widened. For his benefit, a demonstration was staged at Djibouti port (where he was hissed by the dockers) in favor of internal autonomy, but its inspiration was open to contradictory interpretations. Hassan Gouled asserted that "massive peaceful demonstrations including all the indigenous ethnic groups" had occurred not only at Djibouti but also in the hinterland *cercles,* in which the participants demanded internal autonomy inside the Community and a wholly elected government as well as territorial assembly. Kamil, by that time completely at odds with his former political ally, retorted: "It is totally false to claim that all the indigenous tribes demonstrated in favor of autonomy at the time of the Minister's visit. These manifestations were the work of some Somalis, among whom there are numerous foreigners.... The Danakil refuse to accept any precipitate action that would be the work of a minority leading to a Greater Somalia, of which they want no part."[27] The territorial assembly, fearing that such discordant views would perpetuate the stalemate and also might alienate France, passed a resolution on March 23, 1961, to the effect that "all the inhabitants of French Somaliland, no matter what their ethnic origin, are united by the desire to live under the protection of the French flag and to work together for the economic and social development of the Territory." Its members also condemned all attempts to create agitation among the population, "which cannot but harm the economic program."[28]

The French government, nine months after it had declared its willingness to discuss a revision of the Territory's statute, finally invited its assembly to send a delegation to Paris to discuss a draft law on the subject. Just what the official proposals included is not known, beyond a general statement that they would lead to a more equitable division of seats in the assembly between the Somalis and Afars. In sum, however, they were considered inadequate, and the delegation, which included Ali Aref, presented a counterproject that would have left France with control only over foreign affairs, defense, currency, higher education, and the courts of law for Europeans.[29] This was inacceptable to the French authorities, and another attempt the following July to reach an agreement was equally abortive. Ali Aref was reported to have been offended because he was able to discuss the issue only with top-ranking civil servants and not with the highest political authorities. At all events, Paris ignored the subject for some years, despite Hassan Gouled's effort to revive it in the National Assembly meeting of October 25, 1961.

The French government's relapse into inaction with regard to the Territory's statute was based on the not unreasonable assumption that French

Somaliland's traditional rivalries between Afars and Somalis were strong enough to cancel out, or at least neutralize, the contradictory political aspirations of each. Paris also assumed, with less accuracy, that the Territory was immune to serious political agitation because its economic situation was then excellent, but Djibouti's very prosperity was attracting ever more Somali immigrants. Local French officials had little direct contact with Djibouti's inhabitants, and they were lulled into a false sense of security by the absence of overt political activity during the 14 months that followed the failure of negotiations over the Territory's statute. Yet beneath the surface, Somali nationalist sentiments were gathering force, and they found organizational form in the Parti du Mouvement Populaire (P.M.P.), which had been formed in 1960 by local Somali and Arab youths with support from Mogadiscio. It took several years for the P.M.P. to build up organizational strength, and in the meantime the older parties were disintegrating. This left the P.M.P. as the party with the strongest structure and the only one that had a wide appeal for the Territory's youth. It did not come into the open until it had found a Somali leader to inherit the mantle of Mahmoud Harbi, and he became its candidate in the legislative elections of November 18, 1962. This leader was Moussa Ahmed Idriss, a 29-year-old bank employee, who to the general surprise was elected and became French Somaliland's deputy in the National Assembly. Although he received only 4,710 votes and although less than half the registered electorate of 23,862 actually voted, he won four times as many votes as his nearest competitor, the outgoing deputy Hassan Gouled. Despite his repeated efforts to win internal autonomy for the Territory, Hassan Gouled was now regarded as only a moderate Issa leader and not a fervent Somali nationalist.

Another notable if indirect casualty of that election was Senator Kamil, whose current unpopularity was evidenced by the failure of his fellow Afars to support the candidate he sponsored. Not only did the Afars massively abstain from voting, but very few Europeans bothered to go to the polls. The multiplicity of candidates—eight in all—was another factor contributing to Idriss's success. Furthermore, his electoral slogan, cast in rhetorical form, was ambiguous yet up-to-date enough to appeal to a wide range of voters. He asked the electorate: Are you willing to remain in obscurity while Africa is on the march?—but he ended his speeches with the cry, "Vive la Cinquième République!" His election not only marked the entry of the Territory's youth into Djibouti's political arena but reflected a widespread dissatisfaction with those who had long been in power, including Ali Aref, who in the eyes of nationalistic youth had sold out to the French. Less than a month after the election, Ali's appeal to the territorial assembly to have the same firm confidence that he had in the president of the republic further undermined his popularity. It was noted that during the strike at Djibouti's port late in December 1962, Ali Aref was hissed and insulted by the dockers.*

The unexpected turn taken by the November 1962 elections, followed by the growing politicization of the labor movement, as shown by the dockers' strike and the May Day demonstrations in 1963,* led to another politically inspired change in the Territory's voting system. Senator Kamil, with the support and perhaps at the instigation of the French government, placed before the Parliament a proposal aimed at giving the Afars for the first time a majority in the territorial assembly. He proposed a return to the system that had prevailed before the November 1958 elections, in which the party whose candidates won a majority of the votes in a circumscription took all the seats at stake there. More important, his draft law included an increase in the number of electoral circumscriptions from three to seven, on the ground that it was unfair for Djibouti's 9,763 voters, of a registered electorate totaling 27,219, to fill half the seats in the assembly. Under the new arrangement proposed, Tadjoura–Obock would be allocated 11 representatives, Ali-Sabieh two, and Dikhil five, and Djibouti—divided into four electoral circumscriptions—would have 14 instead of 16 assemblymen. To make up for Djibouti's demotion and to give political recognition to that town's exceptional economic importance,† it was to be allowed one representative for every 697 voters, whereas in the rest of the Territory the ratio would be one for every 969.[30]

Moussa Idriss complained, with some reason, that the government council and territorial assembly should have been consulted before the draft proposal came up for parliamentary debate, and he vainly attacked it on a number of grounds. He claimed that it provided further proof of France's progressive infringements of nineteenth-century agreements with the Issa sultans; that Kamil had proposed the law in his own personal interest; that the number of electors in Tadjoura–Obock circumscription was only 3,352, and not the 10,937 officially registered, whereas Djibouti *cercle* had 3,760 more legitimate voters than appeared on the rolls; and he concluded his speech by proposing that all the adult women in the Territory be enfranchised. Idriss was again defeated on another draft law, debated and passed at the same session, which required foreigners to obtain official permission

---

* See p. 225.
† Djibouti *cercle* contributed 98 percent of the territorial revenues to the local budget, Ali-Sabieh 1.5 percent, Dikhil 0.5 percent, and Tadjoura nothing.

to enter the Territory and which imposed penalties on clandestine immigrants. It was no coincidence that this policy of upgrading the Afars was confirmed on September 6, 1963, by the promotion of Obock district to the rank of a *cercle*.

In local politics Moussa Idriss was clearly a promoter and defender of Somali interests, but in regard to external affairs he was not a partisan of the Greater Somalia movement and in the National Assembly he belonged to the Gaullist Union de la Nouvelle République (U.N.R.) party. Furthermore, he signed on September 20, 1963, a statement drafted by Ali Aref expressing loyalty to the French Republic and rejecting all annexationist claims that would jeopardize the territorial integrity of French Somaliland. This statement had been formulated at a meeting held in the hill station of Arta by 80 Afar and Issa representatives, who "frankly and calmly" discussed their old and new tribal grievances and worked out an area of agreement.[31]

The Arta declaration reflected the fears felt by members of both indigenous tribes that so small and weak a territory as theirs would be taken over by their more powerful and aggressive neighbors, as well as the belief that its only hope for survival lay in uniting among themselves under the protection of France. Unfortunately for the Territory's future peace, the declaration brought about only a temporary tribal reconciliation, and it was later undermined by the divisive activities of the nonindigenous communities and of international organizations. However, all the candidates for election to the territorial assembly on November 18, 1963, publicly proclaimed their adherence to its principles and none openly questioned maintaining the existing regime.

The changes made by the French Parliament in the electoral law had been timed to antedate that election, which was contested by 24 lists of candidates in the seven electoral circumscriptions. The campaign was marked by no disorderly episodes, and voter participation was appreciably higher than a year before. Of the 28,728 registered electors, 21,408 actually went to the polls, although the Metropolitan French electors were again conspicuous by their abstention. The number of voters having doubled since 1958, the new territorial assembly had a more widely representative base than at any time before. It also had a very different membership, for 21 of the 32 elected not only were newcomers but were, on the average, much younger than their predecessors. The diversity of their political views was reflected by the election of Ali Aref, Moussa Idriss, Hassan Gouled, Mohammed Kamil, and Barkhat Gourat, and all of these men won by large majorities over their opponents.

Perhaps the most outstanding development indicated by this election was the decline in strength of the P.M.P, which received only 13 percent of the total vote, or 50 percent less than in 1962.[32] One cause of the P.M.P.'s decline was the defeat suffered by its president, Obsieh Boeuh, in his trial of strength with the governor, René Tirant. In a letter to the governor on December 18, 1962, Obsieh Boeuh asserted that France had failed to honor its commitments to the Territory by giving control of the railroad to the government of Addis Ababa in the Franco-Ethiopian treaty of 1959. To this letter the governor replied on January 5, 1963, defending the treaty and citing the economic benefits that the Territory had derived from it.[33] However, in the March issue of *Le Populaire,* the monthly organ of the P.M.P., Obsieh Boeuh claimed that the governor had never replied to his letter, and added that Ethiopia had become such a threat to French Somaliland that "we have the duty of defending our country even at the cost of bloodshed." Despite a warning from Governor Tirant, Obsieh Boeuh persevered in his aggressive statements, with the result that he was brought to trial on the charge of disseminating false news likely to trouble the peace and of harming the Territory's relations with a friendly country. In September 1963 he was tried on the far more serious charge of working to harm the security of the state. The financial difficulties and internal dissensions that beset his party during its president's imprisonment undoubtedly played a part in the P.M.P.'s poor showing in the November 1963 elections, which netted it only six seats in the new territorial assembly.

The Afars, on the other hand, presented a strong and united front at this time, being held together by their common fear of the P.M.P. and Somali nationalism. The great majority of them belonged to the Union Démocratique Afar (U.D.A.), which was headed by Ali Aref, Mohammed Kamil, Ahmed Dini, and Barkhat Gourat. Generally speaking, one-party electorates as determined by the dominant tribe characterized the hinterland circumscriptions, whereas in Djibouti there were 12 different lists of candidates. The ethnic composition of the new assembly and of the government council that emanated from it showed the success of the French government's stratagem of reducing the Somalis' predominance and enhancing that of the Afars in general, and of their leader, Ali Aref, in particular. Twenty assemblymen and four ministers were Afars, seven assemblymen and two ministers were Somalis, four assemblymen and one minister were French, and there was one Arab assemblyman. Ali Aref was reelected vice-president of the government council by a vote of 27 to five, and two of the ministers he appointed were the former deputy Hassan Gouled (Youth and Sports) and a former vice-president of the council,

Ahmed Dini (Agricultural Production and the Plan). Other government councilors were Egué Bouraleh (Interior), Omar Mohammed Bourhan (Civil Service), Barkhat Gourat (Health and Social Affairs), and Abdi Ahmed Warsama (Labor). Ali Aref again took the Public Works and Port portfolio, and was the real leader of the U.D.A., even though its official president was Orbisso Gaddito, a primary-school teacher.

During the first half of 1964, French Somaliland enjoyed a period of unusual political peace. Beginning in August of that year, however, external developments caused a fresh rift in the P.M.P. between the partisans and opponents of the Greater Somalia movement, and dissension also developed among the Afar victors. The traditional jealousy between the Afars of Obock and those of Tadjoura reasserted itself, and in November 1964 Ali Aref maladroitly forced the resignation of two of his ministers for failure to maintain party discipline. The dismissed ministers were Ahmed Dini and Egué Bouraleh, and they were replaced by Idriss Farah Abane and Abdoulkader Moussa Ali, respectively. Six months later, another minister, Omar Mohammed Bourhan, resigned and joined the anti–Ali Aref forces. Similarly in the assembly, the vice-president's majority melted away, and in 1965 he was clearly placed in a minority position. Nevertheless, taking advantage of a loophole in the *loi-cadre,* which did not require the government council to resign even if it had lost the assembly's confidence, and sure of the French government's continued support, Ali Aref clung to his post. In September 1965 he even enjoyed a belated success when he helped his loyal supporter, Barkhat Gourat, to defeat Mohammed Kamil in the latter's candidacy for reelection to the Conseil de la République. That year the break-up of the Afar bloc was confirmed when Ali Aref left the leadership of the U.D.A. in the hands of Kamil and Ahmed Dini and formed a new party, the Rassemblement Démocratique Afar (R.D.A.), whose main support came from Afar conservatives. Rather surprisingly, Hassan Gouled, who had renamed his D.I.E.S.T. party the Union Démocratique Issa, did not join the ranks of those who defected but remained a minister in Ali Aref's government.

One of the chief reasons why Ali Aref was able to survive the disintegration of his Afar bloc was the even more serious crisis through which the P.M.P. was passing. Whereas the rift among the Afars was the result of purely internal dissension, the split in the P.M.P. came from its members' sharply differing reactions to external events. These first made themselves felt early in 1964 when the newly formed Liberation Committee of the Organization of African Unity (O.A.U.), itself founded as recently as May 1963, began to show interest in the situation in French Somaliland. Its attention had been drawn to the Territory by a group of refugees from Djibouti who were living in Mogadiscio and who, in June 1963, had organized the Liberation Front of the Somali Coast (F.L.C.S.). It was composed of the former followers of Harbi, who had been present at the meeting of August 30, 1959, at which the Greater Somalia movement was launched, and of more recent émigrés belonging to the P.M.P., who had fled from the Territory after the arrest of Obsieh Boeuh. Although the government of the Somali Republic claimed that the F.L.C.S. operated in "complete independence," its publications and the numerous memoranda it sent to the U.N. General Assembly and to the O.A.U. were given increasing publicity over Radio Mogadiscio.

These activities of the F.L.C.S. so alarmed the territorial assembly at Djibouti that it unanimously passed a resolution on February 7, 1964, denying the right of any person or organization outside French Somaliland to intervene in the internal affairs of the Territory. The unanimity between the indigenous tribes evidenced by this resolution, which was a reaffirmation of the Arta declaration, was shattered in mid-August 1964 when the P.M.P.'s moderate president, Ahmed Farah, was replaced by Obsieh Boeuh. The latter's imprisonment had increased rather than dampened his Pan-Somali sentiments, and he had managed to smuggle out of his cell a cable to the O.A.U. Liberation Committee supporting the F.L.C.S. as representing the true sentiments of French Somaliland's inhabitants. Obsieh Boeuh's alleged acceptance of directives from Mogadiscio and his reelection as president of the P.M.P. prompted the resignation from that party of five Issa territorial assemblymen, including Ahmed Farah, Hussein Ali Chirdon, and Ali Elmi Yonis. The last-mentioned, after publicizing the reasons for his resignation in an open letter to Obsieh Boeuh on August 30, 1964, formed a new pro-French party composed of Issas and Gadaboursis, which was given the name of Alliance pour le Progrès du Territoire.

The advent of this party apparently divided the moderate Issas into the groups led respectively by the assemblymen who had resigned from the P.M.P. and by Hassan Gouled. This largely coincided with and duplicated the division of the Afars between the Kamil-Dini faction and the R.D.A. headed by Ali Aref. Among the Somalis, the most radical fringe was to be found in the F.L.C.S. at Mogadiscio, but many hard-core Somali nationalists preferred to stay in the Territory and to remain members of the P.M.P. As for the Afars, Hamed Bourhan, a prominent civil servant, led a group of dissidents who for political or personal reasons were so at odds with the territorial administration that they went into exile at Diré Daoua. It was among members of this group that the Ethiopian government covertly organized the Committee for the Liberation of Djibouti (C.L.D.), which demanded the "reunification" of the Territory's Afars with their ethnic brothers in Ethiopia.

In organizing the C.L.D. in December 1964, the Ethiopians obviously followed the precedent of the F.L.C.S. at Mogadiscio, but the C.L.D.'s creation had been precipitated by the support for the Somali extremists that had been expressed two months earlier in a new international quarter. The meeting of nonaligned nations at Cairo early in October had passed a resolution asking the French government to take all "necessary steps to make the Territory free and independent." Not only did this move alarm the Ethiopian government, but it aroused some concern among the French authorities, though not to the point where they felt impelled to satisfy at least some of the Somali nationalists' aspirations.

Between October 1964 and March 1965, three members of the French cabinet visited Djibouti, ostensibly to "study" the situation there but actually to reaffirm France's determination to remain in French Somaliland and to defend its frontiers. Each minister recited a list of the benefits that French rule had brought to the Territory and promised its people more aid for their economic and social development. Against the background of growing international support for the Somali nationalists from committees of the O.A.U. and the U.N. General Assembly, the French unimaginatively pursued their existing policy throughout 1965 and most of 1966. Its basic assumptions were that for both economic and political reasons of self-interest, Ethiopia would never take the first step to dispute French rule of the Territory; that the recent splits among the Afars and the Somalis showed that tribal and personal rivalries between them remained so strong that they could never cooperate, much less unite against France; and that an increase in the Territory's port and railroad traffic through French financial and technical aid would lead to a prosperity that was the population's main desideratum. As for the U.N. and O.A.U. committees, as well as the Somali Republic, none of them was financially or militarily in a position to challenge actively the status quo. All they could do was talk endlessly at meetings, appoint missions that would not be allowed to visit the Territory, pass resolutions condemning French policy, and broadcast propaganda that was so obviously exaggerated and tendentious that it could not possibly be taken seriously by those it was supposed to influence.

Such was the French government's view, which lay behind its immobilism in regard to revising the Territory's statute and behind its policy of supporting Ali Aref long after it had become obvious that he had lost the confidence of the population and of the assembly. The authorities did not comprehend the intensity of the Somalis' resentment against the Afars, especially after the Kamil electoral law of 1963 had downgraded them politically. Nor did the French realize that the schism in the Afar bloc had given the Somalis the upper hand in the assembly. Ironically enough, it was the U.D.A. leaders, Dini and Kamil, who launched the attack in the assembly early in 1963, by charging the government council with "financial mismanagement." In this maneuver they were joined by an influential recruit to the U.D.A., Mohamed Ahmed Issa, who had become, thanks to his intransigent nationalism and his charisma, the idol of Djibouti's youth, and it was the element under 20 years of age that accounted for 43 percent of that town's population. Moreover, the P.M.P. under Moussa Idriss was gravitating toward the U.D.A. in their common determination to get rid of Ali Aref, who nevertheless still felt secure because he enjoyed the support of the business community and the local administration.

The Somalis' hostility to the Afars, the disaffection of several hundred Afars themselves, the frustration felt by the youth of Djibouti against the authorities, and the U.D.A. leaders' personal rivalries—all these coalesced so that in late May 1966 a vote of no confidence was adopted in the assembly. Yet this did not bring about the government's downfall, because Sahatdjian, president of the assembly, declared the motion of censure invalid. This interpretation was exactly the opposite of that which he had given the motion of censure instigated by Ali Aref in June 1960, which had led to the overthrow of the Ahmed Dini government. The governor, by upholding Ali Aref in his refusal to resign, showed clearly where the sympathies of the administration lay, and also its intention of manipulating the democratic processes in behalf of the existing regime. This impression was confirmed by the ease with which Ali Aref's candidate carried a by-election in July 1966 in one of the hinterland circumscriptions, thus convincing the U.D.A. and the P.M.P. that they could never win at the polls.[34]

Subsequently, Ali Aref's opponents came together and formed a coordinating committee headed by Cheicko, as Mohamed Ahmed Issa was known, and they decided that the impending visit of General de Gaulle to Djibouti offered a unique opportunity to stage a public protest. Probably the organizers of that protest intended simply to get rid of Ali Aref and to remind the General of his role as liberator of Africa. Nevertheless, the youth of Djibouti and the unemployed Somali laborers who formed the great bulk of the demonstrators had different ideas, and they transformed the protest rally into an emphatic demand for immediate independence. Also unexpectedly, De Gaulle reacted in much the same way as he had done at Conakry after listening to Sékou Touré's impassioned appeal for a negative vote in the referendum of September 1958.

On August 23, 1966, two days before General de Gaulle arrived in Djibouti, Moussa Idriss issued a manifesto demanding independence for the Territory.[35] Yet the president of the republic received no advance warning of this development from his subordinates. Indeed, General Billotte, Minister for the Overseas Departments and Territories, who had been in Djibouti the preceding May, had reported in Paris that the local inhabitants strongly desired to remain French. There is no doubt that the local officials, like General de Gaulle, were taken by surprise at his reception. To a large extent, Governor Tirant was victimized by carrying out his instructions from Paris to support Ali Aref unequivocally.

His stopover in Djibouti was De Gaulle's first visit to the Territory in seven years, and he was welcomed at the airport in the customary manner. All the outstanding members of the European community were present, as well as the native notables, and Moussa Idriss was among those who shook the General's hand.[36] Troops lined the road leading from the airport to the city, not only to do honor to the General but presumably also to hold back the enthusiastic crowds. Suddenly, when the presidential motorcade reached the Magala, the slum section of Djibouti where many immigrant Somalis lived, the armed forces found themselves facing demonstrators brandishing banners which read "Vive l'Indépendance Totale." These were seized by the gendarmes, but as the cortège advanced, more and more such banners were raised to the accompaniment of shouts demanding independence. The ensuing clashes between the demonstrators and the armed forces took an alarming turn.

Although General de Gaulle insisted on stopping to mingle with the crowd and on visiting the port, his program was hastily changed and the site of his speech was shifted from the public square to the assembly hall. With what reporters described as "icy reserve," he told his audience that France would take into account the assembly's desire for a change if it was expressed by regular democratic methods and not by violence and the shouting of slogans. In brief, he implied that the Territory could become independent if such was the wish of the majority of its population, but he did not state when or by what means. De Gaulle left General Billotte behind in Djibouti to pick up the pieces when he departed the next day to make a state visit to Ethiopia. The rioting continued after his departure, and the official tally for the 48 hours of violence was four dead and 70 wounded, of whom half were members of the armed forces. Among the 29 persons arrested—18 of them reportedly from Somalia—were Moussa Idriss and Cheicko, but after being interrogated by the police they were released. General Billotte strove valiantly to conciliate the opposition: he announced that there would be no repression, and he had talks with the main opposition leaders. Repeating General de Gaulle's assurances that the Territory's statute could be changed by constitutional means, he said that France would not stay in Somaliland by force, and he agreed that the government council should be "better balanced." He talked Ali Aref into leaving for Paris on September 1, ostensibly to attend a meeting of the Economic and Social Council there, and persuaded the four Somali ministers who had resigned to stay on and help run the government. He got the council to appoint as its acting vice-president Hassan Gouled, who, though currently allied with Ali Aref, was regarded as a moderate Issa nationalist.

General Billotte's conciliatory policy was not actively continued by the local administration after he returned to Paris. Governor Tirant seemed more intent on restoring order and on blaming alien agitators for the riots than on effecting the reforms that might have eliminated or attenuated local discontent. Late August and early September saw intense political activity among native politicians who were seeking a solution for the crisis in the government council. The Coordinating Committee of the opposition advocated dissolution of the assembly and the holding of new elections, but its major demand was for the immediate resignation of Ali Aref. The governor, however, temporized and took refuge in the law, which authorized only the French Parliament to dissolve the assembly and dismiss the government council. His announcement that the existing government council would continue in office to conduct current business was so ambiguously worded that it impelled the Coordinating Committee to renew its trial of strength with him. On September 7 the opposition called a general strike, combining a demand for wage increases with one for the resignation of Ali Aref. The Coordinating Committee decided to postpone the strike after learning that Tirant was to be replaced by a new governor, Louis Saget, on September 9. Saget was a career overseas administrator who had adroitly handled the ultranationalists in Madagascar and who had gained the reputation of being a liberal.[37] Djibouti's dockers, however, were not to be deterred, and they went on strike the day of the new governor's arrival.*

On September 10 there was a renewal of disorders in the native town, though not on the same scale as on August 25–26. The administration blamed them on "uncontrolled elements," a term that referred to the band of adolescents that set fire to some houses, looted them, and manhandled a few Europeans. Sporadic clashes continued for three days and left a toll of five dead, many wounded, and numerous arrests. Saget showed that he was determined first of all to assert the administration's authority. He established a curfew, forbade all meetings of more than five persons, temporarily

* See p. 225.

prohibited the sale of *khat,* and ordered the troops to cordon off the native town. The gendarmes then conducted house-to-house searches for hidden firearms and for persons illegally living in Djibouti. By September 16 the identity of over 5,000 persons had been checked, at least 350 had been escorted under arms to the frontier of Somalia, and hundreds more had left the Territory voluntarily. After order had been restored, the new governor began a series of consultations with various influential local leaders, who inevitably expressed differing views. Their unanimity, however, in denouncing the "brutal, inhumane, and vexatious methods" used by the armed forces induced Saget to order his troops to temper their zeal.[38]

At Paris, meanwhile, General de Gaulle showed that he had grasped the significance of the demonstration to which he had been subjected, even if the local officials had not learned its lessons. Although he blamed some of the agitation on outsiders, his practiced eye recognized the symptoms of genuine local discontent. Nevertheless, the General had global preoccupations which transcended the Djibouti scene and which weighed heavily in determining his policy. The most important of these considerations were his anxiety to preserve his image as liberator of French Africa in the eyes of the Third World, his concern not to permit France's other overseas dependencies to adopt Djibouti's precedent of street rioting as the means of winning political concessions from Paris, his desire to retain Djibouti as a center for the radiation of French influence in East Africa and the Middle East, and finally his need to keep the Territory as a relay station for the men and matériel being sent to France's nuclear-testing area in the Pacific. On the other hand, the Territory's minuscule dimensions, the insignificance of France's economic stake there, the financial burden its subsidies placed on the French taxpayer, and the possibility that it might become a bone of military contention in the Horn of Africa all lowered the price he was willing to pay for its retention. After consulting with his cabinet, therefore, General de Gaulle announced on September 21 that the population of French Somaliland would be able to express freely its wishes in respect to the Territory's future in a referendum to be held before July 1, 1967. France, he said, was quite able to live without Somaliland and would not remain there by force or by fraud. If the people chose to remain with France, "she would assume her obligations," but if they opted for independence they would receive no further French economic or military aid.

De Gaulle's rapid decision to hold a referendum in the Territory within nine months caused grave concern among its European and Arab businessmen, and it surprised and disconcerted the native politicians. It was generally recognized that the referendum device had served the General's Algerian policy well and that it would be applauded internationally as the most democratic method of ascertaining the people's will. Virtually all of the local leaders, however, said that they would prefer negotiations between Paris and the Territory's elected representatives in regard to French Somaliland's future statute. Only the R.D.A., now headed by Senator Barkhat Gourat in the absence of Ali Aref, came out unequivocally in favor of the Territory's remaining united with France, and this was also substantially the view of the president of the assembly, Albert Sahatdjian. Widely varying opinions were voiced by members of the Coordinating Committee, ranging from the surprisingly moderate stand taken by Moussa Idriss to the strongly pro-independence attitude of Orbisso Gaddito and Cheicko. Mohammed Kamil, who had been embittered by his defeat in the senatorial elections of 1955, now aligned himself with the advocates of independence, although he was not formally a member of the Coordinating Committee. But almost all who said they would vote for independence, if the only alternative offered by France was maintenance of the status quo, wanted the French government to continue providing economic aid and military protection. The general reaction was that no final decision could be reached before the choices to be offered in the referendum were more precisely known.

The claim made by Haile Selassie, immediately after De Gaulle's announcement of the referendum, to the effect that the Territory was an integral part of Ethiopia met with hostility on the part of all party leaders in Djibouti. His statement, as well as the more predatory activities of Mogadiscio, aroused local resentment and fear of the possible consequences of total independence. This rejection of the annexationist intentions of neighboring governments and the insistence on Ali Aref's resignation were almost the only areas of agreement among the Territory's politicians at the time. Such unanimity of local political opinion finally convinced the French government that it must insist that Ali Aref resign, which he reluctantly did on October 17 on the alleged ground that he wanted to devote all his time to explaining to his compatriots the full meaning of the forthcoming referendum.[39] At the same time, the governor dissolved the government council to make way for an apolitical caretaker government. Soon afterward the territorial assembly met and elected Mohammed Kamil as vice-president of the new council. His cabinet, like that of his predecessor and current archenemy, was predominantly Afar in its ethnic composition and was not the coalition that had been hoped for. Nevertheless, the French policy of appeasement, demonstrated by Ali Aref's surrender of his post and the return to normal constitutional processes of government, satisfied to a large extent the wishes of the politically conscious elements of the population.

If the *détente* thus effected had not been widespread and genuine, there might well have been renewed disorder in reaction to three events that transpired almost simultaneously. The first of these was the return of Ali Aref to the Territory on October 18. The second was the arrest on October 25 of 14 persons who were charged with responsibility for the riots of August and September, among them being Cheicko and two other prominent members of the Coordinating Committee as well as two former ministers, Egué Bouraleh and Hassan Liban. Finally, there were General de Gaulle's lengthy comments on French Somaliland in his semiannual press conference on October 28. In great detail the General dwelt on the aid that France had lavished on this "deprived and threatened land," but he also paid a warm tribute to the valiant conduct of the Somali battalions during the two world wars. He then referred to the referendum of September 1958 and the large majority that it had shown to be in favor of the status of an Overseas Territory, despite which the question of independence had been "noisily and urgently" raised during his visit to Djibouti in August. In the forthcoming referendum, therefore, France wanted to learn whether or not the Territory's inhabitants, "in full knowledge of what it entails," wished to stay with her or not. He spelled out what the Territory could expect if its people voted in the negative, but was vague about the benefits that would result from an affirmative vote:

If the response is negative, France will of course withdraw her representatives, her aid, and her forces, leaving those who are asking the people to claim independence to take over their responsibilities. Apparently some of them imagine that after they have chosen separation and become in theory a sovereign state, France would continue to contribute toward their expenditures and other needs, and would use her troops to prevent invasion by neighboring countries. It is necessary to dispel this dangerous illusion. France will certainly not employ her means or men to uphold a pointless façade of statehood which would not be practically viable for many reasons: the small size of the population and the division between them; its slender resources; its defenseless frontiers; its watchful neighbors, Somalia and Ethiopia, which are giants compared with such a future state; the appeals to the one or to the other that will be made from within the territory; and finally, the general situation in that part of the world . . . which is very disturbed.

On the other hand, if the response is positive, then France will continue to regard French Somaliland as being bound up with her own destiny. She will go on giving the aid and protection that she owes to those who form part of herself. She will gradually bring to pass what is possible with her help—the training of men, economic growth, social improvements, and external relations, on the understanding . . . that the internal government and administration will continue to develop according to the wishes of the people as revealed by the questions that will be asked of each and every one of them.[40]

The ambiguity of De Gaulle's promises in the event of an affirmative vote, which contrasted with the clarity of his warning should the Territory vote for independence, did not conceal from well-informed observers the change that had been taking place in the thinking of French policy makers in regard to French Somaliland's political evolution. The day before the General made his cryptic utterances, Philippe Decraene, writing in *Le Monde,* noted that his initial intention had been simply to offer a choice between secession and the status quo, but that subsequent developments in the Territory had convinced him that this would almost certainly result in a vote for independence. Consequently the government decided to deprive the word independence of its allure in offering as the alternative a more liberal statute granting to the Territory almost compete internal autonomy. France would retain control of foreign affairs, defense, currency, and the maintenance of order, and the repository of these powers would be a French official called high commissioner, rather than governor. The native head of the government council would become the prime minister, and he would be responsible to a Chamber of Deputies elected in such a way as to give fair representation to the main tribes. To obviate undue European influence in these elections, the transient element that had lived in the Territory for less than three years would be excluded from voting. These proposals were to be submitted in Paris to a delegation from the Territory made up of politicians representing a range of political opinions and then debated in the French Parliament during December 1966. If the draft law authorizing a referendum and embodying the new statute in general terms was passed by the Parliament, it would be supplemented by more specific legislation organizing the referendum and providing details of the new statute proposed.

On November 17, 1966, a plane carrying such mutually uncongenial men as Ali Aref, Mohammed Kamil, and Hassan Gouled arrived in Paris, where the Territory's deputy, Moussa Idriss, joined them. Ali Aref's unpopularity in Somaliland because of his nepotism and his hostility to the Somalis was well known, as was his unqualified stand for an affirmative vote in the referendum.[41] Hassan Gouled was regarded not as a statesman but as a weak politician who lacked a reliable personal following. The intransigent nationalists were in prison or in exile, so the key position in the negotiations was held by Mohammed Kamil. Not only had he been recently elected by the assembly to be vice-president of the government council, but he was the leader of the anti–Ali Aref Afars, who, as the majority tribe, might well tip the scales in the referendum. More important, perhaps, he advocated cooperation between members of the two main indigenous tribes. Before leaving Djibouti, Kamil had made known his opposition to France's retaining control of internal security under the new statute, and the fact that he favored setting a definite date for the Territory's accession to independence. Moreover, he insisted on the release of the 14 political prisoners sentenced for their activities in the August-September riots as the prerequisite for any discussion of the government's proposals. Moussa Idriss accepted the holding of a referendum on condition that it be supervised not by the local administration but by a committee composed of assemblymen and government councilors. Inasmuch as the Paris authorities were unlikely to agree to the terms laid down by Kamil and Moussa Idriss, the outlook for the success of negotiations was unpromising.

On December 2 and 21 the National Assembly and the Conseil de la République respectively debated and passed without a dissenting vote the draft law authorizing the referendum. It was to offer the people of French Somaliland the choice between total independence and remaining with France under a revised statute. To be sure, there were many absentees in both chambers, and among the 199 deputies who abstained from voting was Moussa Idriss. The Communist Party spokesman, Léon Feix, described the referendum as "intolerable blackmail, incompatible with genuine decolonization." One deputy, Aimé Césaire, the Antilles Negro writer, asked why a third alternative of association with the French Republic had not been offered to the Territory as it had been to the West African and Equatorial African territories. Yet, in the final count, both men voted in favor of the law. In mid-January the French cabinet set March 19 as the date for the referendum, and January 28 as the last day for registration of the political parties intending to participate in the vote. The balloting would be supervised by a French commission composed of magistrates and high officials, and official campaigning by the authorized parties was to take place between March 5 and 17. Voters casting an affirmative vote were to use a white ballot, whereas blue ballots (significantly the color associated with the Somali Republic) would be used by those voting "no." The question to be asked of the electorate was phrased thus: "Do you want the Territory to remain part of the French Republic with a revised governmental and administrative status, the essential elements of which have been brought to your attention?"

The procedure laid down by the French government after the draft law was passed in December called for negotiations between it and an elected official delegation from the Territory concerning the new statute to be offered to French Somaliland. On January 1, 1967, the composition of the official delegation was announced; it included the Territory's deputy (Moussa Idriss), two government councilors (Hassan Gouled and Mohammed Kamil), and nine assemblymen, including the assembly's president (Albert

Sahatdjian), but no member of Ali Aref's R.D.A. The negotiations that took place in Paris during January did not materially alter the terms proposed by the French government in the preceding November. The delegates did not obtain the release of all of the political prisoners, but their second main demand was acceded to. This was that the military measures taken to prevent "foreign elements" from participating in the referendum campaign be relaxed. The French remained adamantly opposed to the presence of U.N. observers before and during the referendum, as demanded by the P.M.P., on the ground that they would falsify the outcome as they had allegedly done during the plebiscites previously held in the mandated territories of Togo and Cameroun.

The chief reasons why the territorial delegates were so ineffectual during these negotiations were their inability to present a united front and the sudden and disconcerting reversals of the political positions they had previously taken in regard to the referendum. By early February, Hassan Gouled had emerged as an advocate of independence, whereas Ahmed Dini and Mohammed Kamil had joined Ali Aref in favoring an affirmative vote. In view of such inconstancy on the part of party leaders, it was not surprising that their followers also began to change sides, and that divided allegiances broke up some of the parties. Of the four officially registered parties, only the R.D.A. and the P.M.P. maintained a consistent policy at each end of the political spectrum. Kamil's Somali followers deserted him after he had come out against independence on the ground that it would lead to an invasion by Somalia or Ethiopia, or both, also to a civil war between the Afars and the Issas. The younger members of the U.D.A. split away and proclaimed their loyalty to the imprisoned Cheicko, who was still the hero of the intransigent nationalists. In effect they took their stand alongside the P.M.P., which gained more recruits when it was joined by members of the hitherto "moderate" Alliance party. Others to jump on the P.M.P. bandwagon were Hassan Gouled and his loyal followers. The remaining members of the U.D.I., however, continued to support its president, Omar Farah, and his announced policy of voting "yes" in the referendum.

In view of the kaleidoscopic political changes that occurred during the early months of 1967, it was impossible to estimate even roughly the relative strength of the Territory's parties.[42] On the whole, it seemed to be the P.M.P. that was the main beneficiary of the many transfers of party loyalties, but estimates of its strength ranged widely between 10,000 and 15,000 members. On the other hand, it was certain that the massive deportation of alien Somalis and the stringent qualifications laid down for the electorate had eliminated a large segment of the population that favored independence.

The electoral rolls, as announced on February 21, contained the names of 39,024 French citizens over 21 years of age who had lived in the Territory for more than three years and thus were qualified to vote. According to this count, the Territory had 37,850 foreign inhabitants, nearly one-third of a total population estimated at 125,050. By electoral circumscription, there were 10,920 registered voters in Djibouti, 4,976 in Ali-Sabieh, 9,526 in Dikhil, 9,121 in Tadjoura, and 4,481 in Obock. As to the ethnic composition of the electorate, there were 923 Europeans, 1,408 Arabs, 14,689 Issas and other Somalis, and 22,004 Afars. Predictably the European and Arab voters would vote for the continuation of French rule, and because the Afars were known also to favor an affirmative vote and clearly formed a large majority of the electorate, the outcome of the referendum seemed to be a fore-gone conclusion. Since virtually all of the Afars were nomads, however, and some of them had gone into Ethiopia because of the drought, it was uncertain how many of them would exercise their franchise.

Tension naturally mounted in Djibouti as the day of the referendum neared, and contributing to it were both tangible and intangible elements. Among these were the impassioned oratory of opposition leaders and the presence of over 3,000 members of the armed forces. The most potent of the intangible elements was the steady stream of propaganda poured out by the Somalia radio and news agency, which reached a high pitch during the three weeks preceding the referendum. By the choice of the reports and rumors that they disseminated, these agencies—without directly implicating the Mogadiscio government—fostered enthusiasm for Greater Somalia. This of course intensified the feeling of frustration on the part of the thousands of alien Somalis living in Djibouti who were not permitted to vote, and led many youths of that group to chalk up on walls of the Magala exhortations to the people to vote for independence. Some of these inscriptions began appearing in English and were evidently the handiwork of immigrants from former British Somaliland, and on March 10 the troops were ordered to cordon off the town against further clandestine infiltration. Two hundred Foreign Legionnaires were stationed in front of the house where Moussa Idriss lived, after he was reported to have said: "The French are engaged in trickery, but after Sunday we shall be free."[43] The P.M.P., after being warned that the stadium was not to be used for a political rally, held a meeting there nevertheless, under the eyes of truckloads of police. Some hundreds of secondary-school students refused to attend classes at the *lycée* during the week before the referendum was held. After Governor Saget at a news conference had stressed the danger of war should France leave Djibouti and had repeated assurances that the elections would be free and fair, he was "jeered by scores of ragamuffins shouting 'No, no, no, goodbye, Monsieur!' "[44] The tracts distributed and the inflammatory speeches made at this time were aimed in part at impressing the 50-odd foreign journalists who had come to Djibouti to cover the referendum. It was self-evident, even before the votes were cast, that regardless of the announced outcome of the referendum, it would be contested, probably in a violent manner.*

On March 19 the voting was orderly and calm, and the massive participation by both of the main ethnic groups showed that their respective leaders were conscious of the implications of the referendum and had impressed its importance upon their followers. According to the official tally, 22,523 persons (60.74 percent of the electorate who went to the polls) cast affirmative votes and 14,734 turned in negative ones.[45] This division among the voters clearly followed ethnic lines. In Djibouti and Ali-Sabieh, the circumscriptions where a great majority of the electorate were Issas and Somalis, there were respectively 6,862 and 4,654 negative votes to 2,798 and 93 affirmative ones. In Dikhil circumscription, two-thirds of whose inhabitants were Afars and one-third Issas, those who voted "yes" numbered slightly more than twice those who opted for "no." In Obock and Tadjoura, where Afars constituted almost the entire population, only a handful of negative votes were cast in each circumscription. Regardless of the disenfranchisement of many residents who claimed French citizenship, the referendum proved that the Issas had succumbed to the glamor of "independence," whereas the Afars had voted for French rule as offering their surest protection against Somali domination and their best hope of economic and social development.

With the announcement on March 20 of the official vote count, there was an immediate explosion of disorder in Djibouti. Young Somalis set fire to houses, furniture, and cars belonging to Afars and Arabs they suspected of having voted "yes," and threw stones at the armed forces, who retaliated with grenades. At least 12 persons were killed and 22 wounded, many arrests were made, and a curfew was established. Djibouti was placed under a virtual state of siege, the armed forces restored and maintained order by harsh methods, the troops guarding the southern border were reinforced, and the authorities began rounding up hundreds of "troublemakers and illegal residents" for deportation to Somalia. The Somali politicians echoed Mogadiscio's claim that the elections had been rigged and, as a protest, stated that they would have no part in any government formed after the referendum. Their attitude was stiffened by Ali Aref's jubilant statements, which showed that he intended to exploit the Afars' victory to the hilt.

* A tract signed "La Voix des Patriotes" stated that "since France knows only violence, we shall shed blood." See Le Monde, Mar. 18, 1967.

The referendum and especially its aftermath placed Governor Saget in a delicate and difficult position. He was well aware of the unfortunate impression created among the foreign journalists by the large-scale deportations and the brutal methods used by the armed forces, but he was also responsible for maintaining order among a turbulent population which had often shown its proclivity for violence. Furthermore, he had to devise some political formula by which the Afar victors could be persuaded to share their power and the vanquished Issas to cooperate in the election of a new government council. The refusal of Somalia to accept any more deportees forced him to concentrate them in a camp installed near the border, so as to obviate the risk that they might carry on guerrilla warfare, like the Somali *shiftas* (rebels) operating in Ethiopia and Kenya.

Saget adroitly induced Ali Aref to renounce his original intention of expelling all who had voted "no" in the referendum and of replacing by Afars all Somalis who were serving in the administration, the armed forces, and even private enterprises. Although Ali Aref, who succeeded Kamil as vice-president of the government on April 5, would not give any portfolios to Somalis, he was sufficiently aware of the danger of a renewed schism in the Afar bloc to divide the posts judiciously between members of his own party and the U.D.A. Then Saget turned to the Issas, who had called for a general strike, which, in conjunction with the expulsion of so many Somalis, had almost paralyzed the port of Djibouti. After a series of talks with the P.M.P. leaders, he persuaded them to give up their systematic abstention from participating in territorial politics, in return for his pledge to ease the drastic military restrictions and to maintain a better political equilibrium between the two main indigenous tribes. The Somalis even agreed to sponsor a candidate in the legislative elections to be held on April 23, although Moussa Idriss refused to be a candidate for reelection and it was obvious that the Territory's next deputy would be an Afar.

Despite the governor's success in establishing a base for conciliation between the Issas and the Afars, prospects for genuine cooperation between them were almost nil. In France, there was a widespread impression that the referendum had settled nothing and had been followed only by a truce in which any incident would provoke new clashes. Long-standing opponents of the referendum were confirmed in their belief that such a consultation had no value in a dependency where 90 percent of the people were illiterate and where none of its leaders favored either of what seemed to them two undesirable alternatives, their common goal, instead, being negotiations with Paris for a more liberal statute. No one accused the administration or the supervisory commission of technically falsifying the vote by ballot-box stuffing or fraud. Indeed, precautions had been taken to see that each party could post representatives at all of the 70 polling booths, and journalists were free to observe the voting procedure. The French government was criticized, nevertheless, for creating a situation in which tribal pressures and the intimidating presence of an inordinate number of troops prevented the true expression of the population's wishes as individuals. As Philippe Decraene aptly put it,[46] an Afar living in the Issa quarter of Djibouti would have shown superhuman courage if he had cast an affirmative vote, and the same was true for an Issa voting "no" in an area dominated by Afars. Undeniably the referendum had deepened the hostility between the two main ethnic groups, and had increased the Issas' distrust of the French administration.

On the other hand, the outcome of the referendum had eliminated the danger of an immediate invasion of the Territory by either of its neighbors and of civil war between the Afars and the Somalis. France's friendship with Ethiopia was reinforced, and Addis Ababa felt reassured that the port of Djibouti would not soon fall into Muslim hands. In Africa, except for Somalia, the Arab states, and the "revolutionary" countries, the referendum seemed to elicit approval because it had prevented the outbreak of war in the region, if for no other reason. Whether or not it had accomplished another of its purposes—that of being an object lesson to the other Overseas Departments and Territories—remained to be seen. Moreover, the referendum had not closed the door to eventual independence of the Territory, which was widely assumed to be inevitable. What use France would make of the breathing spell gained for it by the referendum was the question that aroused most concern and speculation.

The legislative elections of April 23 yielded the first evidence that France's policy of conciliation was succeeding, although the seven candidates included none of the Territory's outstanding politicians. As foreseen, the winner was an Afar, Abdoulkader Moussa Ali, the assemblyman from Obock, who—though a devoted follower of Ali Aref—was sponsored by the whole Afar bloc. Another encouraging feature was that 34,376 persons, of a total electorate of 39,990, actually voted, and this indicated a heavy Issa participation. Although the Somali vote was split between three Issa candidates, the most important one—Idriss Farah Abaneh—received half as many votes as his successful Afar opponent. Moreover, Idriss Farah ranked third in the P.M.P. hierarchy and was known as a moderate who favored cooperation between Issas and Afars. This show of greater cooperativeness on the part of the Issas was probably due to two recent developments. One was the more conciliatory spirit shown by Ali Aref when, early in April, he appealed to his "Issa brothers" to help him revive the Territory's economic prosperity. The other was the reported disillusionment of the P.M.P. directorate with the policy of the Somali Republic. Not only had Somalia's leaders, after encouraging the P.M.P. to move to direct action, failed to follow through with material aid after the referendum, but they had also refused to permit the Somalis expelled from the Territory to return to the Republic.[47] France's effort to drive a wedge between the Issas and the foreign Somalis culminated successfully in the declaration issued on May 27 by 18 Issa *okal,* tribal elders, and functionaries, which ran as follows:

We protest against the fallacious political propaganda which our neighbors broadcast, either by means of the radio or through their agents in this Territory. We beg all who are not directly involved to desist from further interference in regard to the future of our country. Here we recognize only the rights of the descendants of those who signed agreements with France when France arrived in our country—that is, the Afars and Issas. We believe firmly in mutual understanding between the Afars and Issas as the sole way in which we can evolve toward political and economic stability. We ask France for equality and justice.[48]

On June 13–14, 1967, the French Parliament debated the new statute for the Territory, as amended and ultimately accepted by the territorial assembly exactly one month before. The most controversial proposal made by the Afar-dominated assembly was to change the name of the Côte Française des Somalis to the Territoire Français des Afars, and it was one that the Parliament would not accept. The National Assembly debate showed that the deputies were fully cognizant of the danger that would result from allowing the Afars to give free rein to their traditional tribal animosity toward the Somalis, although they were willing to accept changes on minor points. The French acceded to the territorial assembly's request that management of the port remain under its existing administration, over which the assemblymen exercised some control, rather than be made wholly responsible to the Minister of Overseas Territories. They also granted to the territorial assembly, to be renamed chamber of deputies, the exclusive right to initiate budget expenditures and to invest and dismiss the government council by the vote of an absolute majority of its membership. The government council, to be composed of six to eight ministers not necessarily chosen from among the deputies, was no longer to be presided over by the governor but by its own elected president. In other respects, however, the French Parliament showed that it intended to keep a firm grip on the reins and even to reinforce France's role as an arbiter between the two main ethnic groups.

The territorial assembly's request to control the registration of vital statistics was refused, lest the Afar majority deny enfranchisement to a significant portion of the Somalis, and for the same reason the assembly's proposal to revise the electoral law (so that the new chamber's membership would exactly reflect the size of the two principal ethnic groups) was denied. In addition, the Parliament insisted on retaining control of the Territory's foreign policy, defense, internal security, currency, radio and television, and the qualifications for acquisition of French citizenship. The Parliament reserved to itself, too, the power later to alter the Territory's statute after consultation with its chamber of deputies. Although the governor was thenceforth to be designated high commissioner, he was still the repository of the powers of the French Republic: he promulgated the laws passed by the chamber, on which he could ask for a second reading; he was responsible for their execution; and he need not accede to the government council's demand that the chamber be dissolved. In the future, French aid to the Territory would be regulated by precise agreements between the governments of Paris and the Territory, which would specify the amount, the method of financing, and the utilization of French funds and technicians in carrying out specific programs. France retained the right of access to the port of Djibouti at all times.

Whether or not the new statute for the Territoire Français des Afars et des Issas, which became law on July 3, 1967, is liberal enough to meet the basic demands of the Territory's inhabitants remains to be seen. The calm that followed the legislative election of April 23 and that has been prolonged by the economic stagnation caused by the closing of the Suez Canal on June 5 should not give rise to illusions. That the Issas suffered so much from the severe repression which followed the referendum that they harbor hopes of revenge was shown on July 8, 1967, the day after the new government council was elected. Ali Aref, having made a speech designed to reassure Djibouti's business community, announced that his government was composed of five Afars, two Issas, one Arab, and one European. The willingness of the two Issas to accept ministerial portfolios in Ali Aref's government, three days after that government had arrested seven members of the P.M.P., including Hassan Gouled, angered the Somalis. One of the Issa ministers, Djama Abdi Bakal, barely escaped an assassination attempt, and the other, Chirdon, was in fear of his life. On Bastille Day, all those arrested were released, and calm was at least temporarily restored, although the government council at the same time dissolved the P.M.P. During the autumn of 1967, those accused of fomenting trouble during the riots of September 1966 and March 1967 were brought to trial. Some were given very severe sentences, while others were acquitted. Among the latter were the seven leaders of the former P.M.P., including Egué Bouraleh and Cheicko.

The lessening of tension after the Territory's new statute became effective in July 1967, and especially after amnesty was accorded Issa opposition leaders in the autumn, proved to be only a lull in the storm. Early in 1968, the strong terms in which Hassan Gouled denounced the persistence of "racial discrimination" in the Territory, as evidenced by the Afars' continued predominance in the government council and chamber of deputies, betrayed the revival of tribal animosities. Subsequently, three incidents in the spring of 1968, including an attempt by three young Issas to assassinate Ali Aref on May 7, showed that the threat of civil war was a continuing danger to the Territory.

It should be remembered, in evaluating the future of the Territory, that the emotional climate of Djibouti, like its economy, has always been one of instability and extremes—exaltation alternating with depression and feast with famine. The indispensable prerequisite for the Territory's accession to independence under favorable conditions is the attainment of a harmonious working relationship between the two main ethnic groups, and this still remains to be reached.

Chapter Five

EXTERNAL RELATIONS

Foreign relations, in the strict sense of the term, cannot of course exist between independent states and a territory that is not fully self-governing. But external relations and contacts exist informally, and to some extent clandestinely, between French Somaliland and nearby sovereign nations. Although French Somaliland is only a tiny area in the Horn of Africa, the question of its status has increasingly preoccupied its neighbors. At the same time, its relations with them have become of prime importance in the Territory's own evolution, as the wave of nationalism has progressively swept over the area.

The economic weakness of all the states of northeast Africa, especially those that only in recent years have come of age politically, has made them receptive to the competitive aid offered by powerful, industrialized foreign nations. The United States has given considerable assistance to Ethiopia, and the largest American military base in Africa is situated at Asmara in Eritrea. Direct American influence on French Somaliland has been minimal, although the United States was blamed—by implication though not by name—by the native president of the territorial assembly for complicity in the independence demonstrations of August 1966.[1] Although officials in Washington may have been secretly pleased at the discomfiture of General de Gaulle, who was then on his way to Cambodia (where he was to urge cessation of the war in Vietnam), they did not rejoice at the prospect of a French withdrawal from Djibouti. Indeed, in view of Britain's imminent departure from South Arabia, continued French rule over the Territory seemed to them to offer one of the few stabilizing elements in the Red Sea basin.

As for the communist powers, the Soviet Union has given economic and military aid to Somalia in competition with the government of Peking, but the U.S.S.R. has also helped Ethiopia by, for example, building an oil refinery at Assab. In French Somaliland itself, communist influence has been felt only indirectly through the activities and propaganda of some of Djibouti's labor organizations. The Arab countries, on the other hand, have moved more directly to win over the population of Djibouti, where the overwhelmingly Muslim majority is to some degree sensitive to Cairo's propaganda. Because of the inherent appeal of its incitement to revolt and take over the positions now held by Europeans and their elders, the Territory's young people of all ethnic groups are receptive to the Arab countries' call for action. Nasser's economic weakness, his difficulties in Yemen, and more recently his spectacular defeat at the hands of Israel have diminished his appeal, but the forces to which the dissidents can turn for help are nevertheless limited.

There remain, of course, the international organizations that have intervened directly throughout the area. Many of the countries, and especially the restive elements within those countries, which are not strong enough to attain their objectives unaided, have called upon the U.N. and the O.A.U. to help them shake off the control of their present rulers, indigenous and alien alike. In the case of French Somaliland, the governing power there has refused to admit the U.N. Committee on Decolonization and the O.A.U. Liberation Committee, because both groups obviously were going to exert their influence on behalf of the anti-French elements inside and outside the Territory. Consequently, those international bodies have had to make their presence felt in Djibouti from bases in Ethiopia and Somalia, which are the African countries that have always exerted the strongest and most direct influences on the Territory's economic and political life.

The United Nations, as the agency chiefly responsible for the independence of Somalia, has perhaps naturally taken a sympathetic view of that country's aspirations, so that the republic's leaders have mainly turned to its Decolonization Committee in seeking support for their goal of Somali unification. Although this committee thus far has not given them much concrete assistance, the Somalis continue to use it as their principal channel for protesting against the continuation of French rule in the Territory. The O.A.U. is the other international organization most likely to help the republic realize its ambitions, but Haile Selassie's dominant position in the O.A.U. has barred Somalia from making the maximum use of its Liberation Committee. All the countries of the Dark Continent have felt the magnetism of Pan-Africanism and a growing sense of African solidarity, but in the region of the Horn of Africa this nascent unity is undermined by the conflicting claims to leadership put forward by Ethiopia and the Arabs. As a result, the O.A.U. hesitates to intervene there in inter-African disputes and has been checkmated by the opposition of Ethiopia and Kenya to Somali unification. The continuation of French sovereignty in the Territory is tacitly supported by Ethiopia as preferable to that of Somalia, and this is probably also the sentiment of the Afars, who form the majority of its population. Furthermore, because of the close ties that the French-speaking West and Equatorial African states maintain with Paris, they turn a deaf ear to Somalia's grievances. It was reported that the controversial passages in the O.A.U. report to the Kinshasa summit meeting in September 1967 on the referendum in the Territory and its aftermath of riots and deportations were deleted at the behest of those states.[2]

International intervention, exercised either in collective form or by individual powers, has complicated the area's problems. If Somalia, which has displayed the most aggressive policy of any country in the Horn, has received no satisfaction from international organizations, neither has France found the referendum device useful for its purposes. The referendum of 1967 was designed to satisfy the Third World's insistence on the right of a people to self-determination and—in the event of an affirmative vote—to legitimatize the continuation of French rule over the Territory. Both Ethiopia and Somalia accepted the principle on which the referendum was to be based, but well before it took place there was no doubt that its outcome would be challenged by one of them and accepted by the other. The referendum certainly has not settled the future of French Somaliland, and the most that can be said for it is that it has given France the time needed to prepare the Territory's inhabitants for independence and also has prevented, at least for a time, the outbreak of war between Somalia and Ethiopia.

Ethiopia

Franco-Ethiopian friendship has been a constant factor in the Territory's relations with its neighbors except for a 20-year period before, during, and after the Second World War.

Mutual self-interest prompted the first treaties signed by Emperor Menelik and Governor Lagarde in 1897.[3] The Emperor sought French aid to offset Italy's claims to Ethiopia and also the use of Djibouti's port for his country's foreign trade and especially for the importation of firearms. The French needed Menelik's cooperation in realizing their hopes of establishing a foothold on the Upper Nile, as well as his permission to build a railroad from Djibouti across Ethiopian territory to Addis Ababa. To win the ruler's consent they were willing to cede to him a large but vaguely delimited portion of the western region which they had claimed for their Somali coast colony. By the end of the nineteenth century, the failure of the Marchand expedition at Fashoda ended France's interest in Ethiopia as a potential eastern gateway to the Nile, but completion of the railroad to Addis Ababa in 1917 greatly enhanced the economic interdependence of Ethiopia and the Territory.

For many years, the imprecision of the frontier gave no cause for concern to the government of either Ethiopia or the Territory. During the interwar period, when raiders based in Ethiopia began to attack the Territory's nomad herds in the Dikhil region, the French took steps to assert effective control over the frontier area. North of Lake Abbé, however, the tribes continued to trek at will between the Territory's plains and the Ethiopian highlands. The Italian conquest of Ethiopia in 1936 changed this nonchalant official attitude toward the boundary line. Italy's aggressive interpretation of the 1897 treaty led to some skirmishes and the establishing of Italian and French military posts in the Hanlé plain. Soon the Italians began to develop transportation facilities in their colony so as to lessen their dependence on Djibouti's port and railroad.*

Italy's policy might have led to open conflict in the region had not France's defeat by the Axis powers in June 1940, followed by the Djibouti administration's adherence to the Vichy regime, brought about what was in effect a regional truce. But in the spring of 1941, Great Britain's conquest of East Africa once more altered the Territory's relations with Ethiopia, especially after Haile Selassie returned to his capital again as ruler of a sovereign state. Still another change occurred in February 1943 when Bayardelle, then Free French governor at Djibouti, decided that the Territory's security necessitated the reoccupation of Afambo, in the lake country at the western extremity of the frontier zone. The Ethiopian government described this move as an "aggressive act," and doubtless regarded it as France's first step in the seizure of the Aoussa sultanate. Relations then became so tense between Djibouti and Addis Ababa that the French authorities soon realized that the price for reestablishing amicable relations with Ethiopia was a demarcation of the frontier that would be satisfactory to both the countries concerned.

The negotiations were long and difficult, largely because they also involved restoration of the railroad company's prewar rights, but ultimately, with the help of Britain and the United States, they were successful.[4] As a first step, diplomatic relations between France and Ethiopia were resumed in April 1945, and on September 5 of that year, two agreements between them were signed at Addis Ababa. The first of these recognized the railroad company's prewar rights, and the second provided for a delimitation of the frontier by a mixed Franco-Ethiopian commission according to the

* See p. 12.

principles laid down in the 1897 treaty. Because of the inaccessibility of the frontier terrain and the contradictory maps on which the respective French and Ethiopian claims were based, the commission's work was arduous. Agreement was finally reached, however, and embodied in an exchange of official letters in 1947, whose contents were not immediately made public. Nevertheless, enough became known about the terms of the agreement to arouse considerable opposition to them in France. The conservative Metropolitan weekly, *Climats,* published a series of articles whose various authors contended that the French government, without any adequate *quid pro quo,* had surrendered one-tenth of the Territory's total area and, above all, had jeopardized its security by giving Afambo to Ethiopia.[5] The most hostile of the agreement's opponents went so far as to accuse the Ethiopians of trying to stir up the nomads to revolt against French rule and of being unable to govern their own country or even to maintain the infrastructure and plantations they had inherited from the Italians.[6] French resentment reached such a pitch that in the late 1940's the Ethiopian State Bank was refused permission to establish a branch at Djibouti, and needless to say, Ethiopia's claim to Eritrea received no support from France in the United Nations. In 1949, two strikes by the Ethiopian railroad employees at Diré Daoua, in one of which some of the company's European personnel were injured, further intensified French hostility to the Addis Ababa government.

Because of the French attitude, as well as the high-rate policy of the railroad company and the port of Djibouti, the Ethiopians decided to develop alternative facilities at Assab after Eritrea became federated with Ethiopia in 1952. Within two years it became obvious that competition from Assab was seriously harming the Territory's economy, and that some arrangement must be made with Addis Ababa, especially in regard to Ethiopia's use of the railroad. According to E. Chedeville, in an article published in the January 30, 1954, issue of *Le Monde,* the directors of the railroad company had successfully exerted pressure on the French government to sign the 1947 agreement and, in return, to get Ethiopia's pledge not to build a competitive rail line to Assab. Chedeville's "revelation" had been inspired by a communiqué from the Ministry of Overseas France on January 16 confirming France's agreement to evacuate Afambo and cede other areas along a 300-kilometer length of frontier to Ethiopia. At once the Territory's representative council passed a resolution strongly opposing these terms, and its three delegates to the French Parliament lodged formal protests against the agreement. They claimed that it was contrary not only to their people's wishes but also to the constitution of the Fourth Republic.[7]

On two occasions, French government spokesmen defended the agreement in the National Assembly (where it was never submitted to a vote), asserting that France had "surrendered" no territory, because the frontier had never been precisely demarcated. Afambo, they maintained, was not essential to the Territory's defense, and, in any case, France had received compensation in the more economically and strategically important mountainous massif of Moussa Ali. Furthermore, Ethiopia was now pledged not to build a competitive railroad and to permit France to construct a road from Dessié to Assab.* The new boundary, they said, would put an end to the frequent "incidents" between nomad tribes in the area. The main argument in favor of the agreement, however, was that it would restore good relations with Ethiopia, and this was essential to the Territory's economy.

That the last-mentioned argument was sound was proved by an easing of the tension between Ethiopia and the Territory and by an increase in the volume of Ethiopia's foreign trade handled by Djibouti's railroad and port. When Haile Selassie made a state visit to Paris late in 1954, the French press, which had only recently criticized his autocratic rule and the ineptitude of his government, paid him enthusiastic compliments. French press comments became almost paeans of praise when he gave his country a new and more liberal constitution in 1955. The French began to recall the friendly relations between Menelik and Lagarde; the 54 years of missionary work in Ethiopia by Mgr. Jarosseau, the Bishop of Harar who had been Haile Selassie's teacher; the scholarly writings on Ethiopian archaeology and languages by Griaule, Breuil, Azais, Cohen, and Grébaud; and the existence of a French *lycée* and Pasteur Institute at Addis Ababa. In January 1955, Governor Petitbon paid a courtesy visit from Djibouti to Addis Ababa, and a new era of friendly cooperation between the Territory and Ethiopia was inaugurated. Soon negotiations were begun with the aim of ironing out the remaining difficulties between Paris and Addis Ababa.

The Franco-Ethiopian treaty of November 12, 1959, revised the status, management, and ownership of the railroad company in a manner that was highly advantageous to Ethiopia. It was also satisfactory to the French government in its limitation of French liability for the company's financial losses.† Its terms were such that the Ethiopians had every interest in promoting the traffic carried by the railroad to and from Djibouti's port, and this of course benefited the Territory's economy. The new arrangements that it embodied were presented to the Parliament as a practical economic

---

* It should be noted that France never built such a road, although it was regarded at the time as one of the major Ethiopian concessions in the agreement.
† See pp. 208–9.

necessity, lacking which Djibouti's very survival would be jeopardized by Assab. Hassan Gouled, French Somaliland's deputy at the time, complained that the treaty conceded too much to Ethiopia, that it had been negotiated without adequate consultation with the Territory's elected representatives, and that it would open the door to a horde of Ethiopian immigrants.[8] To the last-mentioned point, one of the French deputies replied ironically that, since most of the few Ethiopian residents in Djibouti were prostitutes, they were unlikely to become agents for their country's territorial ambitions. It was clear that the specter of an expansionist Ethiopia, which had alarmed the French public only a few years before, had been largely though not wholly replaced by a new image of that country. To the members of Parliament, which quickly ratified the treaty, Ethiopia now seemed not warlike and aggressive but a beleaguered Christian nation that was courageously defending its integrity against internal disruptive forces and its independence from Muslim encirclement. What had largely contributed to this new and sympathetic view of the Territory's western neighbor was left unsaid in this debate—that is, the belief that the imminent independence of Somalia and its union with British Somaliland represented a threat to both Djibouti and Addis Ababa.

The Ethiopian government, like that of Djibouti, has had to cope for many years with indigenous Afars and Issas who are mutually hostile albeit Muslim tribes both living under Christian rule. With regard to their supervision, however, Addis Ababa enjoys an advantage over the French in that the Issa Ougaz lives at Diré Daoua and the two major Afar sultans, those of Aoussa and Rahayto, reside in Ethiopian-controlled territory. Until the mid-1930's the Ethiopians had fair success in handling this nomad problem, partly because the Afars and Issas were not closely controlled by the central government. In particular, the Afars accepted Ethiopian suzerainty as a lesser evil than Issa domination, just as their far less numerous brethren in the Territory, for the same reasons, had been amenable to French rule. The Issas, for their part, resented the Ethiopians because of the restrictions the latter had imposed on their expansion at the Afars' expense, but they disliked even more the Somalis of Hargeisa and Mogadiscio. The Italian occupation, even though it lasted only from 1936 to 1941, permanently altered the Ethiopians' relationships with both indigenous tribes. On the charge that the Afars had sided with the Italians, the Ethiopians began trying in 1942 to subdue the semi-independent sultan of Aoussa, and two years later they succeeded in capturing him and in transforming his sultanate into a tributary province.[9] Conversely, because the Issas had helped the Ethiopians against the Italians (in contrast to the activities of other indigenous Somalis), the government of Addis Ababa treated them with more indulgence than in the past and encouraged their "individualism."

The Ethiopians' efforts to separate the Issas from the Somalis of Somalia increased because of the irredentist turn taken by Somali nationalism in the 1950's. That irredentism took organized form in a Greater Somalia movement, created in August 1959, and was intensified by the union of British Somaliland with Somalia in the independent Somali Republic in July 1960. Although the new republic's main objective insofar as Ethiopia was concerned was to acquire Ogaden and the Haud with their Somali inhabitants, it also hoped to absorb the Issas and other Somalis living in northeastern Africa. French Somaliland was the smallest of the areas coveted by Mogadiscio, but it contained Ethiopia's two vital lifelines, the railroad and the port of Djibouti. When for the first time, therefore, it appeared possible that French Somaliland might become independent as a result of the referendum of September 1958, the Ethiopians massed troops along the frontier, ready to move in should the vote there go against the maintenance of French rule. Thus, even though Ethiopia's problems concerning its nomad tribes were far more complex and incomparably larger in scale than those of the French, they had basic similarities, and the interests of both powers converged when it came to the question of the control of Djibouti.

Ethiopia's situation was further complicated by a sweeping reorientation of its foreign policy in the mid-1950's. Ethiopia was a minor power in the Near East, but after Nasser emerged from the Suez crisis of 1956 with greatly enhanced prestige in the Arab and Negro world, the Negus began to turn his attention more to Africa. He realized that when the Gold Coast became independent in 1957 there would be a resulting upsurge of nationalism throughout the Dark Continent and also of Egyptian ambitions there. He therefore redoubled his efforts to gain international support and enlist foreign aid not only for his country's economic development but also to improve its defenses, and he was notably successful in obtaining military assistance from the United States.

At the same time, Haile Selassie began a series of moves in Africa with a view to making Ethiopia, if possible, the leader of the newly independent nations and, surely, secure in the region of the Horn. In 1958 he succeeded in his efforts to have Addis Ababa made the headquarters of the United Nations' newly formed Economic Commission for Africa, and the next year he signed the treaty with France that gave him practical control of the railroad and free access to the port of Djibouti. To prevent Arab encroachments on the ports of Massawa and Assab, the Negus demoted Eritrea in 1962 to the status of a province directly under the control of the central

government. As visible confirmation of Ethiopia's status as leader of independent Africa, its ruler persuaded Africa's newly sovereign states to
hold at Addis Ababa in May 1963 the meeting at which the Organization of
African Unity (O.A.U.) was formed. Haile Selassie's position as head of
Africa's longest-independent nation, and his personal prestige as a proved
adversary of fascism, offset the disapproval felt by revolutionary African
and other governments for the feudalistic and autocratic character of his
rule. One consequence of his unique position was that the 24 members of
the United Nations Committee on Decolonization and the nine members
of the O.A.U.'s Liberation Committee carefully avoided taking sides in
Ethiopia's dispute with Somalia, after it had taken a bellicose turn in 1964.
They did not hesitate, however, when a European colonial power was concerned; indeed, they encouraged the independence movement in French
Somaliland. Haile Selassie, as the O.A.U.'s original sponsor, could hardly
do otherwise than welcome to Ethiopia in 1965 the Liberation Committee's
fact-finding mission, which had been refused admission to their Territory
by the French.

Mogadiscio's real if unofficial encouragement of the Somali nationalists
in Djibouti was most clearly evidenced by the organizing of the Liberation
Front of the Somali Coast (F.L.C.S.) in Somalia's capital* and by the Somalia government's granting of facilities for spreading its propaganda. Beginning late in 1963 the F.L.C.S. issued a steady stream of petitions and
memoranda which it sent to the two international committees mentioned
above, and the government of Addis Ababa felt obliged to counter this by
similar moves. In December 1964, therefore, the Ethiopians formed their
own Committee for the Liberation of Djibouti (C.L.D.) at Diré Daoua,
under the chairmanship of Hamed Bourhan. The following month Bourhan
duly assured the visiting mission of the O.A.U. Liberation Committee that
the majority of French Somaliland's inhabitants wanted union with Ethiopia. Later, in a memorandum of July 22, 1965, to the Decolonization Committee, he demanded immediate independence for the Territory and described the claims of the Somali Republic as "unrealistic."

Hamed Bourhan's assertions were repeated in more detail by the Addis
Ababa newspaper, the *Ethiopian Herald,* in an editorial on January 23, 1965.
It is worth citing because it was an early statement of the arguments later
used with varying emphasis by high-ranking Ethiopian officials and even
by the Negus himself in rejecting Somalia's irredentism and in staking
out Ethiopia's own claims to the Territory:

* See p. 84.

The future of the Djibouti area lies in the hands of the people inhabiting the Territory, but France can play a vital role as honest broker in guiding the people in the crucial days before independence.... The present political boundary is artificial and has been imposed against the will of the people.... By history, demography and economy the inhabitants on the coast and on the mainland are the same people. The present boundary cuts across Afar and Issa tribes, the overwhelming majority of which are within Ethiopia.... Chieftains representing this overwhelming majority have petitioned the mission stating that their people want freedom from colonial rule and union with Ethiopia.

This claim was immediately rejected by the Territory's main political leaders and also by members of the territorial assembly. Moreover, the choice of so weak a reed as Hamed Bourhan to voice the alleged aspirations of the Afars was a tacit admission on the part of Addis Ababa of its inability to appeal strongly to Afar loyalties. It even used the sultan of Aoussa to make contacts with lesser Afar chiefs so as to enlist their support for a proposal to create a Greater Danakilia as a semiautonomous unit inside the Ethiopian realm.[10] It is hard to believe that responsible Ethiopian officials could seriously sponsor a proposal originating from other than spontaneous aspirations voiced by influential Afar leaders. Addis Ababa's Afar policy was wholly imitative of Somalia's approach to the emergent Somalis, and it showed an astonishing lack of realism. If it indicated how little the Ethiopians had to fear from the Afars, it also showed how little the Afars felt they had to gain from closer association with the Ethiopians. Moreover, by driving a wedge between the older and younger Afars, it risked creating a new element of division among members of that tribe, which at best had never been able to present a united front. Only the withdrawal of France from the Territory could effect a *rapprochement* between the traditional Afar chiefs and Addis Ababa, but merely by proposing such a union the Ethiopians increased the possibility that Afar youth—naturally susceptible to the appeal of independence—would join forces with the Somali nationalists.

It is unnecessary to dwell upon this development, because the Afars counted for little in Ethiopia's overall political calculations. There were far more serious minority problems inside Ethiopian territory, one of the most troublesome being the growing restiveness of the Eritreans, which found expression in an organization called the Eritrean Liberation Front (E.L.F.). The three foreign Christian nations that have tried successively to govern Eritrea have found its inhabitants very difficult to handle. It became an Italian colony in 1884, and later was a protectorate in which Italy invested heavily to develop its communications network and agricultural production. After the Italian defeat in World War II, Eritrea acquired a temporary British administration, but its ultimate disposal proved to be one of the thorniest questions tackled by the United Nations in that body's early years. Although its day-to-day administration required a sizable subsidy, and large investments would be needed to develop its economic potential, two countries of modest resources—Egypt and Ethiopia—vied with each other for its possession.

The Great Powers being at loggerheads on this question, the U.N. sent two missions of inquiry to Eritrea, in 1947 and 1950, to ascertain the wishes of the inhabitants in regard to their future government. Among Eritrea's various political parties and the several tribes that made up its population of 1.5 million, the members of these missions could find no consensus. Some wanted independence, others union with Ethiopia or Sudan, and still others a British trusteeship. Although only about one-third of the Eritreans were Coptic Christians eager to join their coreligionists in Ethiopia, world opinion tended to favor the Ethiopian claims.[11] Ethiopia refused to accept a division of Eritrea that would give it only the area inhabited by Christians, for it was generally felt that the Ethiopian demand was based on strategic and economic necessity. Eritrea had served as a base from which the Italian conquest had been launched, and landlocked Ethiopia badly needed the Eritrean seaports of Massawa and Assab.

The solution finally reached was embodied in the U.N. resolution of November 2, 1950, which provided for a prolongation of the British administration until September 15, 1952. At that time, Eritrea would be granted internal autonomy but be placed under a federal government, in which Ethiopia would be sovereign in regard to its defense, currency, tariffs, and foreign relations. During the two-year transitional period, the U.N. High Commissioner, in collaboration with the British administration and the Ethiopian government, drew up a draft constitution which was submitted for approval to an elected assembly composed of an equal number of Muslims and Christians. This solution was considered acceptable by the Ethiopians, who proceeded to "colonize" Eritrea by appointing their own officials, but it was unsatisfactory to many Eritreans.

The fear and resentment of being ruled by Coptic Christians which were felt by the Muslim majority of Eritreans, and by some non-Muslims among them as well, was heightened by the Ethiopians' tactless methods of direct rule and by the concentration of their development efforts on the ports of Assab and Massawa for their own needs. By 1955, Eritrea had lost so much of its autonomy that both its prime minister and the secretary-general of the Union Party, which had advocated federation with Ethiopia, resigned their government posts. When Ethiopia in 1962 unilaterally annexed Eritrea as a province, the ranks of the Eritrean Independence Party, led by a Tigre Christian named Michael Woldemariam, grew rapidly, and guerrilla warfare was organized by a newly formed group called the Eritrean Liberation Front (E.L.F.).

Little is known about the early stages of the revolt in Eritrea,[12] and it was not even mentioned in the Ethiopian press until 1966. Reportedly, the E.L.F. is headed by a Supreme Council under the chairmanship of Idris Mohamed Adam, a former president of the Eritrean Parliament now living in Cairo; and its guerrilla forces, whose headquarters are "somewhere in Eritrea," are modeled on the Algerian rebel army. The E.L.F. claims to have permanent representatives not only in all the Middle Eastern Arab countries but also in Somalia, Sudan, Italy, Sweden, and Switzerland. Its emissaries have certainly been active over a wide area, and they are reported to travel on passports issued by the Somali Republic or Syria. The publicity given to E.L.F. activities by the radio stations of Cairo, Damascus, Mogadiscio, and Khartoum, beginning in 1966, provided political support for the Eritrean rebels, but the exact extent of Arab and Somali material aid is not known. Foreign observers in 1967 estimated the size of the Eritrean guerrilla forces at 1,000 to 2,000 uniformed troops, who were believed to have been trained as far afield as Cuba, China, and Syria and equipped with Russian arms smuggled in from Red Sea ports.

In late 1966 and early 1967, a series of armed attacks, the waylaying of trucks, and the derailing of trains caused clashes between the police and the rebels. Promptly and severely the Ethiopian army retaliated by raids and by the burning of villages where rebels were thought to have been harbored. During that period, as many as 9,000 Eritreans may have fled across the border into Sudan. In mid-March, Haile Selassie commented for the first time on the Eritrean revolt in a press conference,[13] when he said that "foreigners" were trying to create divisions and weaken Ethiopia on the "spurious ground of religion," but he evaded a direct question concerning Egyptian involvement in the revolt. Four months later, the Ethiopians changed their methods of handling the revolt, obviously trying to capitalize on the disarray among the Arab supporters of the E.L.F. in the aftermath of the Arab-Israeli war.[14] The government of Addis Ababa not only intensified its military offensive against the guerrillas but for the first time started a campaign to win over the rebels. In July 1967 a pardon was offered to those who surrendered, and when this produced no results the Ethiopians sent high-ranking officials to conduct a propaganda campaign in the hinterland. No reports have been published concerning the efficacy of either the military or the psychological-warfare campaign, or the degree to which Arab support of the E.L.F. may have been modified by international events.

Without a doubt, however, the E.L.F.'s appeal to Muslim solidarity initially brought a widespread response from Arab countries of such diverse political casts as Syria, Saudi Arabia, Egypt, Sudan, and Iraq. Radio Damascus, on November 10, 1966, charged that the Ethiopians were plotting with the Zionists to assassinate the E.L.F. leaders, who were described as simply struggling for their political, economic, and cultural independence. The Arabs saw the "Ethiopian reactionary conspiracy" as only another phase of "subversive world imperialism," but Western journalists were inclined to view the E.L.F. revolt as part of the Arab socialists' overall strategy to drive Occidental and Christian influences from the Red Sea region.[15] A more simplistic view held that Eritrea was merely the scene of another episode in the confrontation between the United States and the U.S.S.R., who were arming and training their respective protégés, Ethiopia and Somalia. Such an assumption ignored the technical and financial aid that the Russians were also providing to the Ethiopians, as witness their three-year construction of Assab's oil refinery, completed in April 1967, and the lack of evidence of foreign communist inspiration for the armed attacks by the Eritreans and Somalis. The Ethiopians, too, were inclined to link together these two movements on their northern and southern flanks, but for different reasons. The Eritrean revolt, if unchecked, might jeopardize Ethiopia's hold on the ports of Assab and Massawa, whereas the Somalis were trying to dismember the country by stirring up trouble in the Ogaden. These developments revived the old fear of Muslim encirclement which had long haunted landlocked Ethiopia, and they gave a new importance in the eyes of Addis Ababa to the fate of Djibouti and to cooperative relations with France.

The French government, for its part, was well aware that Ethiopia's concern to counteract Somali nationalism—which France also felt—lay behind some of the statements and actions of Addis Ababa that, under other circumstances, might have been interpreted as anti-French. Consequently, the French did not take offense at Ethiopia's claims to the Territory as voiced by the Afar Liberation Committee formed at Diré Daoua, or at the Ethiopian government's consistent references to the Côte Française des Somalis as the "Djibouti Territory." The choice of France's Minister of Defense to go on a mission to Addis Ababa in April 1965, presumably to reach a basic understanding on common problems, was a happy one, for Pierre Messmer had fought for the liberation of Ethiopia from the Italians during World War II.* It was clear to both parties that Ethiopia, as a principal pro-

* See p. 16.

moter of the O.A.U. and of African independence, could not approve openly of the maintenance of French rule in Djibouti. At the same time, both governments obviously had a common interest in the prolongation of the status quo there as the only practical way, under existing circumstances, of avoiding a conflict in the Horn of Africa that might also involve the United States and Russia as well as the Arab countries.

Matters unexpectedly came to a head as a result of the Somali nationalists' demonstrations during General de Gaulle's stopover at Djibouti in August 1966. As planned, he went on from there to make a three-day official visit to Addis Ababa, where he was welcomed with exceptional warmth and where the local press and radio tactfully made no mention of the Djibouti independence riots. The General is reported to have offered the Negus financial and technical aid in the construction of the Sidamo branch railroad,* and the two heads of state exchanged pledges to work together to ensure political equilibrium in the Red Sea basin. Ethiopia found it prudent not to negotiate a treaty of friendship with France at that time, but did sign technical and cultural agreements covering a five-year period.

To those unfamiliar with the significance that France's policy makers attach to the spread of French culture, the second agreement signed at Addis Ababa on August 27, 1966, might seem of slight importance. General de Gaulle, however, was especially pleased by its provisions for the training of more Ethiopian teachers of the French language and for the augmenting of French educational institutions at Addis Ababa. French was the first European language learned by Haile Selassie, and it is still the only one he speaks fluently. In 1925, before he became Negus, he made French the sole linguistic medium for instruction at the Lyceum Tafari Mekennon, which he founded that year at Addis Ababa.[16] Later, the French *lycée* at Cairo inspired him to create a replica of it in his capital, but World War II intervened and the school was not inaugurated until March 15, 1948. Under the name of Lycée Gabré-Miriam, it was provided by the Ethiopian government with large grounds and an annual subsidy of 100,000 Ethiopian dollars. France allocated to it twice that amount yearly and also paid the salaries of 37 professors and a *proviseur* (director), who were placed under the general control of the Mission Laïque Française.[17] (In 1967 the *lycée* was attended by 1,830 students, of whom 1,300 were Ethiopians who competed for the 13 scholarships granted for higher studies in France.) Under the new agreement, funds were to be made available for enlargement of the *lycée* and for the construction of a technical college by the Addis branch of the Alliance Française. At the farewell banquet given in the General's

* See p. 210.

honor, Haile Selassie spoke appreciatively of France's cultural as well as economic aid, which had contributed to the development of Ethiopia as a modern state.[18]

General de Gaulle's sudden announcement in mid-September 1966 of his intention to hold a referendum in the Territory to determine its future status evoked an immediate reaction in Addis Ababa. It was the subject of banner headlines the following day in the semiofficial *Ethiopian Herald,* which editorially described Djibouti as "one of Ethiopia's lost provinces along the Red Sea." In a press conference on September 16, the Negus put forward the strongest claim he had yet made to the Territory, asserting that for historical, economic, strategic, and demographic reasons it was "an integral part of Ethiopia." He maintained that the majority of its population were Afars who wanted union with Ethiopia, and that the Somalis were newcomers who were responsible for the August 26 agitation. He also argued that the seacoast on which Djibouti is situated had been acquired by France from chiefs who were not authorized to cede it, that as an independent country it was not viable, because it was economically dependent upon Ethiopia, and that Ethiopia would automatically fall heir to French Somaliland if France renounced sovereignty over the Territory. Furthermore, he implied that only two sovereign powers—Ethiopia and France—were involved in the question, and that his government would resist by force any attempt by the Somali Republic to take over the Territory.[19] The strong tone of the Negus's remarks met with an adverse reaction on the part of both Afars and Issas, who energetically denied the "legitimacy" of his claims and denounced Ethiopian expansionism,[20] but his statement also caused many of the leaders who had been advocating total independence to have second thoughts on the subject.

In an interview granted to André Blanchet of *Le Monde* on October 11, 1966, Haile Selassie expressed more precisely his views on the referendum and on the Territory's future.[21] From his talks with General de Gaulle, whose record as the liberator of French-speaking Africa inspired confidence, he had deduced that independence would be granted to the Territory in the not-distant future. Meanwhile, he would accept the popular verdict as expressed in the referendum because he had always defended the right of a people to self-determination. If the vote favored independence, his army would not immediately invade the Territory, for Ethiopia had no annexationist ambitions and merely sought the confirmation of century-old ties with the majority population. Nevertheless, if the people, after the French had left, asked for his protection, then the Ethiopians would be the first to arrive and offer help. Asked if it would not be advisable, in the event of a pro-independence vote, for Ethiopia and Somalia to organize a second referendum under O.A.U. auspices to ascertain the population's exact wishes, the Negus quickly replied that there was no reason for Somalia to be involved in the matter. For Ethiopia the Territory had economic and strategic importance, but "Somalia does not need Djibouti and her claims to it are purely political." He also rejected as irrelevant any partition of the Territory or any formula involving an international trusteeship.

During the six months that intervened between this interview and the referendum vote, Haile Selassie gave no indication of modifying these views, and they were reiterated by his government's representatives at all international meetings that discussed French Somaliland's future. Ethiopia's delegates duly denounced the evils of colonialism, but consistently refused to criticize France or to support Somalia's plea that resolutions be passed insisting on the presence of U.N. observers before and during the referendum. However, on March 17, two days before the referendum, Ethiopia closed the railroad to passenger traffic and commandeered all the locomotives and rolling stock. This lent weight to the reports that Ethiopia had also massed troops along the border, poised for an invasion if the population should vote for independence.

Enormous relief must have been felt by Addis Ababa when, on March 20, Djibouti announced that 60 percent of the Territory's inhabitants had voted for continuation of French rule. That same day, the "Voice of Ethiopia" broadcast its conviction that the referendum had been truly democratic and fairly conducted: "There is no conceivable reason why the colonial power should want to prolong indefinitely its association with a nonviable territory like Djibouti for the pure pleasure of subsidizing it. So France had neither the desire nor the need to falsify the vote ... and Ethiopia will stand by its decision to respect the outcome." The Addis Ababa authorities were so relieved that, unlike those of Mogadiscio, they welcomed back the 1,000 or so Somalis who had emigrated to the Territory from Diré Daoua, Jigjiga, and Ogaden, who were deported late in March by the French as illegal residents.[22]

Like the French, the Ethiopians are undoubtedly aware that the vote of March 19, 1967, brought no permanent solution in regard to the Territory's future but are grateful for the respite it procured. Had the vote resulted in the Territory's immediate independence, Ethiopia would almost certainly have felt warranted in moving in on the pretext of protecting its nationals.[23] A few weeks later it would probably have announced "free elections," and—after these had taken place—that the immense majority had voted for union with Ethiopia. The annexation of Djibouti would have added to Ethiopia's already complex minority problems and further embittered its relations with Somalia, and it might also have embroiled Addis Ababa with the Arab countries. Moreover, Ethiopia would have had to undertake the management of Djibouti's port and the railroad, which even in peacetime posed difficult problems that became immeasurably more complex after the closing of the Suez Canal by Egypt in June 1967. Ethiopia therefore has every reason to hope that the Territory will remain as long as possible under French administration, which has been economically beneficial to the government of Addis Ababa and has spared it many a political and perhaps military headache.

Somalia

In many respects the history of Somalia resembles that of Eritrea, but of the two countries, Somalia has had much the greater impact on the political evolution of the Horn of Africa.

Both became Italian colonies in the 1880's, and after Italy's conquest of Ethiopia in 1936, all three countries were placed under a common Italian administration. In August 1940, Italian troops overran British Somaliland and that protectorate was briefly part of the Italian bloc. The following year, however, Great Britain drove the Italian forces out of East Africa and thus fell heir to all the lands formerly governed by Italy. Although the British restored Haile Selassie to the throne at Addis Ababa in May 1941, they continued to administer the Ogaden and a so-called Reserved Area, which included the pasturelands of the Haud and the region traversed by the Djibouti–Addis Ababa railroad. In 1946 the French company regained control of the railroad, but the Ogaden was not restored to Ethiopia until 1948 and the Haud in 1955. During the period when they were governing all the Somalis living in the Horn of Africa except those under French rule, the British tried to carry out what was called the Bevin Plan. This was a project for the unification of all the Somalis in a new nation to be called Greater Somalia, which presumably would become a zone of British influence. Although the British later abandoned the Bevin Plan, it was under their aegis and with their encouragement that Somali political parties were formed and Somali nationalism in its present form was conceived. Nevertheless, the British simply gave a modern organization and terminology to the embryonic sense of nationhood that had developed among the Somalis long before the Europeans came to the Horn of Africa.[24] According to Saadia Touval:[25] "It was nurtured by tribal genealogies and traditions, by the Islamic religious ties, and by conflicts with foreign peoples. It ripened and became

1. Léonce Lagarde, administrator and diplomat in French Somaliland from 1884 to 1899

2. Moussa Ahmed Idriss, an Afar political leader and head of the Parti du Mouvement Populaire

3. Hassan Gouled, a Somali prominent in the Parti du Mouvement Populaire

4. Mohammed Kamil, an Afar, vice-president of the government council from November 1966 to April 1967

5. Ahmed Dini, an Afar and leader of the Union Démocratique Afar party; named Minister of the Interior in April 1967

6. Barkhat Gourat, an Afar political leader and member of the French Senate

7. Governor Louis Saget (*center*), with the government council at Djibouti

8. Djibouti port

9. Packing salt at Lake Assal

Photo: R. Michaud, from Rapho Guillumette

10. Native market in Djibouti

11. Djibouti's principal mosque

12. Salt works at Djibouti

13. Dikhil

14. Peltier Hospital, Djibouti

15. Tadjoura

16. Street scene, Tadjoura

17. The shore at Obock

18. Tadjoura's well

19. Ali-Sabieh

20. A street in the native quarter of Dikhil

21. Issa warriors

22. Issa tribal chiefs

23. Afar camel herder at Kouta-Boufa, on the Plain of Gobaad

24. Young Afar girl

25. Afar chief of Khor-Angar village

26. Dourba nomad. His hair is coated with sheep grease as a sign of rejoicing

27. Djibouti *lycée*

28. A classroom

29. The Plain of Féraré and (*background*) the Plateau of Naïsso

30. A clearing in the forest of Daÿ

31. Date-harvest time in Ambouli

32. C.F.E. train at Addis Ababa station

33. Purchase of *khat* from a sidewalk vendor

34. A *boutre* (typical native boat) under construction

35. Bird's-eye view of Djibouti

a political movement as a result of external influences—the establishment of alien governments, the impact of the Second World War, and the example of the struggle for independence in other countries."

After the end of World War II, the disposal of Somalia, like that of Eritrea and Libya, presented grave problems for the United Nations. The Bevin Plan naturally did not meet with the approval of all the Great Powers, and the U.N. decided in 1948 to send a mission of inquiry to Somalia, as it had to Eritrea, to learn the wishes of the local population. As in Eritrea, the presence of such a mission inevitably stimulated the creation of political organizations, which could not agree on the country's future status, no more than could the United States, Great Britain, the Soviet Union, and France, whose representatives made up the Four-Power Commission of Inquiry. Consequently, the fate of all the former Italian colonies was decided in an overall settlement that emerged after prolonged international bargaining.

The solution found in April 1950 for Somalia was very different from that for Eritrea. Somalia was given an Italian administration under U.N. trusteeship, which was to culminate in independence after a ten-year period. The prospect of eventual independence, together with Britain's project for a Greater Somalia and its encouragement of political parties, gave a tremendous stimulus to Somali nationalism. It also conditioned the Somalis thenceforth to look less to the British than to the U.N. as the champion and guarantor of their aspirations, and to regard Ethiopia and France as the main obstacles to their realization.

Developments throughout the 1950's reinforced all these tendencies. In 1955, Britain's restoration to Ethiopia of the Haud, which like the Ogaden was inhabited almost wholly by Somalis, aroused highly adverse reactions in Mogadiscio and Hargeisa, and it increased the Somalis' long-standing hostility to Addis Ababa. France, too, had antagonized the Somalis by advocating, in the United Nations, the return of the former Italian colonies to Italy. This stand by France and its consistent opposition to a Greater Somalia were due not so much to apprehension in regard to Somali nationalism at that time as to fear of British hegemony in the Red Sea basin. Nonetheless, the Territory—simply by remaining a French dependency— stood in the way of Somali unification. Then, too, the majority of its inhabitants were Afars, traditionally hostile to the Somalis; its parties were developing along local tribal lines; and the Territory's whole political orientation was away from Africa and toward Metropolitan France. It may be noted that, in addition, the French deliberately encouraged the Issas' individualism and thus accentuated the differences between them and the Somalis to the south of the Territory's border.

The resulting isolation of the Issas from the mainstream of Somali life was to some extent offset by the increasing flow of immigrants from British Somaliland. These were attracted to Djibouti because it was far more cosmopolitan and dynamic than either Hargeisa or Mogadiscio. The British indirectly promoted their emigration by refusing to install control posts along their Somaliland's northeastern frontier. The immigrant British Somalis, because of their enterprise and skills, soon came to occupy a far more important place in the Territory's economic life than the Issas. This led them to feel that the Territory—whose very name of French Somaliland encouraged this attitude—was just another part of the Somali world.[26] Not until the mid-1950's did the French begin to sense the dangers inherent in this situation. They took steps to curtail Somali immigration and to require all alien residents to carry identity cards on which was shown the country of their origin. The encouragement that the French proceeded to give to help the Issas and Afars develop their economic and political potential was considered by the immigrant Somalis to be unjust discrimination against them. Their sense of grievance grew with the rapid advance of British Somaliland and, even more, of Somalia toward self-government.

As early as 1951, the Somalis under Italian trust administration acquired an elected legislative council, and in 1956—four years ahead of the U.N. schedule—they had their own autonomous government. The next year, Great Britain took the first step to align its protectorate with Somalia. Even more significantly, the Secretary of State for the Colonies let it be known in February 1959 that Britain would not oppose some form of close association between the two countries in the future. This statement had far-reaching consequences. It alarmed the Ethiopians and the French by reviving the specter of a Greater Somalia. At the same time, it went a long way toward appeasing Great Britain's Somali protégés, who had deeply resented the cession of their trek lands in the Haud to Ethiopia and who held the British responsible for their economic and political backwardness as compared with the Italian Somalis.

Curiously enough, the British Somalis neither feared nor resented the dominant position occupied by their fellow tribesmen in Somalia, but on the contrary felt admiration for it. Although the Italians had done no more than the British to develop educational facilities in prewar days, they did invest more funds in their colony's economy. Above all, by their use of forced labor and their fascist-type racial policy they had inadvertently fostered Somali nationalism. Common Somali ethnic goals and also the respect inspired by Somalia's more advanced political and economic situation explain why that country's far larger dimensions (453,000 square kilometers compared with British Somaliland's 176,000) and greater population (1,250,000 as against 600,000) evoked not fear but emulation among the British Somalis.

On the other hand, the Ethiopians, and to a lesser extent the French, saw in the British pronouncement of February 1959 a threat to their countries' territorial integrity and a spur to the restiveness of their minority peoples. The Somali-inhabited regions of the Ogaden and the Haud in Ethiopia constituted one-fifth of that country's total area. Although the Ogaden is a semi-arid plateau, it was believed to have a considerable, if undeveloped, economic potential, and the Haud comprised rich pastureland vital to the survival of the nomads of both Ethiopia and British Somaliland. The same could not be said of the desolate trek areas of the French Somalis, but the urbanized element among them was the dominant group in Djibouti, the epicenter of the Territory's economy. Defection by the French Somalis would have deprived the Territory of its most dynamic group, but their total number was very small compared with the 850,000-odd Somalis living in Ethiopia. It therefore was not surprising that both Addis Ababa and Paris protested against the British policy and sought reassurances from London. All they elicited, however, was a noncommittal statement by the British government's spokesman in the House of Commons on April 11, 1960, to the effect that "Great Britain neither encourages nor discourages any claims affecting the territorial integrity of French Somaliland, Kenya, or Ethiopia. The question can be envisaged only if such is the desire of the governments and populations concerned."[27]

In the meantime both the Italian and the British administrations moved rapidly ahead with their plans to promote self-government in their respective Somalilands. The election in March 1959 of Somalia's new legislative council had given a large majority of its seats to the Somali Youth League (S.Y.L.). This was the oldest political party in that territory and the one that had longest advocated the union under one government of all the Somalis living in the Horn of Africa. The S.Y.L., anticipating its control of the government after Somalia became independent on July 1, 1960, adopted as the new state's emblem a star with five points, symbolizing the unification of the Somalis then living under five different administrations. It also sponsored a meeting at Mogadiscio on August 30, 1959, to organize a Pan-Somali movement, which was attended by delegates from French Somaliland, the Ogaden and Haud regions of Ethiopia, and the Northwestern Frontier District of Kenya, as well as from British Somaliland.

The last-mentioned territory had to move quickly to catch up with Somalia's more rapid progress toward independence. On February 17,

1960, elections were held in British Somaliland for the legislative council and were contested by four parties, all of which called for independence and a merger with the former Italian colony as the first step toward creation of a Greater Somalia. After the British announced that their territory would become independent on June 26, 1960, delegates from British Somaliland and Somalia met at Mogadiscio on April 17. They voted formally to unite on July 1, 1960, as a sovereign state which would be a republic with an elected president and a central government of the Western parliamentary type at Mogadiscio, as well as a national army.

The union of the Italian trust territory and the British protectorate brought together two impoverished countries, neither of which had a good internal communications system, a flourishing foreign trade, or a good port, and both of which had had to be subsidized by their respective administering powers. Their combined population numbered somewhat less than 2 million, the majority of whom were nomads. However, the political maturity of the new state's leadership was far ahead of its economic development, and among the former African dependencies that are now independent countries the Somali Republic is almost unique in still being a parliamentary democracy with legal opposition parties. Although the new republic's constitution forthrightly announced as its goal the creation of a Greater Somalia, it also pledged that only peaceful and legitimate means would be used to attain it. This policy elicited the aid of some Western democracies, but also support from certain sources that were not disinterested. Even before Somalia became independent, it had received encouragement from the Arab League countries in general and from Egypt in particular, and at two inter-African conferences it had tried to enlist help for the realization of its irrendentist ambitions. After July 1, 1960, it was subject to even greater external pressures and strove more strongly than before to win wider international support.

Another policy enunciated in the new republic's constitution was the encouragement of solidarity among the peoples of the world and in particular among the African and Islamic peoples. Somalia's attainment of independence coincided with the transformation of many other African dependencies into sovereign states, and also with the wave of Pan-Africanism that swept over most of the Dark Continent. The republic was eager to participate in the unity movement, but being uncertain as to which faction would best promote its aims, it hesitated between joining the "revolutionary" Casablanca group or the "moderate" Monrovia one, both of which were formed in 1961.[28] The dilemma was finally solved in May 1963, when those two groups joined to form the Organization of African Unity, but in the meantime Somalia placed its hopes in the creation of an East African Federation in which it might find satisfaction for its claims to the Northwestern Frontier District of Kenya. The federation did not then materialize, but Somalia proceeded notwithstanding to press its claims in such a way that it antagonized Kenya's major political parties and also Great Britain. At the same time its unceasing propaganda attacks on Ethiopia continued—and with no more satisfactory concrete results. However, if Somalia's uncompromising irredentism was alienating its neighbors and the moderate nations in general, it also brought the country aid from communist states. Late in 1963, Peking and Moscow began to vie with each other in offering Somalia technical, financial, and, above all, military assistance.

An internal political and economic crisis caused a lull in Somalia's external activities throughout 1964, but this comparative passivity did not mean abandonment of its long-range policy of Somali reunification. During that year, in fact, Mogadiscio for the first time turned its propaganda guns on French Somaliland. To be sure, the republic had encouraged the formation of the F.L.C.S. at Mogadiscio in June 1963. Long before that time, too, it had welcomed there the Issa politician, Mahmoud Harbi, as a persecuted Somali nationalist, and the S.Y.L. had tried to establish a foothold in Djibouti. Even then, however, the Territory had not been a main target of Somalian irredentism as were Kenya and Ethiopia, and Djibouti still offered the best economic opportunities available to many impoverished emigrants from Somalia. Alain Jacob, in a series of articles entitled "Somalis Tourmentés et Courtoisés," published in *Le Monde* on December 27–29, 1963, noted the republic's nonaggressive attitude toward France, for which he cited two reasons. One was the existence of a non-Somali majority in the Territory and the second was the Somalis' admiration for General de Gaulle's policy of liberating France's West and Equatorial African dependencies. He concluded that Mogadiscio's attitude would radically change only in the event of an Ethiopian takeover of Djibouti.

The relaxed French attitude reflected in these articles soon received a jolt. When the new French ambassador presented his credentials at Mogadiscio in April 1964, the president of the Somali Republic said:

We cannot hide our regret and surprise at the French government's act in excluding the Somali territory of Djibouti from the African countries which it has freed, making this territory the only one in Africa still in French hands. I hope that the friendly relations between our two countries will result in the French government's changing its policy and allowing the Somali people it rules to exercise the right of self-determination.[29]

A frontal attack on France, as on Ethiopia, was out of the question for practical reasons as well as for those of principle. Only through the medium of international organizations could Somalia hope to bring pressure effectively on the French government to relinquish the Territory, which the Mogadiscio authorities invariably referred to as the "Somali Coast."

Somalia launched its campaign at the Cairo meeting in October 1964 of the heads of nonaligned states, who passed a resolution calling on the French government to take all necessary steps to free the Territory. As a follow-up to this vague exhortation, the O.A.U. Liberation Committee sent a four-man mission to conduct an on-the-spot inquiry in January 1965. Denied admission to the Territory, it went to Mogadiscio, where its members received petitions from the F.L.C.S. and heard testimony given by political refugees from French Somaliland who were living there. From Somalia the mission proceeded to Ethiopia, where the same performance was repeated at Diré Daoua with the Djibouti Liberation Committee, which had been formed the month before in anticipation of this occasion.* Ironically enough, the mission's hearings produced such a rash of mutual denunciations by the respective sponsors of the "liberation fronts" that Djibouti —the objective which in principle they were disputing—seemed almost forgotten.

The territorial assembly and government council of French Somaliland at once took pains to recall their existence to the O.A.U. Liberation Committee by denouncing the activities of both liberation fronts as an unwarranted interference in the Territory's internal affairs, and a stalemate ensued. Somalia tried to revive the question at the O.A.U. foreign ministers' meeting at Nairobi in March 1965, but again failed. This was conceded in a Radio Mogadiscio broadcast on March 9, 1965, which announced in part that "Ethiopia, which is one of the nine member states of the O.A.U. Liberation Committee, found the way to blocking this matter, and much against our will the question of the Somali people has also suffered a setback."

Concluding that because of Ethiopian opposition the O.A.U. could not serve as a useful instrument for exerting pressure on France, the Mogadiscio government then turned to the U.N. Decolonization Committee of 24. Not only was the U.N. naturally inclined to be sympathetic to the aims of a country for whose independence it had been responsible, but the resolution passed on December 14, 1960, by its General Assembly had specifically condemned colonialism and created a committee to implement this policy. Somalia first tried to convince members of the Decolonization Committee that conditions in French Somaliland justified its intervention. On June 8,

* See p. 110.

1965, it submitted a memorandum asserting that "beyond all manner of doubt ... this is not a self-governing territory and ... is, in short, a colony." At the next meeting of the General Assembly, the Somalian delegate's assertion that "French domination of the Somali Coast must cease" brought an angry response from the Territory's Minister of Interior. He denounced Mogadiscio's "baseless and absurd claims to my country" and its heeding the "political refugees who claim to represent our Territory. We say to these men, French Somaliland is not for sale or for cession."[30]

In view of these hostile reactions from the Territory's elected representatives, Somalia made little headway until the spring of 1966, when at long last it succeeded in persuading the Decolonization Committee to put French Somaliland on its agenda. In May of that year, the Somali Republic submitted a proposal to the U.N. asking that France grant independence to the Territory and free all political prisoners. It further proposed that—after France had withdrawn its administrators and troops—the U.N. establish a two-year trusteeship in the Territory, after which a plebiscite would be held so that the inhabitants could choose between independence and union with Somalia.[31] The next month the Decolonization Committee sent a mission to Mogadiscio and Addis Ababa which followed the same routine as had the O.A.U. mission 18 months before. At Mogadiscio, members of the committee were told that the policy of the French administration at Djibouti was "to destroy the Territory and to rule it forever," and that it was bent on "imprisoning, killing, or deporting all nationalist elements in the country." As for the French troops, "they number 40,000 men, who raid and loot the local people. Each of their white officers is paid on the basis of the number of persons he arrests, and so to make money they round up people and herd them into jails without trial."[32]

General de Gaulle's visit to French Somaliland in August 1966 was hailed by the Somali Republic's leaders as heralding a change in French policy toward that Territory.[33] The demonstrations that he witnessed in Djibouti were acclaimed in Mogadiscio as proof that all of the Territory's inhabitants wanted independence. Spokesmen for the republic denied the allegation that it had any responsibility for the riots and asserted that they were purely spontaneous. They were further interpreted by the same sources as a protest against the local French officials, who were accused of sabotaging, or failing to carry out, the liberal policies of Paris. Considering that the Territory's population had freely and clearly expressed its wishes, Mogadiscio asserted, the reactionary local administration would be disavowed by the General, who would surely compel his subordinates to implement his established policy of liberating all of France's African dependencies.

De Gaulle's announcement of the referendum that would be held in the Territory and would enable its population to decide its future status was greeted in the same vein by Mogadiscio as further evidence of the French President's determined liberalism. Radio Mogadiscio's broadcasts of late August and early September 1966 consistently stressed the right of the Territory's population to self-determination, but made no mention of its Afar majority and soft-pedaled the anticipated absorption of the independent "Somali Coast" by Somalia. Ethiopia's claims to Djibouti were dismissed as purely *pro forma,* put forward simply to conceal the secret hope of the "colonialist" Addis Ababa government for the continuation of French rule over the Territory. However, after the population had voted for independence and then for union with Somalia, the Mogadiscio authorities would be "willing to provide guarantees that Ethiopia's economic interests in Djibouti were respected." As proof of their good will toward France, the Somali authorities on September 5 arrested the secretary-general of the F.L.C.S. on charges of embezzlement, and closed his office at Mogadiscio.

Throughout the autumn of 1966, the government of the Somali Republic maintained its conciliatory attitude toward General de Gaulle.* It continued to deny that it had had any political agents in the Territory, and, as a matter of fact, the French in Djibouti never uncovered any reliable evidence that Somalia was directly involved in the riots. Somalia's premier[34] asserted that the Somalis who had crossed the border in large numbers prior to the General's visit were simply nomads who habitually trekked in the area, that the slogans in English on the banners brandished before his eyes were not necessarily composed by Somalis from former British Somaliland, and that the Somalia government was primarily concerned that the people of the Territory acquire independence and only secondarily that they should later be united with Somalia. The premier and his foreign minister went to Paris in October for talks with their French counterparts, who assured them that no secret understanding with Ethiopia in regard to the referendum existed. Early in December, Somalia's Minister of Somali Affairs published a document entitled "French Somaliland in True Perspective," in which his government's stand in favor of the principles of self-determination as expressed in a referendum was reiterated. In addition, it urged that all political prisoners and exiles be allowed to vote and that the Territory's independence be guaranteed by international agreement. Inevitably this document included a denial of the validity of Ethiopia's claims, to which Somalia remained adamantly opposed.

* The Somalia leaders were reported to have made numerous but futile attempts to persuade General de Gaulle to go to Mogadiscio after his state visit to Addis Ababa so that they could explain to him their views on the future of Djibouti. Chauvel, "Djibouti."

Both the Somalia and French governments obviously were anxious to maintain friendly official relations, but after the riots of mid-September at Djibouti the tone of Mogadiscio's propaganda began to change. French troops in the Territory were accused of making arbitrary arrests and of brutally deporting *bona fide* Somali residents of Djibouti "simply because they demanded immediate independence." Governor Saget was urged to put an end to these "oppressive measures" and not to repeat the mistakes made by his predecessors. Beginning in October, every issue of the weekly *Somali News* carried stories of the sad plight of the refugees and of the donations for their relief made by even the poorest of their fellow tribesmen in Somalia. Increasingly doubts were aired as to the freedom with which the Territory's inhabitants would be allowed to express their wishes in the forthcoming referendum, and numerous references were made to the "dubious conditions" under which the referendum of September 1958 had been held. Somalia's representatives in international meetings began to press strongly for the presence of U.N. or O.A.U. observers as the only guaranty of impartiality in the referendum.

After the French Parliament approved the law organizing the referendum, and especially after the alternatives to be offered the Territory's population on March 19, 1967, were made known, the criticism from Somalia became sharper and also extended over a wider range of targets. Nevertheless, it should be noted that the Mogadiscio government confined itself to making verbal protests and appeals to international bodies. It left to radio broadcasters, notably those of Radio Hargeisa, and to the F.L.C.S., which had been revived in November 1966, the diffusion of the most extreme (and often absurd) condemnations of the French authorities. These organs denounced the Territory's administration for failing to welcome back political exiles and to release prisoners so that they could vote in the referendum, for refusing to admit U.N. or O.A.U. observers of the voting, and for arresting and deporting nationalists likely to vote for independence. It added to these now almost threadbare reproaches fresh criticism of the French officials for limiting to four the number of political parties permitted to campaign before the referendum, for issuing an excessive number of ballots to docile Afar chiefs and refusing them to qualified Somali voters, and finally for imposing unduly stringent conditions of eligibility for the electorate. General de Gaulle for the first time was held up to scorn as a hypocritical "liberator" of the Third World, trying to deceive public opinion at home and abroad by holding a fraudulent referendum in French Somaliland.

On the positive side, the Somalia propagandists urged the Territory's Arab voters to join the Somalis in rejecting Christian colonial rule, claiming that if all the Muslims maintained their solidarity and voted for independence, it would mean "the end of Zionist imperialism in Africa."[35] Those French parties and leaders, such as the socialists and liberal Catholics, who had protested against the conditions under which the referendum was being held were praised and thanked.[36] Friday, March 17, was proclaimed a day of fasting and special prayers in Somalian mosques, and a two-hour mass demonstration was organized in Mogadiscio, during which shouts of "Down with De Gaulle!" were mingled with vocal denunciations of Haile Selassie and Lyndon B. Johnson.

As a matter of fact, the Somali Republic's government was already so deeply embroiled with its neighbors in Nairobi and Addis Ababa that it did not relish the idea of entering into conflict with the French over Djibouti. Furthermore, a "revolt" in the Somalian army in February 1967, though short-lived and virtually bloodless, had alerted the Mogadiscio government to the possibility of a military coup.[37] It was probably this fear that prompted the premier of Somalia to send an envoy to Addis Ababa to ask the Negus—but in vain—to join him in a hands-off agreement should the Territory vote for independence.[38] When no reply was forthcoming and the Ethiopians massed forces along the Territory's frontier, Somalia seized the opportunity to send a sizable portion of its army to the French border, ostensibly to prevent Ethiopia from seizing Djibouti by force but actually to get the troops out of Mogadiscio. The last thing the Somalian politicians wanted was a conflict with either the Ethiopian or the French army, yet no Somalian official could have hoped to stay in office had he not at least verbally supported the supposedly ardent desire of the Somali peoples for reunification. The announced result of the referendum could hardly have surprised the leaders of Somalia despite their frequent reiteration of confidence in a victory of the Parti du Mouvement Populaire. It was, therefore, largely for internal effect that the government decreed three days of mourning, permitted nonviolent demonstrations and hunger fasts in the principal towns, and sponsored the offering of prayers for the Territory's martyrs who had died during the struggle for independence.

The Somalia government found itself on the horns of a dilemma. After having irrevocably supported the principle of self-determination, it was now forced to denounce the referendum vote as fraudulent and to lodge protests against it with the French government, the O.A.U., and the U.N. Furthermore, it refused to accept the thousands of Somalis deported by the French from Djibouti, on the ground that to do so would be tantamount to acknowledging the legitimacy of the referendum. A more practical reason was that impoverished Somalia could not afford to add them to its population. It is noteworthy that neither then nor later did the republic break off diplomatic relations with France. In fact, the premier and the foreign minister who took office as a result of the July 1967 elections in Somalia let it be known that their government desired to restore good relations with France and with the Territory's administration.[39]

Late in September 1967, the Somalia delegate to the U.N. General Assembly reiterated his government's willingness to negotiate directly with the Paris authorities the question of repatriating the deportees from Djibouti. Yet Mogadiscio continues to permit—if not encourage—the activities on its territory of the F.L.C.S., which in June 1967 was reorganized and renamed the Somali Coast Freedom Party.

In all likelihood, in March 1967 the government of Somalia, like that of Ethiopia, felt a sense of relief at the outcome of the referendum. A vote for independence would have added immeasurably to its already formidable political and economic difficulties. It would have had to choose between an almost inevitable military defeat at the hands of Ethiopia and the acceptance of Ethiopian control of Djibouti. Either alternative would have caused the overthrow of the republic's government and possibly led to a wider international conflict. Moreover, the acquisition of Djibouti and its port would not have offset the difficulties that would be created by the concurrent necessity of absorbing a large and hostile Afar population. And the addition of the thousands of the Territory's Somalis who originated in British Somaliland would have upset the delicate balance between the political forces of the northern and southern regions of the republic—a particularly ominous consequence in view of the presidential elections that were due to be held in Somalia within a few months.

Although the Somalia leaders reportedly felt disillusioned with the O.A.U. and the U.N. for failing to give them strong support—just as the P.M.P. resented the failure of the republic to provide its group with direct aid—they perforce turned to those organizations again. A vigorous campaign was set in motion by the Somali government to discredit the referendum in the eyes of world opinion and to maneuver the international organizations into demanding that France release the several thousands of Somali deportees who were being held in a desert camp near the frontier. If these men were permitted to return to Djibouti, they might be organized into a handy fifth column that could be counted upon to continue "spontaneous" pro-independence agitation there. For every reason the republic of Somalia, in its official actions, could not afford to adopt methods other than the "legal and pacific means" to which it is pledged, nor could it, for internal political reasons, renounce the goal of Somali reunification to which it has equally committed itself.

The Arab Countries: Aden and South Arabia

For many centuries, geographical proximity and easy communications across the Gulf of Aden have made for close relations between the Somali coast and South Arabia. In ancient times the gulf was an invasion route from the Arabian peninsula to the East African mainland, and more recently it carried a flourishing traffic between them in slaves and firearms. After the Suez Canal was opened in 1869, Aden and Djibouti, on either side of the southern entrance to the Red Sea, were developed as bunkering ports and military bases by Britain and France respectively.

Aden became the colony of a Western power earlier than Djibouti, and has consistently maintained a long lead over its rival across the gulf. Although Britain and France both lost their main colonies east of Suez after World War II, Aden retained its importance as a military base longer than Djibouti and has always been a more active port. It is more accessible to shipping and offers more facilities—including an oil refinery—as an entrepôt and port of call. The tariff and currency reforms of 1949 in French Somaliland were motivated by France's vain hope that they would transform Djibouti into a center comparable to Aden for international trade and investment. Almost all of Ethiopia's foreign trade, however, has continued to flow through Aden, and many of Djibouti's export-import firms are still subsidiaries of parent organizations situated in Aden.

In Yemen, France scored a greater success than in Aden. There French enterprises helped to build many of the country's public works, and at Taiz they constructed a spinning mill and a hospital which is staffed mainly by French doctors. Although France has no direct diplomatic relations with Yemen, the Yemenese crown prince was invited to Paris in 1957 to discuss ways of promoting closer relations between his country and the Territory. Regular contacts between the two have been maintained by the many Yemenese residents of French Somaliland, who have contributed appreciably to the economic development of Djibouti.

Anglo-French colonial rivalry remained acute in this region longer than in other parts of Africa and in the Far East. For about a century, the Red Sea was virtually a British lake, and French Somaliland was no more than a minute enclave at its southern end. Not only did Great Britain control a far larger Somali area as a protectorate, but after World War II it also took over the administration of Italy's former East African colonies and promoted the Greater Somalia project. To France's long-standing resentment of Britain's overwhelming superiority in the region was added the fear that

London contemplated including in its expanding zone of influence the Somalis under French rule. In the mid-1950's, however, the sudden intensification of nationalism throughout the region was recognized by both Western powers as a threat to their rule in the Red Sea basin, and it prompted a new spirit of cooperation between them. This culminated in their joint military action with Israel during the Suez crisis of November 1956, which not only brought them closer together but linked both of them with Israel as a main target of Arab opprobrium. When France granted a British request to accept for internment at Djibouti the crew of an Egyptian frigate sunk during the hostilities, the press at Aden launched a bitter attack on the French in Somaliland.

For several years before this incident the Aden trade unions had shown their antagonism to French rule at Djibouti.[40] Mahmoud Harbi, after his defeat in the 1952 elections, went to South Arabia, where he developed close ties with both its conservative and its radical elements. In particular he obtained financial support from the Aden trade unions for the organization of an effective strike that would hamper the competitive operation of Djibouti port.* The long-drawn-out French campaign to crush the Algerian revolt, which began in late 1954, aroused anti-French sentiment throughout the Arab world, and it was intensified by France's participation in the brief war against Egypt two years later. In the concurrent expansion of the fueling facilities of Djibouti port, which made it increasingly competitive with Aden, the trade unions of Aden had an additional motive for their efforts to undermine French rule in the Territory. French officials at Djibouti attributed the growing politicization of the strikes there to the influence and support of the dockers by Aden's nationalist leaders. In 1966 some of those officials went so far as to assert that the independence riots of August and September had been financed from Aden.[41]

The position of the French at Djibouti bore some resemblance to that of the British at Aden. Both Western communities lived aloof from close contacts with the native inhabitants, and both were caught by surprise when violence erupted. The British in 1963, like the French two years later, barred the U.N. Committee on Decolonization from entering their territory on the grounds that it would only cause trouble and be an unjustified interference in local affairs. Yet the similarities between them should not be exaggerated, for the disparities were far greater, in both the scope and the nature of the problems involved.

The Federation of South Arabia, formed in 1959 by an alliance between

* See p. 65.

the British and the conservative sheikhs, and its separation from Aden, had no counterpart in the French Territory. Egyptian influence, which had been a mainspring of the trouble at Aden, had been of minor importance in French Somaliland. France's current troubles in the Territory stem mainly from Somali irredentism and the consequent accentuation of the divisions between the two principal indigenous tribes. To be sure, recent developments in the Territory, like those in South Arabia, can be viewed as evidence of the same overall Muslim determination to oust Christian colonial rule. In the case of Britain in South Arabia and Aden, it is also related to the power struggle inside the Arab world between Nasser and King Faisal. In the case of the Territory, it is compounded by the involvement of the United States and the communist countries with, respectively, Ethiopia and Somalia, the two nations that covet Djibouti.

Britain's decision to withdraw from South Arabia by the end of 1967 involved many difficulties related to the transfer of power. So profoundly troubled is the situation in South Arabia that it seems unlikely that the port of Aden will return to normal operations by the time the Suez Canal reopens to traffic. If that proves to be the case, Djibouti cannot but profit by Aden's continued difficulties, and this prospect has certainly entered into the calculations of the local French authorities. At all events, French policy (in contrast to that of Britain in Aden) is based on the premise of continued French control of the Territory for the time being. As a result, the French will be especially vulnerable at Djibouti, as the sole Western target of Muslim hostility in the Horn of Africa.

Egypt

At the time of the first Suez crisis in 1956, some concern was expressed in France about Egyptian subversion in French Somaliland. It was recalled that Mahmoud Harbi and other politically active dissidents from the Territory had been welcomed in Cairo and given support by the Arab League. In the National Assembly, a deputy queried the government on what it was doing to counter the propaganda being spread by Egyptian teachers in Djibouti.[42] To this the Minister of Overseas France replied that he had been assured by the governor of French Somaliland that there were no Egyptian teachers in the Territory. During the next few years, however, Egyptian activities in Somalia and then Egypt's open encouragement of Somali irredentists and of Eritrean secessionists revived uneasiness about their repercussions in the Territory. Behind the agitation that was affecting all the Muslim minorities under Christian rule in northeastern Africa, France—

like Ethiopia, the United States, and Great Britain—was inclined to see the hand of Nasser, aided and abetted by the Soviet Union. In 1960, however, Ali Aref, then vice-president of the Territory's government council, expressed his conviction that Egyptian pressure and propaganda were making little headway in French Somaliland—and for a very practical reason. In an interview reported in *Le Monde* on August 5, 1960, he said: "We listen to La Voix des Arabes [radio program] but simply to get the news, just as we listen to the Paris radio and to the B.B.C. The U.A.R. does not have much influence in French Somaliland because it doesn't distribute much money there as subsidies."

This tendency to play down the local influence of Nasser was shared by the French officials in the Territory, although they had taken the precaution of forbidding Somali students to attend Egyptian educational institutions in Cairo.[43] For one reason, the Egyptian community in French Somaliland was never large and consisted almost wholly of laborers for the railroad company. Furthermore, the resident Arabs, or at least those who were wealthy and influential, seemed impervious to propaganda or events that were unlikely to affect their immediate interests. Certainly Nasser's interest in Djibouti has been peripheral to his major aspirations, and France's continued presence there is only a trifling obstacle to the realization of his objective of making the Red Sea basin an Egyptian preserve.

Nevertheless, Egyptian policy in regard to Somalia and Ethiopia indirectly influenced the Somali nationalists in Djibouti. Relations between Cairo and the territorial government, like those of Cairo and Addis Ababa, have been officially correct if mistrustful. Nasser's attitude toward the Territory has been conditioned since 1958 by the overall policy of General de Gaulle. So long as the Algerian war continued, the Cairo radio periodically reported unfavorably on developments in French Somaliland, but in mid-1967 this changed as the General's foreign policy became more pro-Arab. In a long commentary on the independence demonstrations of August 1966, the Middle East News Agency stressed that they were not directed personally against the French President but against "the policy of terrorism and oppression" pursued by the local administration.[44] Since Egypt was committed, however, to supporting Somali irredentism, Cairo's propaganda echoed that of Mogadiscio in regard to the referendum and likewise urged the population to vote for independence. Significantly, however, Cairo stopped short of advocating the Territory's subsequent union with Somalia. The Egyptian President probably would have liked to see the Territory emerge as a weak, nominally sovereign state, independent of both Somalia and Ethiopia, which would therefore turn to Egypt for support. If this occurred and Aden were also brought within the Egyptian orbit, Nasser would gain control of the southern entrance to the Red Sea.[45] After the referendum took place, the Egyptian radio had few and moderate comments to make on the outcome. Nasser's defeat in the brief war with Israel in June 1967, and General de Gaulle's pro-Arab stand during that conflict, certainly—if temporarily—eliminated any tendency that Nasser might have had to attack French rule in Djibouti.

The question naturally arises as to what have been the reactions of Muslims throughout the Horn of Africa generally, and in the Territory particularly, to Egypt's policies there. Doubtless the common religion and widespread respect for Arab culture have made Islam and the Arabic language propitious media for transmitting Cairo's nationalist appeals. By these means, Nasser has unquestionably strengthened Muslim solidarity and opposition to Western and Christian rule in the area, but this does not necessarily mean that the Muslims of northeastern Africa accept Egyptian hegemony or even want to create genuine Islamic states of their own. Insofar as Egypt provides them with economic and cultural aid, its assistance is welcomed by the indigenous Muslims, but it must not go beyond the help needed to realize the various locally determined nationalist goals.

To pinpoint such reactions in the Territory, one might examine the response of the Arab community in Djibouti to Egypt's direct and indirect attempts to influence its members. Theoretically this community should be highly receptive to Nasser's influence because it is in a minority position vis-à-vis both the French Christian authorities and the two main indigenous tribes. In general the French have favored—though not outstandingly—the domiciled Arab merchants and laborers. But the attitude of the Afars and Issas has complicated the situation. The respect they feel for the Arabs as the purveyors of Islam and Arabic culture is partly offset by the resentment and envy of the Arab merchants' power and wealth, and especially of the means by which both have been acquired. These same emotions are felt also, though less intensely, toward the Arab manual laborers. Although they are less rich and more transient in the Territory than are the Arab merchants and landowners, they are the best-paid members of the working class and also are aloof, living as a community apart. The Arabs, for their part, do not share this complex of emotions and have felt only rather contemptuous of the native tribes until recently, when a new element—that of fear—has been added. This fear has inspired some repatriations to Arabia and, depending on the course of events in Djibouti, may well become the dominant emotion of the Arabs there.

For some weeks before the referendum, Mogadiscio radio conducted a campaign to persuade the Arab residents in the Territory to vote for independence. A typical broadcast, on January 25, 1967, combined political and religious arguments:

Friendly relations have always existed between Arabs and Somalis, all Muslim brothers, who must unite and struggle against the enemy. Colonialists have tried to divide the Muslims, and so we appeal in advance to the Arab residents of the Somali Coast to support the Somali demand for independence. The Somalis living in Aden, as is well known, support the Arabs there in their independence struggle. We assure the Arabs of the Somali Coast that the colonialists' propaganda—to the effect that they would be robbed of their rights and their property when the Somali Coast becomes independent—is false. We truly believe that the Arabs would lead a better life after the local people have attained their sovereignty. Both Arabs and Somalis must remember God's holy commandments in the Koran that all Muslims should unite and allow nothing to separate them.

To what extent the Territory's Arabs responded to this appeal in the March 19 vote is not precisely known, but the damage done to their property during the riots on the following day suggests that the Somalis believed that they had voted almost solidly for the continuation of French rule. That Mogadiscio felt concerned to prevent a rupture between the two communities at Djibouti was indicated by a conciliatory message broadcast to the Arabs on March 28: "All the Arab countries gave strong support and assistance to the Somali Coast freedom fighters. It is also an established fact that the majority of the Arab people who voted in Djibouti wanted to share independence with the Somalis and voted 'no' in the referendum. However, if one of them happened to vote 'yes,' this should create no problem since it was a matter of personal choice."

In all probability, it was the wealthy and long-established Arabs in Djibouti who voted affirmatively in the referendum, because experience had proved that as a minority they were relatively more secure, in both life and property, under French government than under native nationalist rule. The younger generation of Arabs, on the other hand, may well have voted for independence, to the appeal of which they were highly susceptible. In recent years, facilities for contacts among young Arabs, Somalis, and Afars have greatly increased, particularly in Djibouti. The growing cleavage between the generations, which is a phenomenon common to all the ethnic groups, may serve to counter the present accentuation of tribal emotions, and might eventually bring about a new alignment of political forces in the Territory.

Part II

THE SOCIAL AND ECONOMIC FIELDS

Chapter Six

SOCIAL DEVELOPMENT

Religion

Beginning in the twelfth century, Islam was intensively propagated in the settlements along the Somali coast, probably by merchants or members of the Brotherhoods of South Arabia. From there it spread to the animist tribes of the hinterland, where it was profoundly modified by traditional agrarian rites and customary law. Both Issas and Afars have a great respect for Islam and feel themselves to be deeply Muslim, but their harsh lives leave them little time or leisure to practice it and they have no knowledge of Islamic dogma. Most of the nomads ignore the Koran, only a small minority prays five times daily, the fast of Ramadan is not widely observed, and the sole religious injunctions that are faithfully observed are the Islamic prohibitions against the drinking of alcoholic beverages and the eating of shellfish, pork, or the meat of animals not ritually slaughtered.[1] When Koranic law differs from or conflicts with tribal custom, as is the case with the Afar ceremony for the dead (*rabena*), custom usually triumphs.

Nevertheless, certain *fractions* and some individual chiefs and Marabouts (religious teachers) are renowned for their knowledge of Arabic and of Muslim law. The children of the tribe are sent to them for religious instruction, and they are rewarded by gifts in kind and even in money. The tombs of learned and saintly men are the sites of frequent pilgrimages, some at fixed times of the year, when prayers are offered for the health and prosperity of the individual and his herds. Some Marabouts are believed to possess supernatural powers, and the aid of these "medicine men" is sought for treating illnesses.

Among the sedentary population, especially at Djibouti, religious practices are more regular though not necessarily more fervent than among the nomads. Very few Djibouti residents do not go to the mosque at least for the Friday prayer. The Afar and Somali town dwellers go to any nearby mosque, but the Arabs will pray only in their own mosques because a purer Arabic is spoken by their own imam. After World War II, there was a falling-off in urban attendance at the great ceremony of Beiram, which closes the Ramadan fast. Even at Tadjoura, which has seven mosques for a population of little more than 1,500 Muslims, religious practices seemed less assiduously observed than formerly. On the other hand, the Mecca pilgrimage has gained enormously in popularity. Whereas before the war only a few dozen Muslims in the Territory, despite the proximity of Islam's holy places, made the pilgrimage to Mohammed's tomb, today there are several hundred. In 1949 the French administration began to facilitate the pilgrimage, and in that one year 50 Muslims from the Territory journeyed to Mecca.

The highest Muslim authority in the Territory is the Cadi of Djibouti, who celebrates marriages, registers divorces and wills, administers Islamic properties, and presides over the *shariah* court.

The Muslim Brotherhoods, with the possible exception of the Qadriya, have never exercised great influence in the Territory. An attempt in the late 1940's to introduce Wahabism failed, largely because of the vigorous opposition of the Territory's imams. The great events that stirred the Arab world in the first postwar decade left the Issas and Afars indifferent, until the Anglo-French-Israeli invasion of 1956 stirred their interest in Pan-Arabism and Pan-Islam. Islam has never served as a bridge to unite the Afars and Issas, nor has it inspired fanaticism or xenophobia among them.

Aside from the 700-odd Protestants and members of the Greek Orthodox Church living in the Territory, its Christians are Roman Catholics. The first Catholic mission was founded at Obock in 1885 by the Capuchins of the Province of Strasbourg. Since that time various other missionary orders have installed themselves in the Territory, which was raised to the rank of an Apostolic Prefecture in 1914 and to that of an episcopal diocese in 1955.

The size of the Catholic community fluctuates with the number of European residents, and at the end of 1966 it was estimated at approximately 7,000.[2] Mass is celebrated in each *cercle* headquarters: Dikhil is served by a priest resident at Ali-Sabieh, and Obock by a priest living at Tadjoura. In all there are some 60 priests and nuns stationed in the Territory, and about as many laymen actively organized in the Secours Catholique. The nuns provide most of the nurses for the Djibouti hospital, and they are also in charge of orphanages, clinics, and schools, as well as three *foyers* for African women. It is through such charitable and educational establishments that the Catholic missionaries come closely into touch with the native population, and the greatest influence they exert is through the mission schools. They make virtually no converts among the non-European population, except among the children reared in their orphanages. Indeed, in French Somaliland conversion to another religion rarely occurs, and the various religious communities remain stable and largely aloof from each other, each under its own spiritual leadership.

Education

Education in the Territory developed along much the same lines as in other French tropical dependencies, although schooling in French Somaliland progressed at an appreciably slower tempo, and the university level will probably never be reached. This situation is not surprising, in view of the remoteness of French Somaliland and the small size of its population.

Pioneer work was done by the Catholic missions with minimal subsidies from the government. The public school system only began to get under way during the interwar period, and until after World War II the missions continued to provide most of the formal instruction given in French Somaliland and to receive state subsidies along with official control. After World War II the curricula of the state schools were aligned with those of France, and the mission schools followed suit. Then the public primary schools caught up with and soon surpassed those maintained by the missions. In the fields of secondary and technical instruction, the government led the way and the mission schools lagged behind.

Education in the Western sense was hampered for many years in the Territory by the population's indifference if not hostility. The political changes wrought by the *loi-cadre* and the spread of nationalist sentiment have not only completely reversed this attitude on the part of parents and children alike, but have also created new difficulties politically and economically. There are now more applicants for admission to the Territory's schools than can be accommodated, and the positions open to graduates of the local school system have not kept pace with their number, which increases every year. Other major problems of the growth of the Territory's educational facilities have arisen from the need to combine religious with secular instruction and to close the widening gaps between the schooling offered in the hinterland and in Djibouti, to the Afars and Somalis in the capital city, and to boys and girls throughout the Territory. A difficulty that has come up only recently is that of the adverse effect of political developments on student discipline and the level of academic attainment among Djibouti's secondary school students.

French Somaliland's first school was founded at Obock in 1884 by Father André Jarosseau, later Bishop of Harar. It was modeled after the orphanage he had established in Ethiopia, where children were taught French (both written and spoken), craftsmanship, and some modern agricultural techniques. After Father André's school on the Somali coast was moved with the government to Djibouti, it was taken over by the Capuchin monks.[3] In the new capital, another mission orphanage school was established in 1888, but it was exclusively for girls. It was operated by the Franciscan Sisters of Calais until 1906, when the nuns in charge of the orphanage were placed under the supervision of the Djibouti branch of the Alliance Française. Another religious order, the Brothers of St. Gabriel, started a third mission school at Djibouti in 1901, and its curriculum—like that of its two predecessors—combined a rudimentary primary education with manual training. These "schools" accepted free of charge all children regardless of race, creed, or color, and for many years Catholic priests and nuns were the sole instrument of education in the Territory. To help meet the operating expenses of their schools, the government allocated them a small subsidy of 200 (gold) francs a month.

Since World War II, the missions have extended their educational activities and have received more substantial financial aid from the government, and at the same time they have been subjected to closer official control over their academic operations. In 1948 another mission primary school, the Ecole Charles de Foucauld, was opened at Djibouti by the Capuchins. After 1951, when it was taken over by the newly arrived Frères des Ecoles Chrétiennes, its curriculum was widened to include secondary and commercial courses. By 1958 it had a teaching staff of eight priests and four laymen, who were giving instruction to 340 pupils.[4] Much the same curriculum was then being offered by the Franciscan nuns in their orphanage school at Djibouti, where the faculty comprised three Sisters and 13 lay teachers and the pupils numbered 456. A crafts school opened at Tadjoura in 1956 also owed its existence to Catholic mission enterprise.

The pupil attendance at mission schools has grown steadily, and these schools have maintained their lead as the principal educators of native girls. Until 1948, when they were giving instruction to a total of 300 students, compared with 400 in the state primary schools, they had remained in the forefront of the whole academic scene. This was due not only to the confidence they had been able to inspire in parents over the years, but also to their schools' being the only ones to provide an education for orphans. However, in the late 1940's the state schools forged rapidly ahead of the mission institutions owing to the larger sums placed at their disposal by the Fonds d'Investissement pour le Développement Economique et Social (F.I.D.E.S.). Each year the gap between the two school systems grows wider, both in number of children attending and range of instruction offered. By 1966 there were 1,600 pupils in mission primary schools compared with about 3,000 in their state counterparts. In the field of secondary education, moreover, the disparity was even greater—180 mission school students compared with 424 in state schools.[5]

It was not until April 12, 1913, that the local administration got around to laying the legal foundations for a public school system, and then it simply followed the principle established by the mission schools of providing education free of charge to all children in the Territory. But the state school system remained on paper during World War I and did not assume concrete form until October 1922, when the first three public primary schools were opened at Djibouti. To staff them, a handful of instructors was brought out from France. Among them were two outstanding teachers, Monsieur and Madame E. Duchenet, who later drew up a syllabus that was used in the Territory's schools for a generation. The type of curriculum and especially its practical orientation were copied from the mission schools, and the certificate awarded to graduates of the state primary schools was not equivalent to the Metropolitan Certificat d'Etudes Primaires (C.E.P.). In 1932 the first attempt was made to extend the public school system outside the capital, small primary classes being opened at Tadjoura and Dikhil. In the mid-1930's Governor de Coppet proposed revising the system so that the local C.E.P. would be brought up to Metropolitan standards, but this was not done until after World War II.

No figures are available on attendance at state and mission primary schools before World War II. The total number of children enrolled in them, however, must have been well under 300, because in 1945 there were no more than 110 pupils in the four mission primary schools and 185 in the eight public primary schools.[6] In 1946, Ali-Sabieh and Obock were given their first primary classes, and the existing schools at Tadjoura and Dikhil were enlarged so that their attendance could be doubled. Although the curriculum was now patterned after that of France, to meet local needs more emphasis was placed on teaching the French language, simple rules of hygiene, and manual training. In 1954, the first primary cycle of six years was extended to include courses leading to the Brevet Elémentaire (B.E.), but until the *loi-cadre* was applied to the Territory in 1957, the considerable efforts made to improve and enlarge the state school system were almost wholly confined to the first primary level. Since that time, secondary and technical education has been emphasized, and, at the same time, the primary schools have also made great strides. In 1958 the number of pupils attending state and mission primary schools came to 2,364, and by 1966–67 it had risen to 5,698.[7] In 1967, there were 100 trained *instituteurs* teaching at the primary school level.

Secondary education in French Somaliland began with the inauguration of a *cours complémentaire* in 1949, but more than a decade passed before it was expanded into a *lycée*. Even in late 1956, Gaston Defferre, who was then not only Minister of Overseas France but also co-author of the *loi-cadre,* turned down the plea made by the Territory's deputy and senator to provide French Somaliland with higher education facilities so that an indigenous elite could develop.[8] What the Territory principally needed, Defferre believed, was a continued expansion of the primary system. Since there were then only 27 pupils in the *cours complémentaire,* he felt that there was no urgency about developing secondary education. Soon, however, French officials changed their minds in this respect, because they heard more and more reports to the effect that a considerable number of the Territory's students had surreptitiously gone to Egypt to acquire an Arabic education. They realized that if France persisted in not providing higher education facilities, Somali youths in growing numbers would be welcomed in revolutionary countries where they would surely absorb subversive political ideas. Furthermore, one of the basic principles laid down in the *loi-cadre* was to promote an Africanization of the administrative cadres, which until then had made no headway in the Territory.

Consequently, public and mission schools began rapidly to enlarge their curricula to include secondary courses, and the *cours complémentaire* increasingly took on the dimensions of a *lycée*. By 1963 it had a *proviseur* and three fully qualified professors on its staff, and a student body of 306 boys and girls. The French government yielded to the plea of the government council and, in 1964, agreed to assume the full costs of secondary education in the Territory and to raise the level of the *lycée* to the Metropolitan standard. To house the *lycée* a new building with modern classrooms was constructed, as well as a dormitory for 144 student boarders. By 1966 the institution had a faculty of 27 professors, a student attendance of 604, twelve graduates with B.A. degrees, and 40 candidates being prepared for the baccalaureate.[9] In recent years some two dozen students, on the average, from the Territory have been awarded scholarships to attend institutions of higher education in France.

At the same time as secondary education in the liberal arts and science was being promoted, the authorities were also developing technical studies in the Territory. From the outset, schools in French Somaliland had stressed vocational training, but because this training had remained at the manual level, it had never been popular with the nomads because of their traditional dislike for such occupations. In 1954 the first step was taken to raise it above the craft level with the inauguration of a two-year course in navigation, and in 1956 commercial classes were started not only in the state and mission schools but also by the Djibouti chamber of commerce. Not until the Centre de Formation Préprofessionnelle was founded, however, was technical education in the strict sense of the term launched in the Territory. Admission to this center was restricted to boys 14 years of age and over who held a C.E.P. and who had passed a competitive entrance examination, and its graduates were awarded a Certificat d'Aptitude Professionnelle, which was recognized as the equivalent of the Metropolitan C.A.P. The center offers a wide range of instruction and trains mechanics and electricians as well as stenographers and accountants. Despite its stringent entrance requirements, it had 180 students in 1966, and by far the most popular courses are those that train students for jobs in the commercial sector. It also prepares candidates for the apprenticeships offered by the Berliet and Peugeot motor companies at their factories in France.

The rapid growth of the Territory's school system has inevitably created new problems, but curiously enough they have not included a shortage of teachers. Almost no attempt has been made by the local authorities to train native teachers, and, in relation to the Territory's needs, they have been generously supplied with enough public funds to import most of their teaching personnel from France. (Under the first and second Plans, the F.I.D.E.S. also provided over 268 million Metro. francs for school buildings and equipment.) Since France assumed the entire cost of secondary education in the Territory, the local budget has been able to allocate all the funds available for education to the primary school system, and in recent years those funds have averaged about 18 percent of the total local revenues.

If the Territory has never had a large education service, it has had the good fortune to attract and retain for many years outstanding educators such as MM. Dechenet, Vincent, and Muzette. It has also benefited by the presence of the wives of some French officials and officers who are trained teachers; in fact, by 1964, there were more such *institutrices* available locally than posts for them, because of the slow development of girls' schooling in the Territory. The position of monitor in the education service was open for the first time to native applicants after courses permitting them to earn

the B.E. were started in 1954. A training program for native teachers was
not begun until 1960, and four years later they were given additional courses
that raised the requirements for a teaching post to Metropolitan levels. The
result of this slow start, compounded by further delays resulting from
raising the standards, is that there are probably no more than a dozen
trained native instructors in the Territory. (However, along with the moni-
tors, who are more numerous, they have formed a Syndicat des Instituteurs
Autochtones, which operates as a special-interest group and is represented
on the Education Advisory Committee.) Thus the rise in the number of
primary school teachers serving in French Somaliland from 68 in 1958 to
136 in 1966, as well as the presence of 35 professors teaching in the secondary
and technical schools, provides evidence of the continuation of the policy
of importing teaching personnel from France. This is a very expensive procedure but one that has prevented educational standards from slipping.
Governor Tirant proudly told the territorial assembly on December 8, 1964,
that French Somaliland was spending on education 12 times more per
capita than Egypt, ten times more than Somalia, and eight times more than
Ethiopia.

All observers of the Territory's education system have been struck by the
disparity between the school facilities available in Djibouti and those in the
hinterland—a phenomenon that paralleled the economic development of
the capital and the neglect of the rural areas. The obvious and highly practical explanation for both policies has been the nomadic character of the
rural population and the small number of residents in the *cercle* settlements.
It is not surprising, therefore, that Tadjoura and Dikhil had no schools
until 1932, and that Obock and Ali-Sabieh had to wait until after World
War II for their first educational facilities. Another and equally cogent
reason for this delay was the nomads' indifference and even resistance to
any instruction other than that provided in Koranic schools. When primary
classes were finally started by the government in the rural settlements, they
had to offer free meals as an inducement to the nomads to permit their
children to attend. To encourage the ablest students to continue their education, the government also created scholarships in Djibouti's state schools.
    Abbé Paul Catrice, a Mouvement Républicain Populaire (M.R.P.) mem-
ber of the French Union Assembly, came to the Territory in October 1950
expressly to study the population's educational needs. Upon his return to
France, he urged the government to found special schools for the nomads
and to make a study to determine which native language should be used

as the medium of instruction for the children.[10] He expressed the hope that the three French scholars, Gainet, Blosse, and Chedeville—who were then compiling dictionaries in Paris of the Afar and Somali languages—would eventually produce appropriate textbooks. But the creation of a nomads' school at Yoboki in 1958 was the only tangible result of the resolution passed by the French Union Assembly on June 3, 1952, asking the government to create educational facilities for children of the nomad tribes. The marked progress made by the Territory's school system continued, as before, to be concentrated in Djibouti.

Koranic schools provided the only education in the Territory other than that offered by the French government and missions, and it was highly valued by nomads and native town dwellers alike. In the rural areas, the few chiefs who had some claim to literacy in Arabic often taught children of their tribe the three r's and a few verses from the Koran. In return for this instruction, the parents gave food and clothing to the teacher, and the children were left free to come and go as they chose. Those who stayed the longest were usually orphans who hoped to acquire sufficient learning to be able eventually to open Koranic schools of their own.[11] In Djibouti, the Koranic schools were only slightly less haphazard and informal than among the nomads. Each *quartier* had one or two *maalim* (religious instructors), who taught children in the street or in open courtyards. As of 1947, more of the children in the Territory were attending Koranic schools (482) than the primary schools run by the state (463) or by the Catholic mission (204). Although French officials deplored the Koranic schools' lack of hygiene and organization, there was no attempt to interfere with them because they inculcated in the children obedience to established authority, and only one effort was made to improve them. Before World War II an Ecole Franco-Arabe was founded at Djibouti which tried to combine in its curriculum the essentials of French and Arabic culture. By 1947 it had 150 students, but it was regarded as an unsatisfactory experiment inasmuch as its graduates had learned neither French nor Arabic thoroughly.

The main official objection to the Koranic schools was that Muslim children were required to attend them between the ages of six and 12; thus they could not enter the state primary schools until they were at least 13 years old. The government tried to alter this situation by passing a law in 1956 requiring that children attending primary schools in the Territory must be between the ages of eight and 12, and only very exceptionally be permitted to enter up to the age of 15. This law proved to be both impractical and inadvisable to apply strictly, because the tribes refused to have their children forgo religious education and in any case were reluctant to send them to the French schools. In the 1960's, however, this attitude toward secular instruction changed radically.

As a result of the considerable efforts made by the education and health services of the Territory, as well as the vast increase in Djibouti's immigrant population, by 1963 there was such a huge number of applications for admission to the primary schools that some solution for the problem of "overage" children had to be found. By 1964 this situation had worsened, and many parents were hostile to the government because their children either were refused admission to the state school system or had to be withdrawn for having passed the age limit. The new zeal for a secular education displayed by parents and children alike drastically altered the assumptions upon which the existing system rested. Hassan Gouled's change of attitude in regard to educational policy clearly illustrates the rapidity and far-reaching consequences of this development. As a deputy in the National Assembly, he had urged the French government to enlarge the Territory's school facilities and above all to show greater flexibility concerning the age limit imposed on primary school children.[12] Yet only three years later, when he became the Territory's Minister of Education, Hassan Gouled applied the age-limit law strictly. He then argued that the quality of the instruction given in the state primary schools had deteriorated because classes were too large and because each class included too many children of widely disparate ages.[13]

To deal with this difficult question, Hassan Gouled in April 1964 formed an Advisory Committee on Education, which included the parents of schoolchildren as well as appropriate officials and teachers from both the state and mission schools. This committee's proposal to provide Koranic as well as lay instruction in the same schools but at different hours was accepted by the government. Apparently this solution has already reduced the average age of pupils in the Territory's primary schools, so that it now approximates the norm set in France. At the other end of the educational spectrum the government council has also introduced significant changes. One of the most important of these aimed at altering the attitude of parents who wanted their children to remain in school until such time as the government found jobs for them. The rapid development of secondary and technical education has already created in embryonic form the same phenomenon found in many other countries of the Third World—the problem of the "unemployed intellectual." As a step toward preventing this problem from reaching unmanageable proportions, Hassan Gouled awarded scholarships for study in France to only four students in 1964. The government council confirmed this policy by a decision taken on September 28, 1966. Scholarships in the Territory's schools were to be increased, but those awarded for higher study in French institutions were to be confined to fields such as technology and medicine, for which the Territory could offer employment.

Catholic nuns were the pioneers in the education of girls, and they have continued to maintain their leading position in this field. They started by creating orphanages where girls were taught sewing and child care and received a very rudimentary general education. To attract a wider attendance, they later opened an Ecole Ménagère, whose curriculum had a similar practical orientation. Muslim parents who were traditionally opposed to a Western-type education for their daughters approved of the kind of training given at the Ecole Ménagère, and it served as the opening wedge for girls able and willing to progress toward more academic instruction. This enabled the public school system, from which girls had been virtually excluded at the outset, to take over from the nuns, who, nevertheless, have continued in the forefront as the educators of girls. Moreover, the lay authorities have followed the mission's lead by creating courses in state schools to train girls for their future role as wives and mothers. As long ago as 1934 the government started a sewing school for girls, which failed, but in 1950 the project was successfully revived. Home economics remains the most popular course in both mission and state schools, and there are now several hundred girls undergoing such training.

In 1966, 1,001 of the 4,778 students in all the public and mission primary schools were native girls.[14] Girls are just beginning to catch up with boys in the regular school system, and the number of girl students attending state schools tripled between 1958 and 1966. Inevitably the proportion of girls attending school was higher in Djibouti than in the hinterland, and it was far larger in the primary than in the secondary schools, where they formed only 13 percent of the total student body. Of the 16 non-European girls attending the Djibouti *lycée* in 1966, seven were Issacks, five Arabs, one Gadaboursi, one Ethiopian, and one Sudanese. The indigenous tribes were represented by one Issa girl student, and there were no Afar girls at all. Only one-tenth of the total student body in the *lycée* was composed of girls, and virtually all of them were foreign-born.[15] Of the five girls from French Somaliland who have achieved the baccalaureate, not one is native-born. Obviously, much remains to be done in this area, but the rapid progress made in recent years is encouraging and indicates that the opposition of parents to the education of their daughters is steadily decreasing.

The recent growth in the number of educated girls should cause a marked change in the lowly position held by native women in the Territory.[16] Among the nomads all the women are illiterate, and their activities are restricted to bearing and rearing children and to performing such tasks as milking small animals, as designated by custom. At the age of seven, girls are subjected to a cruel form of excision which has led to their being called *femmes cousues*. Marriage, divorce, and inheritance are determined by Koranic law, which discriminates against women. Girls are not consulted in the choice of a husband, and once married, a wife leaves her *fraction* to join that of her husband. Practically her only possessions are some small animals given her at the time of her marriage and a few household utensils. Repudiation of a wife is easy among Muslims, and is virtually automatic if she is childless. The most effective deterrent to divorce is the requirement that the bride-price be returned to her family along with the repudiated wife. Adultery leads more often to the payment of compensation than to violence, and in the event that a woman is murdered, the blood price to be paid for her is lower than in the case of a man.

In Djibouti, native women lead a far easier life. They have fewer onerous tasks to perform and are freer to come and go. Judging from appearances, they spend most of their time preparing food, gossiping, and sewing. Only a few of them work for wages. Some are employed in the hospital or as nurses for European children, and even fewer work as stenographers in trading firms or as saleswomen in native shops. In any case their pay is small and certainly insufficient to support a family.[17] The Catholic mission has organized in Djibouti a Foyer Social pour la Promotion de la Femme Africaine, where married women can sell their handiwork. Similarly oriented toward enabling Djibouti women to earn money by selling their craft products is the lay Coopérative Artisanale Féminine, founded in 1966. Early in 1966 a Groupement Féminin Franco-Musulman was also founded to increase contacts among the women of Djibouti and to help them increase their earning capacities. Many such organizations, however, are ephemeral and dissolve amid general indifference.

Only recently have women in Djibouti begun to show an interest in politics, because the *loi-cadre,* which decreed adult suffrage in the Territory, did not extend the franchise to women. Nationalist propaganda has made much of this discrimination against native women, stressing that Frenchwomen resident in the Territory are entitled to vote in local elections. Somali women played an active role during the propaganda campaign preceding the March 1967 referendum, and this may well foreshadow effective political activity by women in the Territory.

Political consciousness among Djibouti's youthful population apparently began in the mid-1950's, although its genesis is difficult to pinpoint. Some light has been thrown on its origins and early development by an Issa official of the meteorological service, Aden Bourale. Having lived in Djibouti as an adolescent, he has written an unusually interesting and unique account of the reactions of youth during that period. He contends that anticolonialism among native urban youths dated from the Bandung conference of 1955, which "began for us a new era."[18] Communists, he affirmed, tried to take over the movement, and it was they who "taught us such terms as imperialists and exploitation, and at the same time our elders began to take more interest in politics." In Djibouti it was at the *mabraz*— meetings where *khat* is consumed*—that political events were discussed in an "atmosphere of brutality and impatience. We felt frustrated, but did not know exactly by what." It was during the Suez crisis of 1956, he went on to say, that "the Egyptian press was read in Djibouti most eagerly, and it stirred up public opinion. It was at that time that we became hostile to the French administration." A year later came the *loi-cadre,* and the radio and press commented upon it at length, as they did on the local elections that followed it:

My friends and I thought that the colonialists had simply changed tactics because this (*loi-cadre*) represented no progress at all in our eyes. It seemed almost inconceivable that we could come to an understanding with the French, and the slightest collaboration with them—even friendly relations—was regarded not merely as an insult but as an odious crime. In my group it was not at all unusual to call the French parasites, living at our expense.

Aden Bourale was awarded a scholarship from the European Common Market development fund, which his friends advised him to reject. They told him he would be "treated like a Negro and would certainly be killed and his body thrown into the river." They almost convinced him, but he finally decided to accept the offer and—fortunately for him—profited by and even enjoyed his experiences in Europe. Upon returning to Djibouti, he said that he found the "same atmosphere of hatred toward the French" among his friends.

It was to this strongly anticolonialist spirit that Mahmoud Harbi and Moussa Idriss successfully appealed. The most thorough organization of the Parti du Mouvement Populaire was among the nationalist youth of Djibouti, and they were responsible for its electoral victories. The younger firebrands, in the 12 to 14 age-group, who could not yet vote, found their

* See pp. 163–65.

own hero in the person of Mohamed Ahmed Issa, better known under his alias of "Cheicko." Not only was he the most intransigent advocate of independence but by being imprisoned for his political activities he had, in their eyes, earned a martyr's halo. During the riots of 1966 and the referendum campaign of 1967, these boys served Cheicko's cause by distributing inflammatory tracts, chalking pro-independence slogans on the walls of the Magala, and "politically educating" their parents by repeating to them the propaganda broadcast by Mogadiscio radio.[19] *Le Monde*'s correspondent, Philippe Herreman, reported[20] that some adolescents also organized themselves during the September 1966 riots into a kind of strong-arm force that tried to control the activities of foreign journalists and photographers in Djibouti.

The rapid educational progress made at Djibouti during the early 1960's was certainly responsible for much of this activity, although possibly some of the agitators had been politically indoctrinated in Egyptian schools. There is no doubt, however, that the most intransigent youth leaders are products of the Territory's school system, and that the majority of them are Somalis, who are three times as numerous as the Afars in Djibouti's student population. (According to the December 10, 1966, issue of *Le Réveil de Djibouti,* there were then 2,257 Somalis attending school, compared with 762 Afars.) Four officeholders in the youth section of the opposition's coordinating committee late in 1966 were young men who had failed to pass their examinations in France and who had had to return home without the coveted diploma.[21] Other members of their generation who had not left Djibouti also felt frustrated and concerned about their future employment, for every year the local schools were turning out more and more educated, or half-educated, youths who had difficulty finding jobs in the capital's restricted labor market. Cut off by their education from their elders and their traditions, they drifted together and met in the 15 or so young people's clubs which had sprung up in Djibouti after World War II.

The oldest of the youth clubs was formed by Arabs in the capital during the late 1930's. They asked Governor Deschamps for permission to organize a club, and it was granted on condition that they permit Somalis to attend the meetings. Similarly, he authorized sports competitions with the proviso that each team include players of the different local ethnic origins. But as the main motivation for forming groups at that time was to express and reinforce ethnic solidarity, the interest of their sponsors in multiracial organizations soon flagged. In the post–World War II period, the trend has turned away from forming clubs along tribal lines, or at least for the achievement of tribal objectives. Many of them now have social-welfare and cultural aims that are not simply a façade. For example, one club started evening classes for illiterates; the Young Issas Club campaigned to persuade conservative parents to send their children to state schools, and the Fédération des Sports carried on propaganda to discourage young people from consuming *khat*. Some clubs have been organized jointly by Arabs and Indians, and by Afars and Issas, and with some notable exceptions all have become oriented toward politics, often along intertribal lines. It is interesting to recall that Abdoulkader Moussa Ali resigned as president of the Young Afars Club three years before he ran successfully for election to the National Assembly in April 1967.

An analysis of the ethnic origin of students attending the Djibouti *lycée* in 1963–64 casts an interesting light on the tribal affiliations of the Territory's future trained leaders, and also on their probable political orientation.[22] The most striking fact that emerges from this study is the small proportion of members of the two main indigenous tribal groups who were then receiving the highest education available in the Territory. Of the *lycée*'s 160 non-European students at that time, only 54 were Afars and Issas. Probably some of the 31 Issa students were not born in the Territory. Even more striking was the poor representation of the largest indigenous ethnic group, the Afars, who numbered only 23. Moreover, in the graduating class of 64 students, there were only two Afars and 14 Issas. However, the presence of increasing numbers of Issas and Afars in the lower classes suggested that in the near future this situation would change radically. A remarkable aspect of the Afar component was that 17 of their total of 23 students came from the southern and middle regions of Tadjoura *cercle* and had all been prepared in the same public primary school.

The largest element among the non-European students was that of the Somali-language group, totaling 95, but the Issas account for only 31 of these. The dominant group among the foreign Somalis were the Issacks, whose families had originated in former British Somaliland. Next in numerical importance came the Gadaboursis, who totaled 18. Of the non-Somali-speaking students, the Arabs provided 33, or 21 percent of the non-European student body. The balance consisted of a handful of Sudanese or Ethiopian nationality and several half-castes.

Certain conclusions may be drawn from the foregoing analysis. One might be the greater zeal of foreign-born youth for a formal Western-style education. Another might be the better academic preparation provided in Djibouti's primary schools, as compared with those of the hinterland. And still another might be the higher living standards of the Arabs and alien Somalis. In relation to the size of the ethnic communities from which these students derived, the Arabs were overrepresented, whereas the Issas and, even more, the Afars were underrepresented. Unless these proportions are greatly modified in the next few years, especially with regard to the Afars, the political leadership of the Territory may pass into the hands of the nonindigenous tribal groups, which already are economically dominant. The most hopeful portent, however, is that ethnic loyalties, which have been primordial in the Territory's politics, are less strong among the younger and better-educated generation.

Among secondary school students there seems to be no group organized along ethnic lines. Although the strike at the Djibouti *lycée* in October 1966 was led by the Somalis—many of them immigrants from former British Somaliland—it was participated in not only by all the Issas but also by two-thirds of the Afar students.[23] All the scholarship holders from the Territory studying in France, regardless of tribal origin, joined together to protest to the government against the arrests and deportations that followed the riots of September 1966.[24] Although tribal cleavages have been widened by recent political developments among the older generation of Afars and Issas, the youthful advocates of independence tend to overlook ethnic differences in the common pursuit of their nationalist goal.

The demand for independence by virtually all the secondary school students in Djibouti seems to be based on a total lack of realism. In a radio interview prior to the referendum, a group of 18-to-19-year-old youths who attended the *lycée* at Djibouti were asked how the Territory could become an economically viable sovereign state and also escape the predatory clutches of its neighbors.[25] One student replied: "The United States needs stone to construct buildings and we could sell it the output of our quarries." If that proved insufficient, there was "plenty of money in the banks of Djibouti which the French have taken from us for nearly 100 years. We have calculated the amount, and by distributing it we can live." They were not worried about Somalia, "because its inhabitants are our racial brothers and wish us no harm. We can stop the Ethiopians by cutting the railroad to Addis Ababa. *On nous aidera.*" Although the "on" was not spelled out, and may have meant to some the United States or Great Britain, most of the students were probably thinking of the Soviet Union or Communist China. Although it is difficult to take such fantastic views seriously, the deep conviction with which they were uttered and the fact that they were expressed by the most educated segment of the local population suggests that they merit long consideration.

The scope and intensity that the political activities of youth have taken on, and their significance for the Territory's future, have finally prompted the French authorities to provide outlets for such energies other than political agitation. The scarcity of diversions is very striking in a town that offers by way of entertainment only a few movie houses and one good beach for swimming. To be sure, scout movements for both boys and girls have existed there for some years, and the government has lent them a building and provided them with equipment on a small scale. While religious and political discussions are taboo and the scout leaders try to inculcate a taste for the outdoors and a sense of civic responsibility, their total membership probably does not exceed 100.[26] Governor Tirant, when he first came to Djibouti in November 1962, was immediately struck by the "lack of even the most modest social amenities for young people,"[27] but his plan to build a cultural and sports center never materialized.

The dimensions of Djibouti's youth problems were at once grasped by Governor Saget, probably because he assumed office during the September 1966 outbreaks, in which young people were playing such a conspicuous part. He took steps to group the members of Djibouti's scattered clubs into larger units and turned over to them a building, renamed the Maison des Jeunes, which now has a meeting hall, reading facilities, and a sports field. His activity caused the revival of similar projects which had lain dormant for months, sometimes years, such as the Protestant mission's plan to build a students' meeting place (*foyer*). This *foyer* should help to overcome a handicap from which Djibouti's students have long suffered—the lack of space and quiet in which to do their homework.[28] On October 1, 1966, the *Réveil de Djibouti* opened a new question-and-answer column in its pages, called the Tribune des Jeunes, and though political commentaries are discouraged, young people have been using it to express their aspirations and air their complaints on many different subjects. In the economic domain, Governor Saget has initiated training courses to help young men who had nothing to offer except brawn acquire the skills that should equip them to find more remunerative employment.

By providing the means for improving their living standards and social life, the government has attempted to deal with the easiest aspects of young people's problems, and it remains to be seen whether the local authorities, native and French alike, have the imagination to cope with their psychological difficulties. The main ones seem to be a sense of loneliness and of enforced isolation from the mainstream of the Territory's life. Djibouti's youth wants not merely more information about the government's plans and policy but a larger share in their formulation and execution.

Cultural Activities and Communications Media

Among peoples such as the Issas and Afars, who have no written language, only two musical instruments, few arts and crafts, and little painting, their culture is inevitably perpetuated mainly in oral form. Legends, fables, and songs embody the essence of their folklore and reinforce tribal solidarity by evoking memories of past exploits. Periodically the tribesmen get together to sing and dance or play games.

A few French intellectuals—officials, missionaries, officers, and teachers—have studied the culture and traditions of the indigenous tribes. Duchenet collected and published a book of Somali stories, and Chedeville has produced an Afar dictionary and grammar. In the mid-nineteenth century and early twentieth century, studies of the Somalis were made by Guillain and Ferrand, but today their works cannot be found in bookstores and have been almost totally forgotten. The best-known and most fruitful scientific mission was that of Aubert de la Rue on the eve of World War II, and the published account of his work contains a useful bibliography of the scientific publications relating to the Territory up to that time.

The French administration has made some attempt to protect the vestiges of the Territory's past that have survived in the hinterland, such as stone monuments, Galla tombs, and pottery shards. Governor Siriex's proposal in 1947 to mark the half-century anniversary of the colony's founding by building a museum at Djibouti was not acted upon because of lack of funds. Although documents and objects of historical interest collected in response to his appeal have been housed in various government offices, they pertain almost exclusively to the periods of European exploration and colonial rule. The Territory has not had a sufficiently rich cultural past to attract many French scholars. In East Africa, such men as Griaule, Cohen, Bailloud, Azais, Grébaud, and Breuil have preferred to work in Ethiopia. Since the early 1950's, Addis Ababa has had a French-language publication[29] and a French Institut d'Archéologie, which broadened its scope to include history and philology when it was renamed Institut Ethiopien d'Etudes et de Recherches.[30]

Because of the political turbulence of 1966–67, the French have been moved to develop more cultural activities in Djibouti. The government has been showing educational films, and it has encouraged amateur theatricals by local European residents and the youth clubs. In June 1967, it opened the first two public libraries and provided them with several thousand books and with reading rooms, but the most noteworthy cultural development can be ascribed to private initiative. Under the aegis of Robert Ferry and other former associates of the C.H.E.A.M. (Centre des Hautes Etudes de l'Afrique et de l'Asie Modernes), a Société d'Etudes de l'Afrique Orientale was formed at Djibouti in 1964.[31] Members of this society have already launched a quarterly magazine, *Pount,* of which the first two issues appeared in October 1966 and January 1967. (Its title derives from the name given to the western region of the Red Sea basin by early Egyptian navigators and merchants.) *Pount* has already published articles by local scholars and scientists dealing with a wide range of subjects pertaining to the Territory, and it is trying to revive the project of building a museum in Djibouti. Apparently it is hoped that all these efforts to awaken local interest in cultural affairs may create a national consciousness on the part of the Territory's heterogeneous inhabitants.

The Territory's first newspaper, *Djibouti,* appeared in 1913. As of 1967, it still had only one newspaper, although in 1961 there was also a short-lived fortnightly called *Le Courrier Africain.* In the early 1950's, *Le Réveil de Djibouti* was issued once a week by the local Information Service. Under the able management of J. P. Poinsot, who took it over in 1958, its format was improved and its coverage enlarged. From that time until mid-1967, when Poinsot left the Territory, *Le Réveil* had grown from eight to fourteen pages and had two full pages each week of clear photographic illustrations as well as feature stories, sports news, and radio and cinema announcements. Meetings of the territorial assembly were summarized, and the texts of speeches made by the governor and vice-president of the government council were carried in full. For its international news it drew on the wire services of the A.F.P. and Reuters, and almost every week several columns were devoted to local news from the Territory's various *cercles.* While its Tribune des Jeunes* attracted youthful correspondents, few of its other readers bothered to express their views in the Courrier des Lettres, and its editorials were weak and unduly given over to deploring traffic accidents in Djibouti. Nevertheless, *Le Réveil* under Poinsot's management had a spectacular success and its circulation rose from 500 copies weekly in 1958 to over 2,500 in 1965.

Radio broadcasts, as in most African countries where the population is largely illiterate and has few distractions, have been from the outset very popular in French Somaliland. They reach a larger audience than *Lé Reveil,* and it is said that every nomad group in the Territory now possesses

---

* See p. 155.

a transistor radio receiving set. In August 1964 Radio Djibouti expanded its operations and began broadcasting on both short and medium wave for 13 hours daily. Its programs in four languages—French, Arabic, Somali, and Afar—could then be heard as far afield as Ethiopia, South Arabia, and Somalia. Its sponsors are especially proud of the fact that it is the only station in the world to broadcast in the Afar language. Radio Djibouti has always been operated by the Post and Telegraph Department. The Arabic and French programs were relayed from Paris, whereas those in Somali and Afar were of local origin. Television was introduced into the Territory in April 1967. For two hours every weekday evening it shows films, including telecasts of international events, but thus far it reaches only a very limited audience in Djibouti. The price of a television set ranges between D.F. 50,000 and 75,000 (plus a sales tax of 18 percent and an installation fee of D.F. 6,000).

In May 1966, General Billotte announced that Radio Djibouti would greatly increase its operations, in accordance with a world-wide project devised by the Paris government and to be executed by the national radio-broadcasting authorities. When completed, the new station would "spread French culture throughout East Africa and the Near and Middle East," and thus supplement the coverage of stations already in operation in Guyane and the French Pacific islands.[32] Djibouti's geographical location was largely responsible for the new role assigned to its radio station by France's policy makers. But in view of the current political turmoil in the Red Sea area, and particularly in the Horn of Africa, the French authorities were certainly also concerned to offset the effect on the Territory's population of the propaganda broadcast by the radio stations of Somalia, Egypt, Ethiopia, Aden, and Yemen.

Because Djibouti's only newspaper and radio station have always been operated by the official information services, the French government controls a large proportion of the news that reaches the Territory's population. As long ago as July 1935 the local administration formed a censorship committee to pass upon the motion picture films shown in the Territory.

Health and Social Welfare

French Somaliland is fortunate in being spared many of the diseases of other tropical countries. In recent years there have been no cases of smallpox or yellow fever, leprosy is very rare, and there is no sleeping sickness, amoebic dysentery, or bilharziasis. Malaria, unknown in Djibouti, has been almost eliminated from the rural areas, owing to a campaign undertaken in 1947. Pulmonary tuberculosis is the main cause of death among the urban population and to a lesser extent among the nomads. An examination of 32,000 persons in Djibouti in 1959—virtually the entire population at that time—disclosed the very high proportion of 10 percent of its adult residents to be so infected. Since then 500 to 600 new cases have been discovered each year, and in 1964 the Paris government established a special fund and sent a specialist to organize an antituberculosis campaign, particularly in the hinterland, where two mobile teams now try to track down the disease among the nomads. The high incidence of tuberculosis is recognized as being related to the wider problems of undernourishment and poor conditions of housing and hygiene among both the urban and rural populations.

The basic diet of the nomads is milk and *dourra* (millet). Milk is abundant, however, only when the herds find good pasture, and *dourra* must be bought with the proceeds from the sale of animals or through wage earning, because the nomads do not raise food crops. They do very little hunting and eat meat rarely. Although they lead a generally healthy outdoor life, the nomads pay scant attention to hygiene and suffer from inadequate protection against the cold. Usually their maladies are treated by tribal "medicine men" who have a special knowledge of herbs.

Town dwellers have access to a more varied diet, and despite the high prices of food in Djibouti, they often eat three meals a day, including meat or fish and fresh vegetables. The main impediment to improvement of the diet is the widespread use of *khat,** which greatly diminishes the appetite. Because Djibouti wage earners spend so much of their pay on *khat,* not only are they themselves undernourished but their families, too, are deprived of the food they need. It has been estimated that the rural as well as the urban populations receive only about one-fourth of the calories they should have, and their diet is particularly deficient in protein and fats.

Insofar as Western medicine is concerned, the attitude of the local population is generally receptive, even though they do not comprehend the necessity for hygiene and dislike prolonged treatment. When they are not immediately cured of their complaint, they tend to become impatient with examinations and tests and simply leave the hospital. Yet Djibouti's medical services have gained such a reputation that aliens from outside the Territory come there for treatment, and as many as half of the indigent patients treated at the Peltier Hospital come from Ethiopia and former British Somaliland.[33]

* See pp. 163–65.

The Territory's health service has always been headed by a medical military officer, and it employs 374 persons. Most of the nursing staff are nuns, although some are native graduates of the local nurses' school. The number of doctors in the Territory—all European—rose from 15 in 1958 to 35 in 1964, of whom four were private practitioners, 16 military doctors, and 15 doctors of the health service.[34] The recently modernized Peltier Hospital at Djibouti has 600 beds, three-fourths of which are reserved for patients of the Assistance Médicale Indigène, who receive treatment free of charge. It also has laboratories, several operating rooms, and pharmaceutical and dental services, and its radiotherapy equipment is unique in the Red Sea region. The city also has several dispensaries and clinics.

In 1962 the government, concluding that too many of the medical facilities were concentrated in Djibouti, decided to further decentralize the health service and to provide more care for the rural population.[35] To the existing clinics in the headquarters of the hinterland *cercles* were added medical posts or first-aid stations at Yoboki, As Ela, Holhol, Dorra, and Randa. The Territory's two mobile teams were reorganized and reequipped so as to enlarge the radius of their activities in tracking down diseases and vaccinating the nomads. Allocations to the health service were increased from 15.5 percent of total revenues in 1955 to 25 percent in 1964. In the latter year Governor Tirant was able to announce to the territorial assembly that French Somaliland's per capita expenditures for medical care were 15 times larger than those of Somalia and eight times more than those of Egypt.[36]

By 1961 the local administration had come to recognize that the spread of tuberculosis in Djibouti was directly related to the deplorable housing conditions in which the great majority of the native population lived. The native quarters, known collectively as the Magala, were an agglomeration of miserable shanties, which had grown up haphazardly as a result of the city's rapid demographic expansion. In the early days, the only effort made by the government to provide living quarters for the newcomers had been to allocate them plots of land, with no apparent concern for such vital facilities as drainage, water supply, and the proximity of schools.

Periodic heavy rains and abnormally high tides often inundated whole sections of the Magala, which was at sea level. (The most recent torrential downpour, which occurred on May 2, 1967, flooded the Magala with water to a depth of 40 to 80 centimeters in some places.) To be sure, two of the Magala's main avenues had been paved and provided with sidewalks as well as night lighting, public fountains supplied abundant drinking water, and a pumping system had been installed to drain off superfluous rain and tidal water.[37] On the other hand, private enterprise had done nothing to improve the housing situation, and only the railroad company had gone so far as to build lodgings for its native staff. The wealthy Arab landowners preferred to build houses for Europeans who could pay high rents, and the great majority of the people living in the Magala were poor and often unemployed and consequently offered no certainty of remuneration.

To cope with this growing problem, the government set up a Société Immobilière de la Côte Française des Somalis in 1961, obtained funds from the Fonds Européen de Développement (F.E.D.) and a loan from the Caisse Centrale de Coopération Economique (C.C.C.E.), and acquired the services of two sociologists and an architect from the Société Centrale pour l'Equipement du Territoire (S.C.E.T.). The initial project decided upon was a housing development to be called the Stade, which would provide 400 dwellings. Because the shanties in the Magala were made of flimsy materials, their removal would cause no practical difficulties, but to acquire land for the project and, above all, to rehouse the Magala's inhabitants did present almost insuperable financial and psychological obstacles. By that time Djibouti was physically enclosed by Muslim cemeteries, which it would have been impolitic to remove, and by the saltworks, the cost of whose expropriation or purchase seemed prohibitive.[38] When this problem had been resolved, the question arose of determining the most suitable type of housing and the amount of rental that would be within the capacity of the inhabitants to pay. The S.C.E.T. therefore conducted a socioeconomic survey, prior to which the radio and press carried on a campaign to prepare the unsophisticated and suspicious residents of the Magala for the inquiry that was to follow.[39]

The three experts devised a questionnaire, which included such data as the means of ventilation, the degree of privacy required for Muslim family life, and the future tenants' financial resources, with a view to enabling them eventually to become house owners. They trained five native investigators, who interviewed the heads of 500 Djibouti families. The results of this inquiry were analyzed and served as guidance in construction of the Stade, which was completed within two and a half years and was inhabited by the end of March 1966. Among the facilities provided by the Stade are a school, a marketplace, stores, clubrooms, arcaded streets, and a shade tree in each family courtyard. After one year's experience, a new inquiry was undertaken in order to ascertain its residents' reactions, and the results will serve as a guide for the next housing project. This is to be constructed on land purchased from the Société des Salines, and will provide 800 to 1,000 dwellings. When it is finished, the authorities plan to begin renovating the Magala itself.[40]

Among the nomads of French Somaliland the practice of adopting orphans is rare, but that of abandoning children is not. The conditions of nomadic life are such that often there simply is not enough food. Every year more and more half-starved children—some from outside the Territory—come to Djibouti, either at the urging of their parents or on their own initiative. The orphanages of the Catholic mission are filled with such youthful derelicts.

For many years, tourists who stopped off at Djibouti have been pestered by youthful ragamuffins begging for money. Barefoot and in rags, they follow any Westerner about with a persistence that is outstanding even in the Orient. As experienced a traveler as Jean d'Esme, after a visit to the Territory in 1930, wrote that "in no other land has begging reached such a degree of effrontery...the youthful Somali's strategy to obtain money has been perfected by the atavism of a thousand years and approximates genius."[41] Other visitors have been less harsh in their judgment, and some have reported that these beggar boys often entice French tourists into giving them money by their engaging recitation of the fables of La Fontaine.[42]

When Djibouti's population began increasing rapidly after World War II, the behavior of these youthful vagabonds assumed another, less picturesque aspect. They began to work in bands and to practice theft at the expense of both residents and transients. In 1955, 31 boys were sentenced by the courts for damaging automobiles and for stealing, and were consigned to the center for juvenile delinquents that had been installed at Obock two years before. The problem took on such disquieting proportions that the French Union Assembly sent a mission to investigate it. Its members visited the Obock center and in 1957 submitted an unfavorable report on that institution.[43] They found about 100 boys ranging in age from 10 to 18 living in cheerless barracks and gardening in a desultory fashion under the surveillance of armed guards. The boys did not complain of ill treatment, and as there was no watering point within many miles of Obock they made no attempt to escape. But out of sheer boredom they had tried to set fire to their dormitory, and they obviously were receiving no training that would enable them to be returned to a productive, normal life.

The authorities were aware of the need for a new approach to the problem and in 1960 set up an Association Territoriale pour la Protection de la Jeunesse. It was a nonpolitical and nonreligious organization, and its president was R. Pecoul, the competent French minister of finance in the government council. Under the aegis of this organization, the inmates of the Obock center were transferred to a terrain of some 12 hectares near Ambouli. The Fonds d'Investissement pour le Développement Economique et Social (F.I.D.E.S.) provided the funds for the new center, many of whose buildings were constructed by the boys themselves.[44] There they are taught a trade and given a general primary education. The fact that few of them have tried to escape and that some of Djibouti's abandoned children have themselves sought admission to the center is a testimonial to its success. The center receives a government subsidy as well as gifts in money and in kind from the Secours Catholique and the American Catholic Relief Service.[45] Because of its limited capacity, the Ambouli center cannot take in more than one hundred or so boys, and obviously it cannot touch the heart of a situation that has its roots in the problems of life in the whole area.

One such problem is that of the growing consumption of *khat* throughout the Horn of Africa. For many centuries the Muslims of the Red Sea area have consumed in one form or another the leaves of a privet-like bush that grows abundantly in the highlands of Ethiopia. Since Islam forbids the use of alcoholic beverages, the Muslims resort to *khat,* which serves as a stimulant and is called in Djibouti *la salade.* The leaves are either chewed or infused for drinking or the inhalation of the fumes. To produce the desired effect of euphoria, *khat* must be used fresh, within 48 to 72 hours of picking. Formerly it was transported to Djibouti by train or truck, but now it moves almost wholly by plane. In fact, *khat* accounts for a large part of the freight carried by Ethiopian Airlines, and it is an important source of income for the Ethiopian government and farmers.

The introduction of a money economy and the development of modern means of transportation have greatly increased the consumption of *khat* throughout the Red Sea area. After World War II, this began to arouse concern on the part of the British and French governments because of the deleterious effects of the stimulant upon the local populations, both physically and financially. At various times the administrations of Hargeisa, Aden, and Djibouti tried to prohibit the importation of *khat* or to raise its price to a prohibitive level by taxation, but in each case they had to admit defeat. In 1957 the Arab League became so alarmed by the growth in the *khat* trade that its leaders asked the World Health Organization (W.H.O.) to study the problem.

The effects of *khat* consumption on the health of the area's populations have been analyzed many times in recent years by a variety of doctors.[46] No consensus has been reached on whether or not *khat* permanently harms the user's constitution. All students of the subject agree, however, that *khat* is habit-forming and, if taken in excess, limits the appetite, causes insomnia, and impairs efficiency. After its initial stimulating effects, the user experiences deep depression, and in the long run suffers from anemia and a markedly lower resistance to disease. Specifically, *khat* consumption can lead to malnutrition and tuberculosis.

There is also no disagreement on the harmful economic and social consequences of habitual *khat* consumption. Each year the population of Djibouti spends approximately D.F. 800 million, or the equivalent of about half the Territory's revenues, in buying *khat*. It is purchased in the form of a *botte,* or bunch, weighing three and a half kilograms and costing D.F. 250. Djibouti's Muslim inhabitants regard *khat* not as a luxury item but as a necessity, and it is estimated that a wage earner spends as much as 40 percent of his pay for the stimulant. The user experiences temporarily the illusion of happiness and virility, and *khat* creates sociability among groups of friends who gather in cafes. It is said that no political meeting is held in Djibouti at which *khat* is not used.

The Paris government has not intervened to regulate the use of *khat,* leaving the matter up to the local governor as part of his responsibility for maintaining order in the Territory. It was not until April 1952 that the Djibouti administration imposed for the first time a tax on the sale of *khat,* but this simply stimulated smuggling. Within three years the consumption of *khat* in the Territory had tripled, and it grew with each increase in the minimum wage. Governors Compain and Tirant both inveighed against the evils of *khat,* but felt helpless to prevent its importation and sale. It was argued that to prohibit it might lead to a rise in alcoholism and alienate the government of Ethiopia, and that the taxation of *khat* yielded revenues to the Territory that would otherwise go into the pockets of smugglers. As for the territorial assemblymen, they would not risk their political future by voting to forbid the importation of *khat*. Yet in principle all agreed that steps should be taken to discourage its consumption, especially by young people.

As local nationalism has developed, and with it a certain puritanism, the educated native leaders have come to oppose the consumption of *khat* on the ground that it is harmful to the people's welfare. In May 1965 some of the youth clubs, led by the Fédération des Sports de Djibouti, organized a week's campaign, aided by propaganda from the press and radio, to persuade young people to abstain from using *khat*. But the habit, far from diminishing, is now spreading to the women of Djibouti and to some of the hinterland tribes, and it is thought to have a direct bearing on the political situation. On September 23, 1966, Governor Saget forbade the importation and sale of *khat* in the Territory because he believed that the exhilaration it produced was in part responsible for the riots that had occurred in Djibouti a few days before. He had to rescind this drastic measure, however, because it caused so much popular discontent. Probably the most that can be done at this time is to forbid the sale of *khat* during crucial periods (as the sale of alcoholic beverages is banned in the United States on election days, and as occurred in Djibouti during the referendum of March 19, 1967). As yet no satisfactory substitute for *khat* has been found, and the public support indispensable for any considerable restriction of its importation and use is lacking.

Chapter Seven

THE TRADITIONAL ECONOMY

Water Resources

Water is the element that conditions human, animal, and vegetable life throughout the Territory. Its scarcity poses a problem that has been resolved only for the town of Djibouti, which in this, as in almost all other respects, has been given preferential treatment. As Djibouti's population rapidly grew, so did its residents' requirements of water. Furthermore, as it became increasingly a port of call for passing ships, their demands for water provisioning grew, though for some years there were objections that Djibouti's water was too salty for drinking purposes. Djiboutians, for their part, had additional complaints about the inadequacy of the water supply and of its distribution system. During the first postwar decade, Djibouti was supplied with water brought from Ambouli, four kilometers away, in underground tunnels lying about ten meters below the surface, to a daily total of about 3,000 cubic meters. Not only was this quantity increasingly insufficient for Djibouti's fast-growing population, but the pressure available for its distribution was so weak that water rarely reached above the ground floor. Obviously, new sources of water had to be found that would at least double the amount supplied.

In the late 1950's, research undertaken with French public funds and technicians was rewarded by the discovery of water on a fairly abundant scale, also at Ambouli. This made possible an increase in the town's water supply from 3,150 cubic meters daily in 1961 to 9,000 cubic meters by the end of 1965, and it also reduced the proportion of salinity to the relatively low amount of one gram per liter.[1] Djibouti's residents and passing ships now have an adequate supply of water, and the renovation of the town's obsolete distribution system has been undertaken with funds supplied by the European Common Market countries (Fonds Européen de Développement). By this means the pressure has been improved and many leakages repaired, but the waste of water has increased. Many of the indigenous inhabitants, only recently transplanted from the arid hinterland, are so enchanted by the relative abundance of Djibouti's water that they let it flow from the public fountains day and night, and the authorities have made little headway toward convincing them that the supply is not inexhaustible and must be carefully conserved.

In the mid-1950's, at about the same time that the study of Djibouti's water resources was begun, a similar program of research was drawn up for the rest of the Territory by the B.C.E.O.M. (Bureau Central d'Etudes pour les Equipements d'Outre-Mer). Because of the vast scale of this problem and the inadequate knowledge of the hinterland water-table and the variations in rainfall, it has not met with the same rapid success. Although the Territory's water resources are not negligible, many consist of hot springs and impermanent ponds, and virtually all have a high mineral content. Obviously the best-known sources are the permanent wells used by the nomads, most of them dug in the beds of wadis. The use of these wells by certain tribal and family groups is carefully determined by custom, and around some of them have grown up small palm groves and tiny settlements. Under the 1957 program, the first work undertaken was the improvement of the wells.[2] Next, in 1961–62, small dams were built to catch floodwater and thereby create permanent ponds. This part of the program was concentrated in Dikhil *cercle,* northern Tadjoura, and the plain around Obock, where the nomad herds suffered acutely during periods of drought. In Tadjoura the dams built at Moudo, Dawao, and Dorra proved satisfactory, but the one at Bouya gave way after a severe flood, and the Hourrougo dam in Dikhil *cercle* met with the same fate.[3] This partial failure led to a reorientation of the program away from dam building to the digging of deep wells, and to this end a Bureau of Hydraulics was set up in March 1962. From the outset, however, its operations have been hampered by the lack of a qualified staff to undertake the indispensable task of drawing up a detailed inventory of the Territory's existing water resources. Some success has nevertheless been achieved by the few technicians at the Territory's disposal, working with funds supplied on an increasing scale by the Fonds d'Investissements pour le Développement Economique et Social (F.I.D.E.S.) of the French government. Between 1960 and 1966, the F.I.D.E.S. spent D.F. 100 million on such projects for the hinterland, a sum roughly equal to the amount it expended on the improvement of Djibouti's water supply, and in 1966 it allocated the majority of its funds to hydraulic research in the rural areas. Water in fair quantity has been struck in the Obock region, and a series of wells is being dug at Dorra and in Ali-Sabieh *cercle.*

The results of this expenditure of money and effort have been disappointing, on the whole, but the government intends to persevere in its plan to create a network of watering points sufficient throughout the year for the Territory's animal herds. Governor Saget, in his tour of the hinterland *cercles* in September 1966, learned that the most keenly felt need of the rural population was for more water. Such a network not only would prove beneficial to the administration in terms of popular gratitude, but would also greatly advance the official program of stabilizing the nomads in small agricultural settlements.

Agriculture and Forestry

It seems paradoxical to speak of agriculture and forestry in a country where 90 percent of the surface is covered by desert, 9 percent is poor pastureland, and only 1 percent is wooded. Yet the existence of 6,000-odd hectares of forests on the slopes of Mounts Gouda and Mabla suggests that the scarcity and salinity of the Territory's water rather than the sterility of its soil is responsible for the sparse and poor vegetation. The forest of Daÿ, which is composed mainly of juniper, ficus, and jujube trees, contains some magnificent specimens. It is a botanical oddity harboring unique vegetation watered exclusively by mist and dew, and has been described as an ideal setting for science-fiction films. The area's inhabitants claim that it was created by malevolent spirits who gave free rein to their imagination, and it has inspired many local legends. Its conservation—for lack of a forestry service—is entrusted to the commandant of Tadjoura *cercle*. Mangroves are fairly abundant at isolated points along the coast. There are also spontaneous growths of doum palms on portions of the plains of Hanlé and Gaggadé, and indeed wherever water occurs near the surface. The nomads use their fibers to weave mats and utensils and their sap to make wine, but they treat the trees so roughly that even these palms are in process of disappearing. Nevertheless, enough trees have survived the depredations of man and beast to produce annually some 15,000 *stères* (cubic meters) of firewood and 1,000 tons of charcoal, of which most is used by the rural population and the balance is exported to Djibouti.[4] Long and costly experiments at Ambouli have enabled a nursery there to provide enough saplings to line Djibouti's main streets with trees.

Traditionally the utilization of land and water in the Territory has been regulated by intertribal agreements based on clearly defined customary rights. Among the Afars, the noble tribes control the largest areas. In return for the services formerly rendered them in time of war, they ceded a portion of their land to vassal tribes or, in the case of other tribes, exacted payment in kind for their use as pasture. Yet areas have apparently always remained where herds can graze freely, as, for example, in the Alta region near the Ethiopian frontier, where many nomads gather with their herds every year after the rains. Furthermore, where water is comparatively abundant, tribal custom does not restrict its use, but wherever water is scarce only certain tribes may draw on it.

As elsewhere in its tropical African dependencies, the land legislation introduced by France in Somaliland was based on Western concepts and practices. In 1924–25 two laws were passed that divided the whole Territory into public and private domains.[5] All public land described as "vacant and ownerless" was assigned to the state, and whatever revenues it produced went into the territorial budget. As to the private domain, temporary grants might be made by the governor for plots of less than 5,000 square meters, but larger areas must be sold at public auction. Those holding temporary grants might acquire permanent title if they fulfilled the conditions laid down in their *cahiers de charges*. In the case of urban plots this usually meant erecting a building within two to three years, and in the case of plantations crops had to be planted within five to six years. Certain plots were reserved for sale to native inhabitants on easy terms, while veterans of the French army could acquire them free. The *loi-cadre* of 1956 substituted the Territory for the French state as owner of the public domain, and the territorial assembly replaced the governor as the ultimate authority for granting permanent titles to holders of temporary grants.

So unsuited was such legislation to French Somaliland and its nomadic society that it might have caused confusion, if not trouble, had it ever been seriously applied. Vast concessions were indeed granted to a few big companies at the turn of the century, but except for the salt-producing regions, the rural areas were regarded as so unproductive that these concessions were never developed. Only in Djibouti and Ambouli, where real estate rapidly gained monetary value, was a land-tenure system set up, and then in only rudimentary form. As of 1961, the entire area to which permanent title had been granted totaled no more than 67 hectares of urban and 489 hectares of rural land. At Ambouli, a mere handful of the Hakmi Arabs were the legal proprietors of the garden plots they farmed.

Date culture and market gardening are the only activities in French Somaliland that may properly be described as agricultural. Altogether some 25,000 date palms grow in the Territory, with an annual yield of about 200 tons of dates. The largest grove, covering 5 hectares, is at Ambouli, but the best known is that at Dikhil because of its comparatively attractive surroundings. Dikhil's production amounts to only two tons a year because its palms are either too old or too young for maximum bearing. The same oases that grow dates also have market gardens because of the availability of water necessary for the irrigation of both. Most of these market gardens are very small, not only because the water supply is limited but also because few of the villagers are willing to perform the backbreaking toil required for their cultivation. Only at Ambouli is truck gardening done on a larger scale and by professional gardeners. There some 2,000 Hakmi Arabs grow 100 to 300 tons of vegetables and fruit a year for sale in the nearby market of Djibouti, whose residents are otherwise wholly dependent on imported foodstuffs.

Ambouli's 150 or more garden plots range in size from 2,500 to 5,000 square meters, and most of them are farmed by primitive methods. The Hakmi use no fertilizers and either wait for flood waters to deposit alluvial soil on their plots or transport it by hand from the bed of a nearby wadi. Although 41 percent of the gardens now have motor pumps, bought on credit through the local farmers' cooperative, the majority are irrigated by water carried in goatskins from one of Ambouli's wells.[6] For all their labor, the Hakmi do not earn enough money to maintain their families throughout the year, because production is irregular, the farming season very short, and the distribution system time-consuming and inefficient. Cultivation is limited to the cool months between November and May, and because Djibouti's merchants handle only imported foodstuffs the farmers must go from door to door peddling their wares. To survive during the six months of the hot season, they must hire out their services to the Europeans who have flower gardens.

For many years agriculture was neglected by the French authorities in Djibouti, who believed that the Territory's economic productivity, such as it was, lay in the development of livestock. The sterility of the soil and scarcity of water, not to mention the nomads' antipathy to farming, made the outlook for agriculture highly discouraging. In fact, the Agriculture Service as such was suppressed in 1949 and its small staff transferred to the department of animal husbandry. The government, however, continued to maintain gardens and nurseries at Ambouli and Randa, although experiments there have yielded largely inconclusive results.

The origin of the government's Ambouli gardens and nursery, which now cover an area of 150 hectares, was a small farm started by an elderly Arab in 1935. After his death the government bought it and turned it over to the Agricultural Service with a view to the acclimatization and propagation of useful fruit-bearing trees and vegetables, as well as of ornamental flowering bushes. In 1966 the Ambouli nursery distributed free of charge 25,000 plants and cuttings throughout the Territory, and more than half the recipients were native farmers. Its own surplus in foodstuffs was donated to charitable institutions, such as the mission orphanages and Djibouti's hospital. In recent years its work has included research on the control of plant diseases, the planting of selected date palm trees along the coastal lands, and especially the development of market garden and fodder crops as a vital part of the administration's program to settle the nomads.[7]

In the early 1950's the rapid growth of Djibouti's population led to considerably increased food imports from Ethiopia and Yemen, and this development aroused the administration to give further consideration to the Territory's agricultural potential. Beginning in 1956 the F.I.D.E.S. financed a two-year study by an agronomic engineer of the Territory's arable lands. He selected a total of 3,000 hectares, or only 0.03 percent of the Territory's total area, where he believed cultivation possible under certain conditions. About half of the designated hectares were in the Hanlé area, the plains of Gobaad and of the littoral south of Djibouti contained 500 hectares each, and the remainder consisted of smaller patches of lowland scattered throughout the Territory. The same expert also demarcated 3,500 additional hectares that might conceivably be made arable if wells could be dug deep enough to reach the water table. Obviously more research concerning the available water resources was needed, so the B.C.E.O.M. sent a mission composed of hydraulic engineers to carry out detailed studies of the three main areas selected.

To meet the most urgent need, which was to increase food supplies for Djibouti, the first experiments were conducted on 90 hectares of the littoral to the south. The Ambouli market gardeners were also organized into a cooperative society, to which sufficient credits were allocated by the F.I.D.E.S. to enable its members to partially mechanize their operations. More funds were also made available to the two existing experimental stations and a third was started in the Gobaad plain. The Randa station concentrated on the development of citrus-fruit and grape cultivation, whereas the one at Ambouli widened the scope of its experiments to include 48 different species of plants and trees. As part of the official program to stabilize the nomads and improve their living conditions, the new station in the Gobaad plain was assigned the very difficult task of popularizing agriculture among them.

Before this part of the program could be undertaken, the government had to create the conditions that would make possible the development of small farming communities. In 1959–60 work was begun in the Hanlé plain and in the region of the Saddaï wadi between Obock and Tadjoura. In Hanlé, five deep wells were to be dug at the points indicated by the mission of hydraulic engineers, and the waters of its wadi were to be deflected into a canal that would eventually serve to irrigate a total of several hundred hectares. It soon became evident that the cost of this work would far exceed the original estimate of D.F. 27 million, and in any case its success was far from assured. There was no certainty that water would be found in sufficient quantity, and it was even more doubtful that the nomads could be persuaded to use it to irrigate crops. Consequently, the ambitious program at Hanlé has now been cut back and comprises a mere 12 hectares, which are to be developed on a purely experimental basis.[8]

Despite more realistic views of the amount of time and money needed for even a minimal development of agriculture in the Territory, the Paris government has promised that it will continue its program, albeit on a very modest scale.[9] This conforms more closely than did the original project with the views held by the local authorities, who have never been optimistic about French Somaliland's agricultural prospects. Efforts to settle the nomads will probably continue, but the chief goal in respect to agriculture seems now to have shifted back to increasing Djibouti's food supplies.

Animal Husbandry

For virtually all of French Somaliland's rural inhabitants, animals are the sole source of wealth and food. Without animals, a local saying goes, the nomad is no better than a beggar and will surely die of hunger. Even the possession of animals, however, does not guarantee survival to a nomad, despite the Territory's underpopulation (5.4 persons to the square kilometer) and very low living standards. It has become a widespread practice for the nomads to seek seasonal employment in the town or on the railroad, for it is only in the rare years when natural conditions are exceptionally favorable that the Territory's 40,000-odd nomads can make a living solely from their herds.

No exact count has ever been made of French Somaliland's herds because they are not subject to tax and because they are always on the move. Even today the numbers usually quoted—10,500 cattle, 78,000 sheep, 600,000 goats, 6,500 donkeys, 2,500 fowl, and 25,000 camels—are almost identical with those cited in the French National Assembly debate of October 24, 1961. Whatever their number, there is no doubt about their being too numerous for the Territory's resources in fodder and water and about their being insufficiently productive for their owners.

The poorest nomad family owns perhaps only a dozen goats, whereas a rich one may possess as many as 50 cattle, 20 camels, and several hundred sheep and goats—though herds of this size are rare in French Somaliland.[10] The average herd there consists of 50 to 100 sheep and goats, a few camels, and two or three donkeys, which are used as pack animals. From his herd a nomad obtains milk, his basic food, some butter, and very occasionally meat. In fact, French Somaliland's nomads are not animal breeders in the Western sense, but simply the guardians of their herds.

Their attitude toward the animals is much the same as that found elsewhere among African tribes. They consider animals primarily as a form of capital and only secondarily as a source of food, so that it is the number they possess and not the condition of the herds that is important to them. The nomad prefers to get such meat as he eats from hunting rather than from slaughtering his animals, and since he pays no tax on them and buys few imported articles, he feels no need to sell them. Only when milk becomes very scarce during the dry season will he trade his animals for *dourra* and corn.

Because the nomads live in a largely closed economic circuit, custom and tradition continue to determine their attitude toward their animals. Upon the death of the head of a family, his herd is divided between his sons, the eldest getting only a few more animals than the others. Daughters and wives do not share in this inheritance, although the wives are the caretakers of the animals bequeathed to their minor sons. Women are allowed to milk only sheep and goats, and they may drink the milk of camels and cows only after the men of the family have had their fill. Pasture and water are the main concerns of the head of a nomad encampment, and they pose complex problems for him because not all of his animals have the same needs in respect to fodder. Cattle require good grass, which is found in French Somaliland only on some of the plains and for only a short time after the rains end. Camels, sheep, and goats, however, get nourishment from the leaves of spiny plants which are drought-resistant and exist in many parts of the Territory. Rainfall determines the times at which seasonal migrations take place, but custom usually governs the trek routes. Intertribal agreements worked out over the years and rarely broken still regulate the movements of herds, which seldom extend beyond 200 kilometers and are usually less. In those places where the use of pasture and water has been reserved by custom to specific *fractions* and families, there has developed what might be called an embryonic form of private property.*

* See p. 26.

Official intervention in the field of animal husbandry has been slight, taking the form of protecting the herds and more recently of generally improving the conditions of nomadic life. The Territory's Animal Husbandry Service was created only in 1939, and its small staff has been assigned many tasks. These include the inspection of meat and of the salting of hides produced at Djibouti's abattoir, checking the health of animals in transit through the Territory (mostly from Somalia and Ethiopia to Egypt), vaccinating the local herds against various diseases, and protecting them against parasites. This service has a central station at Boulaos, and secondary centers were opened at Randa and Ali-Sabieh in 1964. (In 1965 it was decided to install others at Dorra and Arta.) Theoretically its veterinarians make periodic inspections of the nomads' herds, but in fact there are too few of them to visit tribes that are perpetually on the move and in inaccessible areas. Most of the nomads have come to value such protection as their herds receive from the veterinary service, but they do not accept its advice to eliminate over-age animals. The shortage of veterinarians and the inadequacy of the means at their disposal became crucial during the summer of 1967, when for the first time there was an epidemic of rinderpest among the herds of Dikhil *cercle*. Although the government council, on August 16, gave emergency powers to the Animal Husbandry Service, its veterinarians found it almost impossible to convince the nomads that quarantining the herds and slaughtering infected animals was necessary.[11]

More successful have been recent efforts of the authorities to improve conditions of nomadic life by a program of well-digging and the introduction of new fodder crops. In 1962 an expert of the Food and Agriculture Organization was asked to make an inventory of the Territory's pasturelands and to study them particularly in relation to the herds' seasonal migrations. He recommended rotation in the use of pastures and their preservation against overgrazing when grass was abundant, and also suggested that fodder reserves be created. At the same time, he urged that such measures be introduced gradually and only after the nomads had been convinced of the need for drastic changes in their customs.[12] This has now been accepted as a long-term project and as part of the overall program to induce the nomads to adopt a sedentary way of life. In the meantime the authorities have shown concern for the welfare of the nomads and their herds in more tangible ways. A severe drought early in 1967 prompted a campaign in which the armed forces distributed food and water to the nomads and air-dropped fodder for the animals in the northern *cercles,* which were among those hardest hit.[13] This timely aid to the Afar nomads may have had a direct bearing on the massive affirmative vote cast by that ethnic group in the referendum of March 19, 1967.

Fishing

Fishing is practiced only at a few places along the coast and more by foreigners than by the indigenous population. The taking of nacre is largely done by Arabs, and it gives rise to a comparatively large export trade amounting to some hundred tons of shell a year. A decree of February 14, 1923, forbade foreigners to fish in the territorial waters of French Somaliland, but like so many other French laws it has been honored more in the breach than in the observance. Furthermore, the artisanal character and small scale of fishing along the coast have made its legal protection seem superfluous.

About 20 Afars fish in the waters off Obock and Tadjoura. It is impossible to estimate the size of their catch because most of it is consumed locally and only part is dried, by traditional methods, and shipped to Djibouti. In any case, production is small and irregular, since fishing is done in a limited area, by primitive means, and only to meet the fishermen's fluctuating monetary needs. At Djibouti the fishermen are more numerous (about 200) and more professional: over half of them are Arabs and the rest are Somalis. In that city townspeople and passing ships provide a larger and more regular market than along the northern coast. Of the 420 tons sold at Djibouti in 1963, 370 tons were consumed by the resident Europeans, Arabs, Malagasys, and Asians.[14] Fish is never eaten by the nomads, both because facilities to distribute it in the interior are lacking and because of Islamic prohibitions.

Before World War II, attempts were made on two occasions to start a fishing industry at Djibouti, and both failed for the same reasons—lack of knowledge about the Territory's fish resources and about markets. French Somaliland's coastal waters obviously teemed with many kinds of fish— including mullet, tuna, herring, sharks, oysters, and other shellfish—but no precise information existed concerning quantity, species, or migratory habits. It was correctly but vaguely assumed that a large potential market for fish, both fresh and tinned, existed in Ethiopia and the Middle East, but French Somaliland then possessed no facilities for processing, storing, or transporting the catch. These drawbacks discouraged the Laporte Company of Boulogne, which sent a study mission to the Territory in 1952, as they did another company, financed by Dutch capital, which also studied the local situation three years later. Nevertheless, this show of interest by foreigners in French Somaliland's fish potential did impel the French Union Assembly to pass a resolution urging the government to undertake a scientific study of the Territory's maritime resources.[15] No such move, however, was made until 1962, when a mission was sent from France to advise the Djibouti authorities on the means of improving local fish production and marketing. Members of this mission found that French Somaliland's coastal waters were not so rich in fish as were those of the Red Sea but nevertheless possessed enough to warrant a marked increase in production.

In the meantime the local Service de l'Elévage had moved ahead without waiting for encouragement from the Paris authorities. In 1958, 110 of Djibouti's 200 or so fishermen were organized into a cooperative society through which credits (supplied by the F.I.D.E.S.) made it possible for members to motorize their craft and buy modern equipment. It also built refrigerated storage space at Djibouti, a fish-drying plant at Tadjoura, and a lobster hatchery at Obock, and collected, identified, and studied the migrations of 60 varieties of fish.[16] Also in 1958 the newly installed government council asked the Office de la Recherche Scientifique des Territoires d'Outre-Mer (O.R.S.T.O.M.) to make a scientific study of the Territory's fish resources, and finally, in 1965, a boat equipped for oceanographic research, with a French expert, arrived at Djibouti to devise fishing techniques and tackle appropriate to the situation. That same year an experiment was undertaken with a view to the possible development of tuna fishing on an industrial scale.[17]

Actually the current goals for the expansion of fishing in French Somaliland are not high. It is hoped that the apathy of the native population toward fishing will be sufficiently overcome to meet the growing demand for fish from the residents of Djibouti and from passing ships. Only when this is accomplished will a small canning industry be installed, the output of which will go mainly to Aden and nearby East African ports.

Salt and Other Minerals

For many years salt was French Somaliland's sole important export. Sea salt was extracted by the Société des Salines de Djibouti, which was founded in 1911 mainly to supply the Ethiopian market by way of the railroad to Addis Ababa. This company started operations in 1912 with modern equipment, and soon began producing on such a scale that it not only provisioned Ethiopia but exported its surplus salt to East African ports and even to India and Japan. During the interwar period, production averaged 60,000 tons a year, reaching a record figure of 77,000 tons in 1936. After

World War II, the Société des Salines signed an agreement with Ethiopia on May 15, 1946, whereby it was granted a monopoly for the purchase, transport, and sale of salt in that country. This agreement was never implemented, and soon the Ethiopians began asking for appreciable modifications in its terms.[18] The reason for this change of front was Ethiopia's good prospects for acquiring Eritrea, along with the saltworks that the Italians had developed at Assab to the point where they had been exporting some 400,000 tons of salt in the prewar years.

The Société des Salines' loss of the Ethiopian market was followed by its merger with a far more important French company, the Salines du Midi, which not only controlled saltworks in the Mediterranean (at Sfax in Tunisia), the Indian Ocean (Diégo-Suarez in Madagascar), and the Far East (Cana in Vietnam), but also possessed vast vineyards in France. The new company, known as Société des Salines du Midi et de Djibouti, opened a branch at Assab and saltworks in Aden, and progressively lost interest in its operations in French Somaliland. (To obtain permission to sell any salt from Djibouti on the Ethiopian market the company had to pledge that it would bring in 30,000 tons from Assab.) Production at Djibouti declined rapidly, falling from 28,484 tons in 1955 to 2,300 tons in 1957. In July 1957 the company ceased operations at Djibouti after a half-hearted attempt to find new markets for Somaliland's salt in the Far East. Indeed, it kept going as long as the mid-1950's largely because the local administration had urged it not to close down lest that aggravate an already bad unemployment situation.[19] The company claimed that it could not continue to operate profitably after the loss of the Ethiopian market and that the ocean-freight rates from Djibouti were excessive for a commodity of such low intrinsic value as salt. More cogent, if unstated, reasons were the tightness of the French salt market and the company's own lack of enterprise in French Somaliland, largely due to more remunerative enterprises elsewhere.

The Territory's salt resources are literally inexhaustible and are located in fairly accessible regions. In addition to the sea salt at Djibouti, there are huge reserves located on the banks of Lake Assal, which have long been known to the nomads of the area. The salt there forms a platform 18 kilometers long, ten kilometers wide, and two meters deep, and it has been described as a "geographic curiosity that is probably unique in the world."[20] Its existence was discovered by the French in 1883, but serious study of it was not undertaken until 1921, by a mining engineer who had been sent to Lake Assal to prospect for potash. He estimated that the salt deposit at that time amounted to about 2 billion tons, and that it was growing at the rate of 6 million tons a year. Before the railroad was built, the salt was cut into slabs, called *amoles,* and loaded on 50 to 60 camels, which came almost daily to carry it from the lake to the Ethiopian highlands. There it was used for cattle herds, and in 1922 the rate of exchange was one cow for an *amole* weighing from 15 to 20 kilograms.

It seems almost inexplicable that a deposit of this size, located only 90 kilometers from Djibouti, should never have been exploited on a commercial scale. The Société des Salines made no attempt to use the concession it held for many years to extract from Lake Assal and did not try to renew it when it expired in 1942. Chiefly responsible for such inactivity has been the tight control over the French salt market exercised by an organization of salt producers, the Comité des Salines de France et d'Outre-Mer, one of whose prime functions is to prevent the importation of foreign salt. Permission to extract salt from Lake Assal would be granted by this committee to any group or individual only on condition that its production would not disturb the existing monopoly. In effect this meant that it could be used only to provision a local chemical industry, which could conceivably yield a profit if sufficient generating power were available.

Concerning other mineral deposits in French Somaliland, limited prospecting has found evidence of only small deposits of copper, Iceland spar, iron, and a few other ores. In the National Assembly on April 27, 1961, the Territory's deputy, Hassan Gouled, complained that France had allocated no credits for a systematic study of his country's mineral potential. In reply the government's spokesman rather vaguely promised that prospecting would be continued, but the conclusions reached by the various scientific missions sent to the Territory since World War II have not been encouraging. Because of French Somaliland's geological formation, its subsoil probably contains no deposits of petroleum, or of ores in sufficient quantity to warrant their extraction.

Chapter Eight

THE MODERN ECONOMY

Electrical Power

Djibouti has had electrical current since 1906, when a private concessionaire was authorized to generate it for the town. This arrangement lasted until 1939, when his small diesel-powered plant could no longer fill the demand for current, and its operation was taken over and expanded by the public-works service. Djibouti grew so rapidly in the postwar years that a new thermo-electric *centrale* was built in 1954. It continued to be operated by the administration until 1960, when it was handed over to the newly created autonomous *régie* called Electricité de Djibouti. Three years later Tadjoura, Arta, and Dikhil were each provided with small generating plants.[1]

Between 1953 and 1966 the current produced and sold by Electricité de Djibouti grew from 2,800,000 kwh a year to 25,300,000. In the latter year it had 5,030 customers, of which the largest users were the port, airport, and administrative services, and its employees numbered 253, including 28 Europeans.[2] The *régie* had increased its clientele by reducing its rates and yet was able in 1964 to make a small profit, which it turned over to the territorial budget.[3] Since then the authorities have been debating the alternatives of enlarging the existing plant or replacing it with a new and more powerful *centrale*. The lack of coal deposits and of waterfalls in the Territory necessitates heavy expenditures for imported fuel. Over the years, various methods of deriving power from indigenous sources have been proposed. The most ingenious was a scheme drawn up by Pierre Gandillon, which he published as a brochure entitled *La Houille d'Or* for the Paris Colonial Exposition of 1931. Its author proposed generating power hydro-electrically by utilizing the differences in level between the bay of Ghoubbat-el-Kharab and Lakes Assal and Alol, which lie respectively at 150 and 20 meters below sea level. This project has been regarded as technically feasible but too grandiose and expensive for French Somaliland's small industrial development.

Industries

French Somaliland's industries are so few that they can be counted on the fingers of two hands, and all of them are privately owned and operated. They include enterprises related to the expansion of Djibouti town and port (the Société des Batignolles for building construction and the Société de l'Afrique Orientale for lighterage and ship repairs), one factory producing oxygen and acetylene (Compagnie de l'Air Liquide), one company making ice and soft drinks (Compagnie Industrielle de Djibouti), and two meat-packing plants (Société Incode and the Djibouti abattoir). Two of these, the Société des Batignolles and L'Air Liquide, are branches of large French concerns, three are local companies whose customers are Djibouti residents and passing ships, and only one produces exclusively for export. The last-mentioned company is the Société Incode, which is financed by Israeli capital and staffed largely by Israelis. Its output is shipped by a small refrigerated freighter to Haifa. Formed in 1954, it was encouraged by the local French administration as the first industry of its kind established in Djibouti.[4] It can handle 150 head of cattle a day, almost all of which are imported from Ethiopia and former British Somaliland. The local abbatoir, which began operating in April 1956, provisions Djibouti in fresh meat. It was hoped that the Israeli company would be the first of a series of industrial concerns, but Djibouti has failed to attract large-scale capital investments despite its special fiscal and tariff regimes, which were unique among France's overseas dependencies.

Finances and Planning

France's Christmas gift in 1945 to its colonies took the form of two new franc currencies, one created for its African territories and the other for its Pacific islands. French Somaliland shared with French West and Equatorial Africa the C.F.A. (Colonies Françaises d'Afrique) franc, which was initially given the value of 1.70 Metro. francs. This reportedly led almost at once to a 30 percent rise in the cost of living at Djibouti, but the resulting discontent was as nothing compared with the uproar that followed France's devaluation of her currency, and consequently of the C.F.A. franc, which occurred on January 26, 1948. French Somaliland's businessmen and residents were particularly outraged because they regarded this devaluation as an infringement of the pledge in 1943 to maintain the value of the franc, following a 20 percent capital levy decreed by the Free French regime on all bank deposits and on the notes then circulating in the Territory. The

Djibouti chamber of commerce cabled a protest to the Paris government, stressing the exceptional hardships that devaluation would bring to a colony 90 percent of whose essential consumer goods had to be imported and paid for in hard currency. Saïd Ali Coubèche, Somaliland's representative in the French Union Assembly, told his colleagues on January 30, 1948, that the franc's devaluation would have "deplorable and disastrous" effects on the Territory's economy, harm its finances—whose soundness was shown by a balanced budget and stabilized prices—and lead to a sharp rise in the cost of living. Indeed, as soon as the devaluation was announced, almost all of Djibouti's shops closed and their merchandise disappeared from the market for several weeks; when the goods finally reappeared, their prices had risen by 80 percent.[5] On October 17, 1948, France increased the value of the C.F.A. franc to that of 2 Metro. francs, but the effect of this re-evaluation was soon overshadowed in French Somaliland by far more momentous changes in the Territory's fiscal and tariff regimes.

Several missions of experts which had studied French Somaliland's economic situation in 1947–48 weighed the advisability of transforming Djibouti into a free port. The Territory was surrounded by countries belonging to the sterling bloc and was buying most of its imports from outside the franc zone. Because French Somaliland was isolated from France's other African dependencies, there was little danger that serious modifications made there might serve as a precedent for the other territories. The main argument in favor of creating a free port at Djibouti was that this would serve to maintain it as Ethiopia's port of foreign trade. A secondary consideration was the prospect of Djibouti's becoming a center for the region's petroleum traffic. At that time its relations with Ethiopia were not cordial and difficulties had arisen in regard to the frontier and the use of Djibouti's port and railroad. Moreover, this was the period when the Sinclair Petroleum Company was prospecting in Ethiopia's Ogaden province, and it seemed possible that oil might be found near French Somaliland's frontier. Consequently, not only Djibouti but the whole Territory was made a single free customs area by the law of January 1, 1949.

As a corollary to this step, French Somaliland was given its own currency on March 29, 1949. It was hoped that these two bold moves would transform an economy that was stagnant and even retrogressive in comparison with the growing prosperity of Aden facing it across the gulf. The Territory was so sterile that it had only one indigenous export of value, and unless profound changes were made it was likely to remain indefinitely a colony of civil servants and soldiers. Some promoters of the reforms even believed that if Djibouti were made a free port, exempted from income and other direct taxes, and given its own money pegged to a strong currency, it might become a financial and trading center comparable to Tangier and Hong Kong. After some hesitation the Paris government decided to peg the new Djibouti franc to the American dollar rather than to the British pound. A deposit in dollars was made with the Franco-American Banking Corporation of New York, which gave it 100 percent coverage, thereby making it freely convertible at the fixed rate of 214.392 Djibouti francs to one American dollar. Then the privilege of note issue in the Territory was transferred from the Banque de l'Indochine to the French Treasury, and finally the Office des Changes at Djibouti was restricted to control over transactions with the franc zone.

The next few years proved that these reforms were not fulfilling the hopes of their sponsors, but they were never rescinded because it was impossible to tell to what extent they or other factors were responsible for the fluctuations in the Territory's economy throughout the 1950's. For example, Ethiopia instituted in 1949 a strict currency-exchange control which had the practical effect of channeling far more of its foreign trade than before through Assab, but it was not certain whether this move had been prompted mainly by Djibouti's monetary reform of that year or by the concurrent devaluation of the British pound, to which the Ethiopian dollar had been pegged. Justifying the reforms in answer to a question posed to the government in the National Assembly on February 19, 1953, the Minister of Finance cited the growth in the Territory's transit trade and revenues between 1949 and 1952. His critics replied that this expansion was due primarily to French public investments under the Plan; in any case there was a sharp fall in Djibouti's exports and railroad traffic in 1954. That year a company was set up there with Israeli capital, and in 1955 a French firm transferred its headquarters from Saigon to Djibouti, but their example was not followed by other private investors.

One French economist who specialized in overseas affairs concluded that the reforms of 1949 had harmed the franc zone and had also been useless to French Somaliland.[6] In reply, P. H. Siriex, who had been governor of the Territory from 1946 to 1950, argued that they had been inevitable considering the circumstances at the time they were made.[7] In his view, the basic error had been to count too heavily on the indispensability of Djibouti's port and railroad to Ethiopia and on "Ethiopia's relapsing into medieval torpor" without the stimulus that the Italians had briefly provided. With remarkable foresight he urged that French Somaliland no longer be treated as an isolated area and that a solution for its problems be sought within a regional framework that would include Aden and Mogadiscio as well as Addis Ababa.

According to an eminent authority on the Horn of Africa, the French Territory on the eve of World War II had become the most prosperous of the three Somalilands.[8] Yet it has never covered its expenditures from local resources, and its mounting budgets have been met only by ever-increasing subsidies from France, in one form or another.[9] The Metropolitan missions that studied the Territory's financial situation in 1947–48 calculated that out of a revenue then equivalent to $11.5 million, $8.5 million came from French military and civil expenditures, $2 million from the Territory's transit trade, and $1 million from Djibouti's port services. Since then the situation has not appreciably changed: the administration and garrison still provide about two-thirds of the Territory's financial resources, and the remaining third comes from the transit trade and the services and provisions supplied to passing ships.

During the first postwar years, most of French Somaliland's local revenues came from export and import duties and port taxes. Of these, the amounts collected by the customs service at Djibouti, Obock, Tadjoura, and Loyada were the more important. In 1947 the regulations governing their assessment and the rates were somewhat lowered.[10] To make up for the ensuing decline in revenues, especially crucial because of a 70 million C.F.A. franc increase in the volume of the 1948 budget, direct taxes on income and profits were raised, as were also the stamp and registration duties. These were insufficient, and France had to provide a larger subsidy than before. To balance the 1949 budget, 28.5 million C.F.A. francs had to be taken from the Reserve Fund. The administration announced its intention of distributing the fiscal burden more equitably and of reducing expenditures, but officials wasted much time and money in trying to impose taxation on the nomads, and it was the townspeople of the Territory who continued to carry the entire tax load. In any case, the major monetary and tariff reforms of early 1949 altered the whole trade picture as well as the main sources of the territorial revenues.

Adapting the budget to the new laws proved to be a long and arduous task, especially as local business interests were very powerful in the representative council. It was not until January 1, 1952, that radical changes were introduced which eliminated all direct taxes, including those on business transactions, commercial and industrial profits, and general income. However, merchants and business firms were required to pay for a license (*patente*), the cost of which depended on the nature of the enterprise and on the rental value of the premises it occupied. The existing special taxes on alcoholic beverages and tobacco were maintained, as were those on real property. The most important innovation of the 1952 fiscal code was the imposition of a 15 percent ad valorem sales tax on all imported merchandise except foodstuffs for the native population.

Introduction of this sales tax seemed hardly compatible with Djibouti's new status as a free port, but it had the desired effect of increasing local revenues, and the year 1953 ended with a budgetary surplus of nearly D.F. 40 million. This happy state of financial affairs did not last long, for the next year saw a trade recession and increased budgetary outlays because of a pay raise for civil servants and application to the Territory of the Overseas Labor Code. In 1954 the authorities took the easy way of reducing expenditures by cutting down the budget for developmental expenditures by D.F. 18 million. Nevertheless, the territorial budget totaled D.F. 1,225 million, or 49 million more than in 1953. Because the economy did not revive in 1955, port duties were reduced by as much as 50 percent on certain merchandise in transit, railroad rates were substantially lowered, and private capitalists were encouraged to invest in the country by a virtual exemption of new enterprises from taxation for the first few years of their operations.

As a result of the application of the 1956 *loi-cadre* to French Somaliland and the closing of the Suez Canal after the Anglo-French-Israeli invasion of Egypt during the last months of that year, the fiscal structure of the Territory changed and its revenues shrank. Those revenues could be augmented only by increasing the sales tax from 15 percent to 18 percent and by imposing a surtax on petroleum products, the territorial assemblymen having refused to institute a head tax. The legislative powers of the assembly were by that time appreciably larger than those of the representative council, and the budget was thenceforth divided into three parts—ordinary revenues and expenditures, investment funds, and operation of the port. The ordinary budget for 1958 was finally balanced at D.F. 840 million, a substantial reduction from the D.F. 931 million budget for 1957, which had required an increase in taxation. The investment budget came to D.F. 204.1 million and that of the port to 280.3 million.

Between 1958 and 1961 the volume of the Territory's budgets did not vary greatly, rising only from D.F. 1,074 to D.F. 1,095 million over the three-year period, but it began to climb steeply beginning in 1962. By that time the territorial assembly had come to accept the inevitability of heavier taxation to meet the larger allocations to the health and education services. The general economic situation had improved, and though the 1962 budget was

TERRITORIAL BUDGET OF FRENCH SOMALILAND FOR 1967
(Millions of Djibouti francs)

Revenues		Expenditures	
Direct taxes	281.6	Public-debt service	57.6
Indirect taxes	1,031.0	Representation in Parliament and	
Stamp and registration duties	88.0	territorial assembly	42.1
Public enterprises and revenue		Government council	24.2
from state-owned land	145.1	Ministries:	
Various government services	148.5	Public Works	153.8
Contributions from France	113.9	Finances and the Plan	440.6
Total	1,855.1	Health and Social Affairs	346.3
		Education, Sports, and Youth	150.8
		Internal Affairs	232.5
		Civil Service	13.9
		Economic Affairs	44.7
		Labor	19.8
		Maintenance operations	88.9
		Security and prison services	134.4
		Subsidies and grants	60.6
		Transfers to investment budget	44.9
		Total	1,855.1

15 percent higher than its predecessor, the Territory ended the year with a surplus of D.F. 88 million. In 1963 the budget totaled D.F. 1,503 million, which was 18.7 percent higher than that of 1962. Income from all taxable sources had grown, but indirect taxes brought in nearly 75 percent of all the fiscal revenues. Three-fourths of the expenditures went for operating costs, in which the pay of personnel made up the most important single item. The year ended with a sizable deficit, which had to be covered from the Reserve Fund, so in 1964 the territorial assembly was compelled to increase taxation. The budget for that year, amounting to D.F. 1,800 million, was marked by far larger grants to the health and education services, which together came to account for one-third of total expenditures. Although the 1965 budget showed only a slight increase (D.F. 1,828 million), France had to provide a larger subsidy than before, amounting to D.F. 160 million, though use of the term "subsidy" had been abandoned by the Paris government in 1963. This took the form of paying the salaries of more of the civil servants assigned to the Territory and the cost of secondary and technical education there.

From the foregoing summary of French Somaliland's financial history during the postwar years, it is clear that the volume of its budgets has grown appreciably, if irregularly, and that local economic developments have largely accounted for the fluctuations in the territorial revenues. The high level of expenditures for the payment of personnel has remained fairly constant, and sums allocated to the social welfare services have risen sharply in the 1960's. The financial aid provided by France, under one name or another, has also shot up, from D.F. 26 million in 1958 to 160 million seven years later. The Territory's growing dependence on France took on new significance during the riotous incidents that occurred at Djibouti late in 1966 and early in 1967. For the first time local political developments affected French Somaliland's economy and were inevitably reflected in its finances, adding still another element of instability to their chronically fragile economic base. The 1966 budget, totaling D.F. 1,912 million, marked an all-time record; that for 1967 declined to about D.F. 1,855 million; and in 1968 an even greater decline may be expected because of the closing of the Suez Canal to navigation.

As of the present writing, more than half of local revenues come from the sales tax. The equipment budget, almost wholly financed by France, has shrunk from nearly D.F. 200 million in 1966 to 49 million in 1967 as the result of uncertainty about the Territory's future political status. The foregoing table provides a breakdown of the Territory's revenues and expenditures in 1967.

French Somaliland became a colony of France only through the enterprise of a handful of determined pioneers, and it has been kept under French control in large part as a reaction against what were interpreted as predatory gestures by alien powers. Detailed knowledge of the colony was confined to the few Frenchmen who had lived and worked there, and even an awareness of its existence was largely restricted to French stamp collectors and readers of Monfreid's books. Every imperial power, at one time or other, has been accused of colossal ignorance of its distant colonies. In the case of the Territory, an apocryphal story concerns the attempt by the French Navy to send a ship up the Ambouli River to explore the hinterland. When upon arrival the captain learned that the Ambouli only flowed underground, the ship was abandoned at its estuary and lay there rusting year after year.[11]

From time to time, books and articles have been published in France by authors trying to convince the government and public opinion of the vital importance of the Territory to France's national interests. This has been difficult to do, although there was a fairly constant interest over the years in Ethiopia and its foreign commerce, and consequently in Djibouti's role as the main port for that trade. That interest, however, could be described as existing only among the railroad company's shareholders and French Somaliland's merchants, and rarely did it figure in the considerations of France's policy makers. It is true that for many years the Paris authorities regarded Djibouti as indispensable to the maintenance of lifelines to distant parts of the French empire. But as the links with those colonies became increasingly tenuous, the significance attributed by France to its foothold on the Somali coast diminished. On the other hand, as Djibouti's status as a strategic military and naval base declined, interest in the port as a trading center increased, in consequence of the growth in oil-tanker traffic using the Suez Canal. Djibouti, one of the southern gateways to the Red Sea, developed more and more into a port of call where passing ships were supplied and serviced.

To a minor extent, political and cultural considerations helped to shape France's complex and changing attitude toward its tiny Somaliland dependency. Especially since 1954, the Territory has provided a livelihood for many civil servants and military men for whom employment elsewhere became progressively harder to find, especially as one French colony after another became independent. If the Paris authorities and the men posted to Somaliland were happy to have it as a safe if unattractive haven, the French taxpayer was not so pleased by the growing financial drain which that Territory came to represent in his eyes. Then, beginning in 1958, when General de Gaulle came to power in France, the Territory as a center—albeit very small—for the radiation of French culture in East Africa and the Middle East entered the picture. This new factor largely explains the strong reaction of the President of the Republic to the reception he received during his 1966 visit to Djibouti. The pro-independence demonstrations at that time threatened to affect adversely his prestige in the Third World as the liberator of French Africa.

All these various and complex considerations were reflected in the successive changes in France's economic policies applied in the Territory. Thus French Somaliland, in common with other colonies before World War II, was left to fend for itself financially, aside from the small-scale aid provided to the railroad company and for the development of Djibouti's port. Similarly France's new sense of responsibility for the welfare of its colonies, first felt during the Second World War, expressed itself in a development plan drawn up in Paris which included French Somaliland. There as elsewhere it was financed by French public funds and was locally executed through the agency of two new state organizations, the F.I.D.E.S. and the C.C.O.M. (Caisse Centrale de la France d'Outre-Mer).

Since 1947, French Somaliland has had four successive plans, of which the last is scheduled for completion in 1970. To the first two plans the Territory made small contributions from its own resources, but since 1959 the funds have been supplied wholly by France. Between 1947 and 1959, the F.I.D.E.S. spent altogether 7,029 million Metro. francs in French Somaliland, most of which went to the improvement of its communications. Specifically, the port of Djibouti received 1,756 million, the Territory's roads 130 million, and the telecommunications network 100 million.[12] The social sector was also allocated the comparatively large sum of 1,054 million, of which 234 million went to the health service, 128 million to education, 313 million to housing, and 377 million to various urban and rural welfare operations. But the producing sector was given only 882 million, and of this relatively small total 729 million were spent on the construction of a new power plant for Djibouti. For the development of animal husbandry, agriculture, and hydraulics merely 98, 28, and 26 million, respectively, were provided. In addition, the Territory received special contributions in emergencies, such as the 90 million francs donated to offset the economic recession that resulted from the closing of the Suez Canal in late 1956. Moreover, the above-mentioned sums dispensed by the F.I.D.E.S. did not include France's sizable expenditures for the Territory's civil service, armed forces, radio station, and airfield.

The new political consciousness that developed among indigenous leaders, in the wake of the application to French Somaliland of the *loi-cadre* of 1956, was in part expressed by their increasing criticism of France's financial expenditures there and of the orientation of the Territory's plans. By that time the F.I.D.E.S. had divided its operations into two sections, of which the one termed "local" was subject to approval or amendments by the territorial assembly. The most pointed criticism of France's financial policy, however, was voiced by Hassan Gouled when he was the Territory's deputy to the National Assembly. His frank comments there on November 6, 1959, and October 25, 1960, were in part inspired by his resentment of the larger sums that France (and the Common Market Development Fund) was then allocating to other overseas territories, but they were also prompted by more objective considerations. Although Hassan Gouled had long urged the building of a drydock at Djibouti and the improvement of its port, he wanted as much money to be spent on development of the neglected hinterland. What we need, he told his colleagues, is more water and native technicians and not so many expatriate civil servants. In brief, he implied that the main beneficiaries of the development plans were the French nationals, not the native population.

Governor Compain indirectly replied to such criticism in a speech he made to the territorial assembly in November 1960. In that year, he emphasized, France was spending in the Territory three times as much as French Somaliland's total indigenous revenues. Other defenders of the official policy stressed the small size of French Somaliland compared with most of the other overseas territories, and its meager natural resources. A cogent difficulty was the failure of private capitalists to follow the lead given by the F.I.D.E.S. in contributing to the Territory's development. The net result was that the F.I.D.E.S. had played an unduly important role in the economy of French Somaliland. Completion of the main program financed by the F.I.D.E.S. in 1957 had led to a sudden rise of unemployment and consequently of popular discontent. Consequently, the Paris authorities came to the decision that a revision of the Plan's objectives was in order.

Some important changes in France's economic policy followed the visit of Robert Lecourt, a member of the French cabinet, to the Territory in 1961. First, he earmarked a sizable sum for the purchase of foodstuffs for the nomad population, whose herds were suffering from a prolonged drought. Of wider significance was the program he initiated for the development of agriculture and watering points in the rural regions. Under the third Plan, moreover, larger credits were allocated for the Territory's health and educational equipment, to such good effect that, with respect to its hospitals and schools, French Somaliland forged even farther ahead of neighboring countries than before.

Progress in health and education has been maintained, but by the time the fourth Plan was drawn up in 1966, a certain disillusionment concerning the reorientation of the Territory's economic program was evident. Experience during the preceding few years had shown that the scheduled extension of the cultivated area could be effected only at enormous expense, and that its ultimate success was most uncertain in view of the poor quality of the soil and the nomads' aversion to farming. Nor were the results of official encouragement of a fishing industry much more hopeful, though in this case lack of success could not be ascribed to the absence of natural resources. Here again, however, the obstacles were similar—shortage of the time and money that were required for the indispensable preliminary studies, and indifference of the population, both as fishermen and as consumers. It was therefore decided to continue experimenting in both domains but to reduce considerably the agricultural and fishing programs. Thenceforth the available funds and technical assistance were to be concentrated on the creation of more watering points for the nomads' herds and on the development of Djibouti's port. A regular and more plentiful water supply was obviously desired and needed greatly by the hinterland population. And enabling the port of Djibouti to handle its increasing traffic was felt to be the only sure way of coping with its unemployment problem—and indeed was the key to the Territory's economic progress as a whole. Ironically, the new orientation given to French Somaliland's development plan coincided with the political agitation that jeopardized the Territory's future stability and led to a suspension of the Plan's application for six months. Then, soon after the referendum of March 1967 had settled the issue, at least for the immediate future, the outbreak of the Israeli-Arab war resulted in the closing of the Suez Canal and a sharp decline in the port's activity. In the summer of 1967, Ali Aref and Ahmed Dini went to Paris to solicit additional financial aid in setting up the new services required because of the Territory's autonomous status and in alleviating the conditions resulting from the stagnation of Djibouti's trade and shipping.

Trade

French Somaliland's internal trade is negligible because of its lack of indigenous resources and the limited number of consumers. The European community fluctuates considerably in size but averages 6,000-odd residents, and the only others who have appreciable purchasing power are a few thousand regularly employed non-European wage earners and a handful of well-to-do traders. The imports for this domestic market, amounting to 40,000 to 50,000 tons a year and valued at 5 to 6 billion Djibouti francs, consist mainly of foodstuffs (coffee, sugar, flour, and wine), textiles and other manufactured consumer goods, and building materials. When the nomads have needs beyond those that they can satisfy themselves, they go to the nearest village to buy food, cloth, and firearms. To make these purchases they sell some animals, hides, butter, and doum-palm leaves. Some of the Assayamara Afars carry the salt of Lake Assal to Aoussa, where they buy corn or *dourra* with the proceeds, and certain Issa tribes make charcoal for sale. Because of their ingrained distrust of paper currency, the nomads accept readily only silver coins, either Maria Theresa thalers or Indian rupees.[13]

Aside from such limited exchanges, the nomads live by subsistence agriculture and have no part in the external trade, which determines the modern sector of French Somaliland's economy. Almost all of the Territory's trade falls into the transit category, because the indigenous market for imported goods is small, and salt—one of the three commodities produced locally for export—ceased in 1957 to be an element in foreign trade. To

MAJOR IMPORTS OF FRENCH SOMALILAND IN SELECTED YEARS
(Tons)

Product	1913	1930	1935	1938	1942	1947	1948
Cereals	1,370	978	1,184	1,473	—	3,331	16,248
Wood	2,059	1,033	660	3,341	—	1,039	1,601
Coal	54,860	167,190	17,525	19,882	1,218	17,599	41,095
Petroleum products	1,261	1,781	1,239	2,690	470	3,485	3,926
Cement	597	15,995	1,860	8,487	—	10,546	4,817
Metal articles	8,556	1,035	303	3,038	—	624	2,421
Cotton textiles	4,365	1,209	1,007	907	—	193	161
Motor vehicles and spare parts	1	26	86	261	—	287	600

Source: La Documentation Française, "La Côte Française des Somalis," *Notes et Etudes Documentaires*, No. 1321, Apr. 28, 1950.

MAJOR EXPORTS OF FRENCH SOMALILAND IN SELECTED YEARS
(Tons)

Product	1913	1930	1935	1938	1942	1947	1948
Sea salt	2,285	26,065	76,522	51,106	200	48,783	59,134
Coffee	3,800	12,582	15,176	3,747	—	1,610	7,277
Cereals	—	174	—	—	—	6,584	25,333
Rawhides	5,500	8,864	7,339	1,070	—	820	1,449

Source: La Documentation Française, "La Côte Française des Somalis," *Notes et Etudes Documentaires*, No. 1321, Apr. 28, 1950.

some extent the administration and population of Djibouti have been able to influence the volume and nature of this trade by the kind of services and other facilities they provide for merchants and shippers. But most of its foreign trade, and therefore the basis of the Territory's prosperity, lies outside of local control, as has been dramatically shown on the occasions when external circumstances have modified its scope and character.

At the turn of the century the value of the colony's trade was somewhat less than 10 million francs annually, of which imports accounted for 7 million.[14] After the first section of the Djibouti–Addis Ababa railroad was opened to traffic as far as Diré Daoua, the volume of trade increased rapidly. On the eve of World War I, it amounted to 81 million francs, more than half of the total being represented by exports. Completion of the railroad, which virtually coincided with the end of the war, further stimulated commerce, and in 1920 foreign trade came to a total of 304 million francs. Thereafter and until 1935 the Territory's imports were stabilized around

21,000 tons a year, except for a brief spurt in 1929, when that tonnage was more than doubled. Exports developed more slowly but also more regularly, rising from 11,000 tons in 1920 to 28,000 tons in 1935, of which coffee and hides accounted for all but 7,000 tons.

As a result of the war between Italy and Ethiopia in 1935, this trade was fundamentally altered. Provisioning of the Italian army in Ethiopia was effected by the French railroad. In 1936 it carried on the trip up from the coast 62,000 tons of merchandise, and the following year the Territory handled 161,000 tons of imports, largely from Italy and destined for Ethiopia. During the same period, however, Ethiopia's exports—which had exceeded its imports during the years before the Italian occupation—declined sharply and in 1938 became insignificant. In 1938, also, the Italians began to deflect their imports away from French Somaliland through development of the port of Assab in Eritrea and the building of a road from there to Addis Ababa.* This pricked the bubble of Djibouti's new prosperity founded on the rapid growth of the import trade. Then, too, the virtual elimination of Ethiopia's exports removed the element of stability they had given until then to the Territory's economy. Yet it could not be said that the trade position of the Territory was unfavorable at the time that World War II broke out and drastically changed the economic picture.

During the first years of the war, the fighting in nearby East Africa and, above all, the political choice made by the French authorities in Djibouti undermined the Territory's economy to such a point that Djibouti's population came near to starvation. Its condition was somewhat improved when the Free French took over the administration early in 1943, and from that time until 1946 the volume of trade was maintained at somewhat under 100,000 tons a year. A marked improvement began in 1947 as the result of a growth in Ethiopia's exports and an even larger increase in its imports. This revival, as compared with trade in the previous years, is reflected in the two foregoing tables.

After the Second World War, the French government imposed rigid trade and monetary controls on the economy of all its dependencies. This policy was motivated in part by the need to conserve its small stock of hard currency, but even more by the determination to preserve its traditional colonial markets while awaiting the revival of French industry and exports. French Somaliland suffered less from application of this policy than other territories that had been far larger consumers of France's products and also

* See p. 12.

nearer that source. On November 7, 1946, the customs duties on merchandise of foreign origin imported into the Territory were temporarily suspended, and the following year textile rationing was ended in time for the Muslim population to revive the traditional practice of buying new clothing at the end of Ramadan.[15] Nevertheless, import duties were reimposed at the high rate of 10 to 40 percent ad valorem on consumer goods, as was a duty of 1.5 percent on merchandise in transit.

The reform of the currency and the changes in the tariff and fiscal regimes,* which became law early in 1949, were designed to stimulate Djibouti's trade, but the local merchants complained that only the names of the existing imposts had been changed. It was true that the former transit duty had been replaced by taxes for the maintenance of the port and airfield, and that the new sales tax (*taxe intérieure de consommation*) approximated the old duties on imported goods. To be sure, the 15 percent ad valorem rate of the sales tax was appreciably lower than that of the former customs duties, but the devaluation of the Djibouti franc in relation to the C.F.A. franc had made the cost of imported merchandise higher and had thus cancelled out the advantage. Despite this, the volume of French Somaliland's trade increased notably, especially with regard to exports, in the wake of the 1949 reforms. The sales tax was not applied to foodstuffs imported for the native population, such as cereals, vegetables, and butter, or to articles likely to attract tourists, such as French perfumes, liqueurs, radios, and cameras. Currency controls were lifted except for transactions with the franc zone, and the Djibouti franc was freely convertible. No longer were import or export licenses required, and without any formalities whatsoever merchants could buy or sell anything they pleased except firearms and narcotics.

Although it was certainly inexact to describe Djibouti as a free port, except in comparison with its previous status, it was far freer than any other French African dependency at the time. Moreover, from that time on, official controls were never reimposed except temporarily during periods of emergency. When on two occasions the Suez Canal was closed, in 1956 and 1967, the government, fearing shortages and speculation, required merchants to declare their stocks and forbade reexportation. Prices of certain essentials, such as drugs, petroleum products, and rents, were then temporarily frozen, as they also had been after the economic recession of 1963.

French Somaliland's exports can be divided into four main categories: indigenous products, Ethiopia's shipments in transit, merchandise unload-

* See pp. 181–82.

ed from freighters for transshipment, and the fuel, food, and water supplied to ships using Djibouti as a port of call.

For many years indigenous exports consisted of sea salt, shell, and hides, and salt provided virtually all the tonnage of value. Because the French market was closed to Djibouti's salt output by a producers' monopoly,* the Territory's product had to be sold elsewhere, mainly to Ethiopia. After World War II, however, it was eased out of the Ethiopian market by competition from Eritrean salt, and failing to find other buyers, Djibouti ceased to export salt in 1957. This reduced French Somaliland's indigenous shipments to a few thousand tons of shell and rawhides of some bulk but little value, and left the Territory dependent on its two other economic activities.

From the time the railroad was opened between Djibouti and Addis Ababa, the transit trade between Ethiopia and French Somaliland became the most important element in the latter's economy. It consisted of carrying Ethiopia's coffee, hides, wax, and musk to Djibouti for reshipment, usually to Aden, and of transporting the manufactured goods and fuel unloaded at Djibouti's port for sale in Ethiopia. The umbilical cord that linked the economies of the two countries was almost severed by a succession of external events. These were, in chronological order, the Italian occupation of Ethiopia, World War II, and the subsequent restoration of Ethiopia's sovereignty.

Inevitably these events profoundly altered the economic relations between Ethiopia and French Somaliland, at first incidentally and as a by-product, and later as the result of deliberate policy. The Italians in the late 1930's and the Ethiopians ten years later became increasingly restive because of their dependence on an alien port and railroad, over whose self-interested management they could exercise no control. At great expense the Italians developed an alternative outlet at Assab, and it was taken over and expanded by Ethiopia after it gained control of Eritrea in 1952. Before they were able to do so, however, the authorities at Addis Ababa had already shown their displeasure with the French in Djibouti. In the late 1940's they imposed import quotas and currency controls, and, reportedly, they also encouraged a strike among the railroad employees, which adversely affected the transit trade through French Somaliland.

It was not until 1954, nevertheless, when the port of Assab became actively competitive to Djibouti, that the French authorities awakened to the danger. Belatedly they reduced Djibouti's port taxes and the railroad's

* See p. 178.

freight rates, and in other ways tried to make the Territory more attractive for the transit trade. Suddenly they came to realize that Djibouti's
facilities were not necessarily indispensable to Ethiopia and, moreover, that
French Somaliland's economy was largely dependent on Ethiopia's prosperity and good will. If, for example, Ethiopia no longer shipped its livestock to Djibouti, that town's abattoir and refrigerating plant would have
to close down and the provisioning of ships would be gravely hampered.

This salutary recognition of the facts led to a series of political and economic concessions to Ethiopia, and in due course to an attitude of cooperation which has enabled French Somaliland not only to retain but to increase its share in the handling of Ethiopia's foreign trade. At the same
time the French became conscious of the danger inherent in a transit trade
that depended wholly on the sale in foreign markets of agricultural products the tonnage of which was determined by climatic conditions. This induced the French authorities at Djibouti to develop far more than ever
before the Territory's only other important economic activity—the fueling
and provisioning of ships that used it as a port of call.

Until well after the end of World War II, Djibouti's trade was dominated by a few big companies, almost all of which were branches of Metropolitan French firms. The oldest of them, the Société de l'Afrique Orientale, was an offshoot of the powerful Compagnie Générale des Colonies in
Paris. It was established at Obock, and when the capital was transferred to
Djibouti it became one of the largest landowners there. It gave birth to two
local subsidiaries, the Compagnie Maritime de l'Afrique Orientale, whose
fleet of tenders and barges monopolized the loading and unloading of
freighters that called at Djibouti, and the Société Industrielle de Djibouti,
which supplied water to the town from its pumping station at Ambouli.
The Territory's exports to France were carried by ships of the Messageries
Maritimes, but this did not constitute a monopoly of the Territory's foreign
trade, since most of its exports went to non-French markets and were transported in ships of various nationalities. At this time the Société des Salines
ranked highest among Djibouti's export firms, and the Banque de l'Indochine had the monopoly not only of the banknote issue but of the credit
facilities as well.

Such a situation was naturally much criticized by French radicals in the
Parliament, but it was less their influence than the pressure of economic
circumstances that gradually loosened the grip of the large companies
on the Territory's economy. In the mid-1950's the shrinkage of markets
forced the Société des Salines to close down at Djibouti, and the establish-

ment there of a branch of the Banque Nationale pour le Commerce et l'Industrie weakened the position of the Banque de l'Indochine, as did the withdrawal of its note-issue privilege. Concurrently, the development of Assab as a major port for Ethiopia's foreign trade and, to a much smaller extent, the creation of Air Djibouti, loosened the hold that the Compagnie des Chemins de Fer Franco-Ethiopiens had long had upon the internal transport of passengers and merchandise.

Because of French Somaliland's geographical position and lack of indigenous resources, France has never played the predominant role in its trade that it did in other French African territories. Until the reforms of 1949, the franc zone held a fairly important place in the import trade of the Territory, but took barely 10 percent of its exports. From Great Britain and the sterling bloc came nearly half of Djibouti's imports, and most of its exports went to that bloc. Ethiopia, both before and after its currency was pegged to sterling, was the Territory's main provisioner and market, and there has always been considerable contraband trade with British Somaliland. England took some of the Territory's shell exports, Israel bought its meat, and Egypt was a main market for the livestock exported from Djibouti. But it was the British colony of Aden, the center of the region's foreign trade, that was the destination for most of Djibouti's reexports and that controlled much of Djibouti's trading organization. Indeed, Djibouti's main import-export firms were branches of larger companies based at Aden or Addis Ababa. Two Frenchmen, Chefneux and Besse, preferred to establish their important firms at Addis and Aden respectively, rather than in Djibouti. The net result has been that many of the merchants of Djibouti, far from offering competition to Addis Ababa and Aden trading companies, have become more or less executors of the business policies determined in those two towns.

The most striking characteristic of Djibouti's business firms is that not one of them, whether European, Asian, or African, is an independent entity. This is especially true of the Arab and Indian mercantile concerns that are subsidiaries of companies whose headquarters are located elsewhere, most of them in Aden or Addis Ababa, but some as far away as Cairo, Jiddah, and India. Various interpretations of this phenomenon have been offered.[16]

One explanation is the inefficacy of the law in giving protection to traders. Credit at great risk is the basis of all local trade in Djibouti, and the number of defaulting debtors who cannot be prosecuted is large. Consequently, Arab and Indian traders prefer to utilize the services of relatives stationed in Djibouti whom they trust rather than to create subsidiary firms there. Furthermore, the instability of the local market is such that these firms engage in widely varying activities in many places, and Djibouti represents only a small operation for them. Multiple enterprises in various areas enable a firm to shift its energies and capital rapidly to a place where it is likely to make the largest and most immediate profits. How quickly this could be done was shown in the mid-1950's when a considerable number of Djibouti firms transferred their agents and funds to Assab as soon as that port began to control a larger proportion of Ethiopia's foreign trade. Another advantage of this system to the traders has been the greater ease of tax evasion that it permits. The lack of any centralized accounting and the distribution of profits over many enterprises have made it impossible for the French authorities to find out how much business a Djibouti firm actually does.

Another effect of the system has been to restrict the operations of Djibouti's banks largely to the control of money-exchange operations. Rarely do the Indian traders in Djibouti have recourse to bank loans, for if they must borrow they prefer to do so from private sources, even from a competitor, because his interest rates are lower. So notoriously thrifty are the Indian merchants that they are said to order monthly food parcels from India rather than pay the high prices charged by the Djibouti importers of foodstuffs. Local Arab merchants, who are kept on a tighter rein by their home offices, occasionally take out bank loans. In general, however, Djibouti's business firms operate in a network in which they are largely self-sufficient. Indeed, Djibouti, like the Principality of Monaco, has in many cases become simply a mail address for companies whose main activities are carried on elsewhere.

The reforms of 1949 did not fundamentally alter the trading organization of Djibouti, although they led to a proliferation of small foreign firms. As of 1923 the companies established there numbered 65, the most important being the European-owned export-import houses. Of these, 24 were French, eight Greek, six Italian, one English, one Belgian, and one Swiss, as compared with 16 Arab and 11 Indian firms.[17] A survey 24 years later gave a count of 132 European and 300 non-European trading establishments.[18] Many of the companies founded during the postwar period were ephemeral, but according to an official analysis in 1961,[19] there were then estimated to be 80 sizable and "furiously competitive" export-import firms. The local newspaper three years later upped this figure to 100.[20] There is little or no specialization in the merchandise bought and sold, and the larger firms sell everything from American cars, Japanese cameras, and Swiss clocks to African wood carvings. Foreign as well as French merchants are well represented in the chamber of commerce, which was founded in 1912. It has 14 regular members and eight alternates, and only five of the former are Metropolitan Frenchmen. As in other French territories, this chamber has a semiofficial status, but despite its reorganization by the administration in March 1947, it has never been very active.

In French Somaliland the spirit of free enterprise has been allowed to play a far greater role than in the rest of French-speaking tropical Africa, and among the results have been chaotic competition and at the same time a curious lack of initiative. So anxious has the administration been to develop the Territory's trade that it has permitted three times as many traders to do business at Djibouti than are needed. Moreover, these traders, whether wholesalers or retailers, prefer to sell little and at inflated prices, and the result is excessively high living costs. The opposite policy is pursued in Aden, Hargeisa, and Asmara, where the local administrations restrict the number of mercantile licenses they issue and relate them to the consumers' capacities.

In an address to the territorial assembly on May 14, 1966, General Billotte, Minister for France's overseas departments and territories, warned that "efforts to improve the port will not avail unless the spirit of enterprise remains alert. In this respect, I urgently appeal to our merchants to revise their methods of sale and their prices, which I find too high as compared with those prevailing at Aden. They must do this if they hope to take over the commercial torch from Aden after 1968."

Even in the unlikely event that Djibouti's merchants should heed this warning, no reorganization of the trading system can fundamentally alter the sensitivity of the Territory's trade to political events and economic circumstances external to it. The sudden closing of the Suez Canal in June 1967 as a consequence of the Israeli-Arab war is a dramatic illustration of the blow that can be dealt the Territory's trade by forces outside of French Somaliland. More cogent because directly related to the Territory have been the effects on its population of the irredentism of the Somali Republic. The local reaction in Djibouti took the form of unruly demonstrations and strikes in August and September 1966, which were followed by an appreciable decline in the volume of the Territory's trade. Even more serious has been the ensuing lack of confidence in the Territory's economic future on the part of the big trading firms and shippers. One month before the referendum of March 1967, ten sizable companies in Djibouti held directors' meetings, at which they were authorized, if the need arose, to move their headquarters out of the Territory and to convert their funds held in Djibouti francs.[21] Between August 1966 and March 1967, about

$10 million worth of Djibouti francs was withdrawn from the local banks by worried depositors.[22]

It is a dismal commentary on the future of the whole region that perhaps Djibouti's most hopeful prospect lies in the even greater loss of confidence by businessmen in the future of Aden and also of Assab. The disorders in Aden during 1967 seem likely to worsen after the departure of the British, and the usefulness of Assab as a port for Ethiopia's foreign trade may be sharply reduced if the authorities at Addis Ababa prove unable to control the revolt of Eritrea. Djibouti's best chance of holding its own, and even of capturing some of the trade and shipping that have been going to Aden and Assab, depends on the Territory's ability to achieve political stability within its own borders.

Transportation

Construction of Djibouti's port and the railroad began so nearly at the same time that their causal relationship resembles that of the chicken-and-the-egg. Djibouti was selected as the territorial capital by Governor Lagarde both for its potential as a port and for its accessibility to the Ethiopian plateau. Building of the first section of the Djibouti–Addis Ababa track coincided with the earliest work done to create a port for the new capital. Thus from the outset the two were linked as complementary media for tapping and furthering the trade with Ethiopia, and they developed together with the growth of the transit traffic between the coast and Addis Ababa.

After World War II, the port began to perform supplementary functions which have become increasingly important in its activities. The railroad, on the other hand, has continued to operate exclusively as carrier for the transit trade with Ethiopia and, furthermore, has played a diminishing role in that respect. Competition from trucks using the road between Addis Ababa and the Eritrean port of Assab has cut deeply into the railroad's revenues. At the same time, because Assab as a port became increasingly competitive with Djibouti's port, the French authorities have taken steps to enable their port and the railroad jointly to meet Assab's competition. Another project that may also bring the two closer together again is the building of a branch line from the railroad to the Ethiopian province of Sidamo, and if it materializes, a considerable increase in the transit trade should result. Nevertheless, the railroad's potential for expansion remains limited, whereas the history of the port illustrates its greater capacity to adapt itself and to grow under changing circumstances.

The port's initial functions were to bunker French ships en route from France to Indochina and Madagascar and also to serve as a minor base for the French navy. Completion of the railroad to Addis Ababa in 1917 added the function of port for Ethiopia's foreign trade (in which capacity it soon replaced Tadjoura and Zeila) and also for the Territory's imports and exports. Yet for many years its equipment remained rudimentary, consisting only of a jetty, a quay for depositing incoming and outgoing merchandise, and limited storage space for coal. Ships touching at Djibouti were able to anchor in a fairly sheltered roadstead, but loading and unloading operations were very slow, and the water, ice, and food available to them were strictly limited.

It was not until 1931, when the world depression caused France to assume more responsibility for its colonies' development, that a long-considered project to create a deep-water port at Djibouti finally got under way. By the time World War II began, the project was only partly completed, but in the last normal prewar year of 1938 the port was able to handle 194,000 tons of merchandise and was used by 1,454 ships of varying tonnages. During the first war years the port was almost totally inactive, but in 1943 work on it was resumed with limited local means. Its rapid revival after 1945 is shown by the following tabulation.[23]

Year	Number of ships	Merchandise handled (tons)		
		Unloaded	Loaded	Total
1920	243	105,115	10,815	115,930
1935	1,093	47,000	97,000	144,000
1938	1,454	150,000	44,000	194,000
1942	275	3,445	3,239	6,684
1946	1,278	74,611	74,713	149,324
1948	1,357	240,800	166,600	407,400

The postwar development plan financed by the F.I.D.E.S.* gave priority to the port in its program for the Territory. Enlargement and modernization of the port were entrusted to the Société des Batignolles of Paris, but progress was so slow that it took the visit to Djibouti of the Minister of Overseas France to put pressure on that company to complete its work by 1950. Almost coincidentally with completion of this project the currency, fiscal, and tariff reforms came into force.† The following decade saw growth in the port's previous activities as well as new ones. By 1960 it was performing three distinct functions. It was the port for most of Ethiopia's transit trade, an entrepôt for merchandise unloaded by ships

* See pp. 187–89.   † See pp. 181–82.

at Djibouti for reexportation, and a source of fuel and provisions for ships using it as a port of call.

Between 1950 and 1952 the transit trade with Ethiopia doubled, and in the latter year Djibouti handled four-fifths of Ethiopia's foreign trade. Also in 1952, the federation of Eritrea with Ethiopia introduced a new element into the situation, for the Ethiopians thereby acquired control of the road between Addis Ababa and Assab and also of the port of Assab. Work on both had been begun by the Italians, and the Ethiopians rapidly completed and improved them. These new assets provided the government of Addis Ababa with a strong bargaining point to exercise pressure on France, not only to cede to it about one-tenth of French Somaliland's territory but also to adjust in its favor the charges made by Djibouti's port and railroad. Although a compromise was reached regarding a division of the transit trade between Assab and Djibouti and although this trade grew in volume, the competition between the two ports increased as Ethiopia progressively enlarged and modernized the port of Assab. By 1955, Assab's share in Ethiopia's foreign trade was 19 percent, compared with 11 percent just three years before, while that of Djibouti fell from 66 percent in 1952 to 55 percent in 1955. This trend has continued, for between 1963 and 1964 Assab's transit trade with Ethiopia increased by 43 percent, whereas that of Djibouti grew by only 4.8 percent.[24]

Assab's main advantages over Djibouti lay in the cheaper rates charged by truckers compared with those of the railroad, and in the absence of any tax on the merchandise handled at its port. In 1966, however, the Ethiopian government imposed a tax of 2.5 percent ad valorem on the imports and exports that passed through Assab, but it was so small that it has not basically diminished the attraction of that port. Djibouti's trump cards are a larger port and more modern equipment as well as the greater variety of services it offers. Assab has been servicing only 40 to 50 ships a month, whereas Djibouti's monthly average has been 210. In 1964, however, fueling facilities were built at Assab, and probably that port will soon begin to compete with Djibouti in a function which has become of increasing importance to the French port. Djibouti still leads Assab as the port for Ethiopia's foreign trade, especially in the handling of bulky imported goods, but its share in Ethiopian exports, particularly coffee, hides, and oleaginous products, continues to decline. Annually this transit trade for Djibouti now amounts to only 45,000 to 50,000 tons and accounts for a diminishing share of that port's total activities. Moreover, it fluctuates in volume and value because it depends on such uncertain elements as climatic conditions in Ethiopia and the policies of the Addis Ababa government. The result has been a tendency for Djibouti to neglect the transit trade with Ethiopia in recent years in favor of the port's other more regular and remunerative operations. For the same reasons there is a growing lack of interest in two of the other traditional activities of Djibouti's port which have also been declining over the past decade. One is the export of indigenous products, which has shrunk almost to the vanishing point since the cessation of salt exports in 1957. The other is the volume of merchandise unloaded by ships at Djibouti for reexport to destinations other than Ethiopia. This reexport trade has been falling steadily since 1960.

The decline in the foregoing activities has been more than offset by a marked growth in the port's third main function—that of fueling and provisioning ships. Between 1955 and 1965 the number of ships calling at Djibouti increased by 81 percent and their aggregate tonnage by 130 percent.[25] In 1965, 3,352 ships, totaling well over 12 million tons, stopped at Djibouti. The international character of this shipping is shown by the fact that they flew the flags of 34 different countries. French vessels headed the list, but they accounted for only 15 percent of the total; they were followed by ships from Greece (14 percent of the total), Great Britain (8 percent), West Germany (7.5 percent), Norway (7 percent), and the United States (7 percent). In 1965, the port handled 2,254,000 tons of merchandise, compared with 801,000 tons in 1950, exports far exceeding imports in both years.

This rapid expansion was due partly to improvements in loading and unloading operations and in Djibouti's increased facilities for provisioning ships in food and water, but it is mainly attributable to the port's fueling services. About 13 percent of all the ships that touch at Djibouti stop there exclusively to unload merchandise for reexport, 40 percent in addition buy fuel, and 47 percent are only refueled. Although the Société des Pétroles de Djibouti built the first oil-storage tank there as long ago as 1937, fueling did not become a major function of the port until some years after World War II. Djibouti's fueling operations quadrupled between 1952 and 1964, and in 1965 it sold about 2 million tons of fuel worth approximately D.F. 5,428 million. If it can be said that as a fueling port Assab may come to rival Djibouti, it is also true that Djibouti is well on the way to competing with Aden in this respect. Aden still has the great advantage of possessing an oil refinery, but its port charges are 15 percent higher than those of Djibouti and ships calling there must anchor in the open roadstead.

A view now widely held by the French is that Djibouti's future as a port lies principally in its becoming a modern service station for the thousands of tankers that each year pass through the Bab-el-Mandeb. Chiefly because the political future of the whole region is so uncertain, however, some larger tankers are being built which will not pass through the Suez Canal but will reach Europe by way of the Cape of Good Hope. Nevertheless, since the Suez route is much shorter, it is felt that Djibouti should constantly improve its port facilities and also not neglect its functions other than fueling.[26]

The French proudly describe Djibouti as the most modern port of the Red Sea and the Indian Ocean. It has 1,800 meters of quays, nine piers available at all tides to ships drawing up to 34 feet, a wharf for barges and tenders, a network of rail tracks totaling 9 kilometers in length, a refrigerating plant, three reservoirs for the distribution of 200,000 tons of drinking water a year to ships, and a fuel storage tank with a capacity of 190,000 metric tons. Djibouti port can handle 3 million tons of merchandise a year and until mid-1967 was working almost to capacity. Since 1955 the port has had its own budget, whose principal source of revenue is the taxes imposed on the merchandise loaded and unloaded there. The port's own budget for 1967 amounted to D.F. 556 million, and its largest single expenditure is payment of the salaries of its 115 permanent employees and 343 day laborers, as well as a reserve of 700 nonpermanent dockworkers.[27]

Despite wide fluctuations in its progress, Djibouti's port is certainly one of French Somaliland's few successful enterprises. Nevertheless, its prosperity is threatened increasingly by Assab and its attractions cannot yet rival those of Aden. The irremediable handicap under which it labors vis-à-vis Aden is geographical, for to reach it, ships using the main sea lanes must make a time-consuming detour of 90 miles. Other serious disadvantages are, first, the growing frequency of politically motivated strikes by Djibouti's dockworkers and the wages paid them, which are higher by a third than those of Aden's dockworkers; and second, the indecision and procrastination of the Paris authorities in regard to projects for improvement of the port. While the government was trying to reach a decision about constructing an oil refinery at Djibouti, Aden built one. Since 1954 the question of building a drydock at Djibouti has been studied and restudied, and even at this late date its construction would provide Djibouti with an asset unique in the Red Sea region. This proposal received the unanimous support of the Conseil de la République in its session of July 26, 1955, and of all the members of the French Union Assembly except the communists, who asserted that the project was simply a cover for the government's plan to conduct aggressive warfare in the region.[28] In 1956 the arrival of a senatorial mission which came to Djibouti to make an on-the-spot study of the drydock question coincided with the early stages of the first Suez crisis and also a violent demonstration by the dockworkers. The unfortunate impression these created could not be effaced by the governor of French Somaliland and the vice-president of the government council, who visited Paris the following year expressly to promote the project. In 1960 the question was revived, but nothing materialized beyond the appointment of a committee to make one more study of the drydock and of alternative schemes. The main stumbling block has always been that, in view of the very heavy cost of its construction, the drydock would not be profitable.

Nevertheless, in the early 1960's, the congestion of the port rapidly became such that the Paris authorities realized that something must soon be done to enable Djibouti to cope with its existing traffic, not to mention the increase in the transit trade foreseen if the branch line to Sidamo were built. In 1964, therefore, a master plan was drawn up and approved for execution over the following years. In 1966 two more quays were built and work on the construction of another fuel tank was begun. But the program was suspended following the outbreaks at Djibouti in August and September, and it was not resumed until after the referendum of March 1967. The latest development plan for the Territory once more gives priority to the port of Djibouti, and the prospect that it may benefit from the troubled situation at Aden is certainly not alien to the hopes of its financiers.

As this book is being written, three months after the closing of the Suez Canal, Djibouti's port is operating at about 25 percent of its normal activity. The government has taken effective steps to control prices and stocks of merchandise, and provisions of essential consumer goods have been brought in by air from France or by ship from Madagascar. In the meantime, work is proceeding on the improvement of the port, in expectation of better times ahead.

It is not usually realized that the initial project for building a railroad from Addis Ababa to Djibouti was conceived by Menelik, modern Ethiopia's first ruler. With his encouragement and with capital supplied largely by French financiers, the Compagnie Impériale des Chemins de Fer Ethiopiens was formed in 1896 by two European engineers who were advisers to the Negus. Construction of the tracks through French Somaliland was facilitated by signing of the Franco-Ethiopian treaty in 1897, and that same year work was begun on the section from Djibouti to Diré Daoua in Ethiopia.

From the outset, building of the railroad was hampered not only by the technical difficulties of constructing the line through desert and mountainous terrain, but also by the shortage of labor and the depredations of the nomad tribes in the region through which the rails passed. The nomads feared the preempting of their pastureland and watering points, and showed their resentment by periodically attacking the labor gangs and pilfering the rails, ties, and any metallic objects on which they could lay their hands.* The severe penalties imposed on them for stealing proved to be no deterrent, for they were rarely caught in the act. Later the railroad company agreed to pay compensation to the owners of any animals killed by the trains, but this arrangement was canceled when the company realized that the nomads were deliberately pasturing their oldest and sickest animals along the tracks. Despite all these difficulties the first section of the line was completed in June 1900.

A more serious impediment to the progress of the railroad was the company's chronic financial difficulties, which required it to raise from any available source several costly short-term loans. Beginning in 1899 the French government took an active interest in the company, partly to compensate for the humiliation of France at Fashoda, which had dealt a fatal blow to its expansionist aspirations in the Nile region.[29] To free the company from its dependence on foreign financiers, the Paris authorities agreed, on February 5, 1902, to pay it an annual subsidy for 50 years in return for a degree of control over the operations of the whole line.[30] The Negus did not welcome the entry of the French government into the picture, and he delayed granting permission to build the Diré Daoua section of the line until April 1904. During the interval the company once more had to resort to raising loans because operation of the Djibouti–Diré Daoua section proved to be unprofitable. Moreover, the whole question of this railroad became involved in the complexities of Ethiopia's relations at the time with the European imperialist powers of Italy, Great Britain, and France. Finally, by the tripartite agreement of December 13, 1906, the right to extend the tracks as far as Addis Ababa was granted to the company on condition that it would not extend them westward toward the Nile. This authorization did not solve the company's financial problems, however, and in June 1907 it went bankrupt. That same year an official French mission was sent to Ethiopia, where an agreement was negotiated and signed on January 10, 1908. Under its terms a new French organization called the Compagnie

---

* "They seemed to believe that these objects had been put there to satisfy their needs, and they somehow made them into spears, bracelets and necklaces." Jean d'Esme, *A Travers l'Empire de Menelik*, p. 32.

du Chemin de Fer Franco-Ethiopien was formed, which inherited its predecessor's 99-year concessionary lease and which received three sizable loans from French banks that were guaranteed by the Paris government.

Even with such large and secure capital funds and with an unassailable legal basis, the new company ran into trouble. World War I depleted its technical personnel and caused delays in the delivery of the matériel indispensable for building the many bridges and tunnels required in its construction. Nevertheless, the tracks finally reached Addis Ababa and the whole line was opened to traffic on June 7, 1917. Although Addis Ababa was only 600 kilometers from Djibouti as the crow flies, the railroad had a total length of 784 kilometers, of which only 92 kilometers lay in French territory, and it had to climb from sea level to an altitude of 2,400 meters. It was a single-track line of meter gauge, and served 32 stations, of which the last in French territory was at Ali-Sabieh, 89 kilometers from Djibouti. At a watering point in Ethiopia called Diré Daoua, midway between Addis Ababa and Djibouti, the company set up a repair workshop. Two trains ran in each direction daily between the two capitals. The one that carried only passengers was optimistically called The White Train, and since it traveled exclusively during the daytime it took 60 hours to complete each trip. The other train, the equally fanciful name of which was The Black Arrow, took twice as long and transported only freight.

The traffic carried by the railroad and the revenues it earned increased rapidly during the interwar period except for the few depression years of the early 1920's and 1930's. Of all the railroads in the world at that time, it was said to bring in the largest returns to its investors. Its monopoly of the transportation of Ethiopia's foreign trade enabled it to charge the highest rates that the traffic would bear, and its operations were strongly supported by the French government. Whenever the railroad's security was threatened, whether by the nomads or by the Italian army of occupation in Ethiopia, the French government sent soldiers to guard the line and to protect the Diré Daoua workshops. The company's greatest period of prosperity occurred between 1936 and 1938, when the Italians perforce used it to carry supplies for their army and for the population of Ethiopia. But the shortsighted refusal of the company to lower its rates appreciably led to its partial undoing. The frustrated Italians decided to build a road between Addis Ababa and the Eritrean port of Assab, which they also then controlled, and to assemble a fleet of 400 trucks for the transport of much of the merchandise that had formerly been carried by the railroad. (General Legentilhomme, speaking in the French Union Assembly on February 23, 1956, stated that this road was so well and quickly built that the motorcycle race held on the day it was inaugurated in 1938 was won by a rider who averaged 85 kilometers an hour between Addis Ababa and Assab.) Certainly, the persistent high-rate policy of the railroad company was largely responsible for Italy's decision either to take over Djibouti or to ruin it economically.* The Italians' declaration of war on France in June 1940 abruptly ended the railroad's artificial prosperity and ushered in lean wartime years for all French Somaliland.

The British, after defeating the Italians in East Africa in April 1941, took over operation of the Ethiopian section of the railroad. When the Free French acquired control of the government at Djibouti in December 1942, they began negotiating with the British and Ethiopian authorities for the return of the railroad to the company's management. These negotiations dragged on inconclusively for some years, however, and it was not until July 1, 1946, that Great Britain turned it back to the company. In the meantime, the company's directors had drawn up a program to repair the damage done to the railroad by the retreating Italian army and to modernize and reequip the line. It took some years to carry out these plans, because of the delays in getting delivery of the equipment ordered and also because the company had to raise loans to finance it, inasmuch as the war-damage compensation it received was small. By 1950, however, the line had been repaired and improved and the replacement of steam locomotives by diesel-powered ones had reduced the time for the trip between Djibouti and Addis Ababa to less than 24 hours.

By the end of 1947, long before the rehabilitation program was completely carried out and despite a strike that had paralyzed the line for two months in the spring, both the passenger and freight traffic carried by the railroad had exceeded the annual average during the years before the Italian occupation of Ethiopia. This expansion was due mainly to the heavy postwar demand for Ethiopia's agricultural products. It also stimulated the government at Addis Ababa, whose nationalistic spirit had been reinforced by the events of World War II, to seek a revision of the railroad company's tariff policy. The strike of March 1947 by the Ethiopian railroad workers at Diré Daoua was followed by another which took a more violent turn in August 1949. To a limited degree these strikes alienated public opinion in France, where it was believed that they had been inspired by the Ethiopian authorities with the aim of taking over the whole railroad, but the more knowledgeable Frenchmen recognized the justice of Ethiopia's complaints against the company. In the Conseil de la Ré-

* See pp. 12–15.

publique several senators harshly criticized the company's management, whose insistence on getting the maximum profits from its monopoly would inevitably result in formidable competition by the Addis Ababa–Assab road.[31]

Within a few years the truth of this forecast was amply proved, especially after Ethiopia acquired control over Eritrea and American funds had enabled it to improve vastly the road to Assab. In 1955 the railroad was carrying only 247,000 tons a year,[32] though it was equipped to transport annually nearly 400,000 tons. Moreover, the imbalance had grown between the far larger tonnages it carried on its run up to Addis Ababa and the ever-smaller amount of Ethiopian exports it transported to the coast because of the growing competition from Assab. On March 8, 1955, the members of the French Parliament, annoyed at being asked year after year to approve successive loans raised by the company, placed a ceiling of 384 million francs on the total that the state would guarantee.[33] These adverse developments finally induced the company to lower its tariffs on certain bulky imported goods and to coordinate them with the reductions made by the port of Djibouti on Ethiopian merchandise in transit.

In the early 1950's France was concerned with improving its overall relations with Ethiopia, which had become strained over issues only one of which was the railroad. The main purpose of the agreement between the two governments on January 16, 1954, was to settle the long-disputed boundary between French Somaliland and Ethiopia. The considerable territorial concessions then made to Ethiopia aroused strong opposition in the French Parliament and the territorial representative council, in part because neither body had been consulted during the negotiations. Only very secondarily was the railroad involved in this settlement, and merely to the extent that Ethiopia promised not to build a rail line to Assab. Not surprisingly the French radicals seized on this opportunity to attack the government on the grounds that it had sacrificed Somaliland's interests to ensure the revenues of the monopolistic, privately owned railroad company.[34] Viewed from that angle, the advantage won by the railroad company hardly seemed an adequate quid pro quo for the territorial concessions made to Ethiopia.

Soon after the 1954 agreement was reached, Paris opened new negotiations with Addis Ababa, and in these the railroad company played the central role. The French government had obviously lost faith in the company's determination or ability, or both, to meet the competition from Assab, and was no longer willing to underwrite its financial losses. Under the terms of the existing arrangement, the French Treasury had to make up the company's annual deficits, which amounted to 372 million francs in 1954, 154 million in 1955, and 339 million in 1956, and the end was not in sight.[35] The negotiations leading up to the Franco-Ethiopian treaty of November 12, 1959, were difficult and protracted. They involved the juridical problem of endowing a private company with a new status under international law, but a solution to the other issues at stake was much harder to find. The French wanted to retain a considerable degree of control over the railroad and also to make it again a profitable enterprise. They also realized, however, that they must give the Ethiopians an interest in the new company sufficient to induce Addis Ababa to assume a large share of the financial responsibility for its operations. The fact that three-fourths of the capital in the old company was held by the French but that seven-eighths of the tracks lay in Ethiopia gave each of the parties concerned strong bargaining points.

A compromise was finally worked out and embodied in the treaty of 1959. Half of the new company's shares were to be held equally by French and Ethiopian nationals and the total capital was Ethiopian $4,325,000. Its general manager would be chosen by three-fourths of the directors, and he was given wide powers including that of casting the deciding vote. The company's headquarters were to be located at Addis Ababa and its "nationality" became Ethiopian, but the technical services and management would remain at Djibouti. The Ethiopians' pledge not to build a competing railroad was renewed, and indeed it was now to their interest to divert a good part of their foreign trade to the railroad and away from Assab, especially as they also agreed to a parity basis regarding the company's financial losses. Its concessionary lease remained the same as before, and could be renewed after its expiration on January 1, 2017. As an extension of its new railroad rights, Ethiopia was given free access to Djibouti's port in time of war as well as in peacetime.

Fortunately for the future of Franco-Ethiopian relations, this treaty laid the basis for a revival of the railroad's prosperity and also for an extension of its operations. Africanization of the company's personnel was accelerated, and other economies in salaries were effected by reducing the number of employees to about 2,400 in 1964, as compared with some 5,000 in 1948.[36] By lowering its rates and making them more flexible, the company achieved a better balance between its import and export traffic, of which the latter's volume was steadily increasing. The management has been careful to point out that this steady growth in the railroad's traffic is not matched by an analogous expansion of its revenues, because of the need to purchase new equipment and also to cut its rates periodically to meet competition from the truckers.[37] Nevertheless, the company's books are now balanced, and its traffic has been increasing annually at the rate of 5 percent for passengers and 7 percent for merchandise.[38] Moreover, both should expand markedly if the project now under consideration to build a branch line to Sidamo province in Ethiopia materializes.

The Sidamo project dates back to 1960, when a French economic mission reported favorably on the proposal, and its recommendation was confirmed by a group of technicians, who studied it again in 1962. The region to be tapped by the projected line covers 150,000 square kilometers and has a population of 4,270,000. Its fertile soil and abundant rains have been pronounced suited to the cultivation of coffee, tobacco, oleaginous plants, and the like. It would, however, take considerable time to build irrigation and other necessary facilities as well as to train the population to use modern techniques of agriculture and herding. The means of financing the line, which would be 330 kilometers long and take from four to five years to build, have been discussed several times by Haile Selassie and General de Gaulle.[39] The French government has offered to finance its construction by a loan and to give full ownership of it to the Ethiopians. Several questions, however, remain unsettled. One concerns the amount of tonnage Sidamo valley can produce and how soon, for it is calculated that prolongation of the railroad would be justified only if the area's production grew rapidly and exceeded 150,000 tons a year.[40] The other question raises the old bogey of road-rail competition, for the International Bank reportedly has offered to finance the building of a road that would follow approximately the same route as the projected railroad.[41]

Unknown economic quantities are not the only ones to cast their shadows over the whole picture, for there are political imponderables as well. The policy of the Somali Republic has drawn and held together France and Ethiopia, and this spirit of cooperation—if it lasts—may prove to be the factor that tips the balance in deciding whether to go ahead with the Sidamo branch-line project.

It seems ludicrous to speak of a road network in a country that has only 90 kilometers of paved roads and 1,820 kilometers of *pistes* (tracks). Of the latter, all but 800 kilometers can be used solely by trucks and jeeps during the dry season. The paved section consists of the streets of Djibouti, including their extension to the Ambouli suburb and the airport, and a 40-kilometer stretch from the capital to the Arta hill station. There is also a highway leading from Djibouti to the southern frontier at Loyada, which has a crushed-stone surface.

French Somaliland's tracks are classified semiofficially as "improved, motorable, and semimotorable." One cluster of the so-called "improved" tracks is in the south, and the other group in the north. The southern section connects Djibouti with Ali-Sabieh and Dikhil, at which point the track divides into two branches. One of these goes to Garbès and Yoboki, and the other leads to Assela in the Gobaad plain. The main track of the northern group links Tadjoura to Mount Gouda, from which there is a shorter track to the reserved forest of Daÿ.

It is obvious from the foregoing summary that there is no serviceable connection between the northern and southern sections of the Territory's tracks. Thus three-fourths of the country, where virtually all of the Afars live, is not connected by a surfaced road with the southern quarter, where the city of Djibouti is situated. Furthermore, the only two settlements in the north—Obock and Tadjoura—are linked by a track that only by courtesy can be called passable. Tadjoura is 40 kilometers from Djibouti by sea, yet the track connecting the two is 300 kilometers long and impassable for ordinary private automobiles. In 1963 the administration asked the F.I.D.E.S. for the D.F. 300 million credit required to improve this connecting track, but nothing came of the proposal. Equally unproductive of results was the vote in 1954 of the representative council in favor of building a road parallel to the railroad as far as Dessie, where it would join the highway from Addis Ababa to Assab.

For many years no proposal has been made for the expansion of the Territory's road system. Various explanations of this state of affairs have been advanced. The more or less official one is that the existing network corresponds to the Territory's needs and that there is not enough traffic to justify the expenditure required to build new roads. Another, more practical reason given is that the construction and especially the upkeep of roads, which is charged to the territorial budget, are especially onerous and expensive because of the damage caused by tornadoes and rainfall. Probably, however, the most cogent reason is the monopoly enjoyed for many years by the railroad in regard to the only traffic of value. One result of the present transport situation is the concentration of the Territory's 3,000 motor vehicles of all types in Djibouti and its immediate surroundings.

Only to a small extent have the inadequacies of the road and rail system been offset by the development of air transport, because of the latter's expense and limited carrying capacity. Nevertheless, after a late start, air transport has been making rapid progress in the last few years.

As recently as 1947, French Somaliland was held in such low esteem by

civil-aviation authorities that Air France seriously considered discontinu-
ing its Paris–Djibouti service.[42] Yet within a few years this attitude had
changed to such a degree that Djibouti's airfield, built for military planes
during World War II, was vastly enlarged and modernized. In December
1961, the airfield was able to receive its first four-engine jet plane. Today
Djibouti's importance as an air crossroads has been confirmed by the regular use of its airport by one French and three other international aviation
companies. Air France and Air Madagascar alternately provide flights
between Paris and Tananarive six days a week, which stop at Djibouti.
Either Ethiopian Airlines or Aden Airways links Djibouti to Addis Ababa,
Asmara, Assab, Diré Daoua, and Aden by regular services.

Of even greater local interest has been the recent formation of a local
private company called Air Djibouti, which offers both foreign and domestic flights.* From a modest beginning with one plane and one pilot in
1963, it had, two years later, six planes and as many pilots, as well as 50
employees, 17 of whom were Europeans.[43] Its external service to Aden,
started in 1964, now has five regular flights a week and is increasingly
profitable. The Yemen line, however, is unprofitable, but it is maintained
to supply the French medical mission at Taiz with provisions and mail.
Air Djibouti's internal services include eight flights weekly to Obock, two
to Ali-Sabieh and Dikhil, and three to Tadjoura and Randa, and they
seem likely to increase still further.

In addition to the five small airfields served by Air Djibouti, there are
a few landing strips, which can be used by military planes in an emergency.
These very indifferently equipped hinterland airfields will doubtless be
improved in the next few years, but at present there is no plan for further
development of Djibouti's international airport. The size of the Territory's
population and the nature of its resources impose clear-cut limitations on
its potential use of air transportation.

Labor

French Somaliland has neither agricultural nor industrial production worth
mentioning, and its economy is one based almost entirely on services. This
economy is in part sustained by subsidies from the French government,
but locally it depends on trade. Thus the essential services on which the

---

* It was founded by Commandant Astraud de Robiglio, an engineer by profession and an amateur pilot, who had been a pioneer of aviation in Madagascar before coming to Djibouti. In October 1967 it was reported in the press that the plane he was flying had been shot down over
South Arabia.

economy mainly rests are those connected with the port and the railroad. Secondary labor markets are provided by the administration, the military establishment, and—at times—the building industry. With so limited an economic base and with very keen competition from nearby trading centers, labor problems in French Somaliland have become exceptionally acute.

The size of the Territory's active population is hard to determine at any given time. This difficulty is due both to the extreme mobility of its inhabitants and to the ebb and flow of large numbers of foreign residents. Except for a few hundred farmers, fishermen, foresters, and herders who hire out their services for pay, the wage-earning community is concentrated in Djibouti. The attraction of that town for the region's nomads has been growing rapidly over the years, with the result that its population contains a large floating element comprising individuals who are only temporary wage earners and who return periodically to their tribes. Since 1960, political as well as socioeconomic considerations have been a determining factor in the movements of the migrant population. Reliable statistics concerning the size of the Territory's labor force are extremely scanty and they must be viewed within a precise time and space context. Usually they apply only to Djibouti and they are valid simply for the months during which the data are being collected.

During the first years after Djibouti became the colony's capital, the indigenous tribesmen who gravitated there sufficed to meet the demands of the small European population for labor. When work began on building the railroad, however, outsiders had to be called in. Laborers came from Egypt, the Levant, and Arabia in fair numbers and many of them stayed on—though not always as manual workers. In any case, the example of these foreign laborers helped to overcome the nomads' aversion to working regularly for wages when they realized that money could be earned which would permit them to lead a more comfortable existence. The wage-earning opportunities offered by Djibouti also attracted increasing numbers of foreign tribesmen from the neighboring regions. But none of these nomads possessed any skills, and the number of jobs open to them fluctuated with the government's public-works program and even more with the volume of trade handled by Djibouti's port and railroad.

Initially there was no coordination between these two sources of employment, but progressively, beginning in the mid-1950's, the government intervened to create public-works jobs when adverse trading conditions had led to severe unemployment. The last year in which the building projects financed by the F.I.D.E.S. offered fairly plentiful jobs was 1954; this was also the first year in which Djibouti's wage earners began to experience the benefits of the Overseas Labor Code. Concurrently, however, port and railroad activity diminished markedly as a result of the competition from Assab for Ethiopia's foreign trade. A report made in 1954, which gave the number of wage earners in the public sector as 2,397 and those in the private sector as 6,240, was probably an underestimate,[44] in view of the data disclosed by the census of 1956, described below. By that year the public-works program had been virtually completed and exports of salt had ceased.

Of the nearly 25,000 persons described in 1956 as the total active population in the Territory, slightly under half were the nomads, fishermen, and oasis dwellers, who lived almost wholly outside the money economy.[45] About one-half of the 2,340 government employees held jobs in the general administration and one-half in other public organizations. Of the 10,230 wage earners in the private sector, 6,444 were permanently employed, 500 were seasonal workers, 1,090 were self-employed, and 900 were described as "family aides." The privately owned enterprises employing the largest number of workers were the trading firms (3,000 employees), the building and public-works industries, and the transport companies (1,441 and 1,306, respectively). The occupations having the fewest wage earners were fishing (350) and agriculture and herding (400). The 3,028 domestic servants were the largest single category of employees. A decade later the number of persons employed in the private sector was estimated at 7,300.[46] This marked diminution in the wage-earning component of the population was in part attributable to the serious repercussions on the labor market of the political events of 1966.

An analysis of occupations by ethnic groups casts considerable light on the labor problems of French Somaliland. The only Europeans who have been employed on any considerable scale in the manual occupations are Italians. They have been described as excellent masons, carpenters, and foremen who are hard workers and not afraid to labor under the tropical sun.[47] The Territory's other European residents hold either government posts or managerial positions. The great majority are French, but there is also a small number of other Western Europeans and Greeks, a few of whom work as clerks.

Of the two indigenous tribes, the Issas are regarded by all employers as the better workers. They form the majority of the manual workers employed by the big local companies such as the railroad, the Société des Batignolles, the Compagnie de l'Afrique Orientale, and—formerly—the Société des Salines.[48] Only a handful of them hold clerical jobs, and the employment that is most congenial to their warlike traditions is in the militia and gendarmerie. As dockworkers they are swamped by the competition of the Arabs and foreign Somalis. The Afars are rated at the bottom of the labor scale, and the fact that they form the smallest ethnic community in Djibouti among the non-European groups is evidence of the difficulty they experience in adapting themselves to wage-earning. When they accept regular employment, they seek jobs as watchmen, domestic servants, and seamen. Neither Issas nor Afars have ever been subjected to forced labor.

In addition to their preference for the nomadic life of warriors and herders, both groups of indigenous tribesmen suffer from two conspicuous handicaps—their addiction to the consumption of *khat** and their acceptance of the tribal tradition that requires them to support idle relatives indefinitely. A survey undertaken in 1956 showed that Issa and Afar wage earners spent about half their monthly pay for the purchase of *khat,* and subsequent reports indicate that this situation still obtains. The result is that they and their families are undernourished and inadequately clothed. In addition, they feel compelled to provide lodging and food for parasitic fellow tribesmen who make up a large part of Djibouti's floating and unemployed population. So long as the Issa and Afar wage earners do not overcome these handicaps, there is little hope that they can raise their living standards.

Among the foreigners who come to work in Djibouti, there are comparatively few Africans. The Senegalese *tirailleurs* are essentially soldiers and remain such even when they are periodically used as strikebreakers on the docks. The Malagasys cannot properly be called Africans, and in any case they are very few in number and are mainly craftsmen. The Egyptians, when they have been employed as manual laborers, work almost exclusively on the railroad. They formed an important element in the labor force that built the railroad and also were employed after the war in rebuilding the bridges and track destroyed by the retreating Italian troops.[49]

As for the Asians, the Indians are exclusively traders and money changers, and the same could be said of the Jews except for the few who are goldsmiths and silversmiths. The most important group of Asian aliens from every viewpoint are the Arabs of Yemen and South Arabia, who have taken up a wide range of occupations in French Somaliland. Although the most prosperous of them are merchants and some others are gardeners, the majority work as skilled and unskilled laborers. In the mid-1950's the

* See pp. 163–65.

Yemenese reportedly supplied half of the Territory's wage labor force and were the majority ethnic group in such skilled occupations as those of electricians, plumbers, and carpenters. They made effective foremen of labor gangs because of the respect they inspired in the Somali and Afar workers. As unskilled laborers, the Arabs were preferred to the Issas and alien Somalis because they were more robust and worked more regularly and conscientiously. Consequently they were paid far more than other laborers in the same occupations. Until the first Suez crisis they were much sought after by employers, but increasingly it has been feared that they are transferring to Djibouti some of the political ferment that has been troubling Aden.

Numerically the largest foreign element, which during the last decade has increasingly contributed its energies, skills, and political agitation to the Territory's labor force, consists of the Somalis from south of the French border. The great majority are unskilled workers, though among them are to be found a handful of blacksmiths, carpenters, and painters. Until very recently employers have preferred them to the Issas because they have more physical endurance and work more steadily, but since they are also undisciplined and erratic, they require closer supervision than the Arabs. Until the massive expulsions of alien Somalis in 1966–67, the majority of them were dockworkers at Djibouti's port, and virtually all of the dockworkers were Somalis. The relative efficiency of the Somalis was confirmed in the spring of 1967, when their replacement by Afars appreciably slowed down the handling of cargo at the port.

Until the Overseas Labor Code was passed by the French Parliament on December 15, 1952, the Territory's labor legislation consisted of unrelated regulations whose enforcement was one of the many responsibilities of a nonspecialized administrator. The 25 edicts by which the 1952 Code was applied to the Territory vastly improved the status of the local labor force and gave it a secure legal basis. They introduced the 40-hour working week, higher pay for overtime work, paid vacations for regular wage earners, and, later, family allowances and accident compensation. They also brought to the Territory a qualified Labor Inspector.

Following the example set in other French African dependencies, the local administration encouraged the trade unions to become authentic spokesmen for labor, created a Labor Bureau which gathered information and provided data about employment conditions, and introduced machinery to handle labor disputes. An arbitration council was formed to regulate the individual or collective conflicts between workers and between laborers and their employers which the Labor Inspector had been unable to settle by conciliation. At about the same time a labor advisory committee was formed in which the number of members was raised in 1958 from 12 to 14 so as to give a greater representation to workers' organizations. In 1955 the government initiated the negotiations that led to the first collective agreements between laborers and private employers, and this formula was later extended to the public sector. Late in 1964 the government council decreed that employers must supply lodging and free medical services to their personnel, and that all applicants must undergo a physical examination before being accepted for employment.[50] The most recent legislative improvements were the regulations of 1966, which govern the general conditions of employment for workers in enterprises not yet covered by collective agreements. These included setting up a fund to provide loans for family and work accidents, one of its purposes being to make it no longer advantageous to employers to hire only unmarried workers.

In view of the abundance of unskilled labor in Djibouti, it is suprising that wage legislation has lagged only slightly behind the workers' demands and has kept pace fairly well with the rising cost of living. The shortage of consumer goods immediately after World War II, and, far more, the franc's devaluation in December 1945, caused the cost of living to soar in Djibouti and, with it, demands for pay raises, especially on the part of the French civil servants. Perhaps because the government was the largest single employer of labor, it was the privately owned enterprises that first offered higher wages. Only after they had led the way did the government follow suit for both its European and native functionaries. Later, it was the government that, often under pressure, set higher wage scales.

Although the strike of August 1953 was motivated mainly by political considerations, its leaders also demanded and were granted a pay increase for labor. As was common practice throughout the French territories, the government determined the minimum wage, referred to as the S.M.I.G. (salaire minimum interprofessionnel garanti), for wage zones on the basis of the cost of living in different areas. French Somaliland was duly divided into two zones, one consisting of Djibouti and the other comprising all the rest of the Territory, but only in the capital did wages have real economic importance. In Djibouti, wages were raised to a minimum of D.F. 22 an hour, but that minimum had no discernible relationship to the existing cost-of-living index. Two years later another strike also resulted in a rise in the minimum wage, but the circumstances and the bases for this increase were different. Private employers rejected the strikers' wage demand that year on the ground that prices had not risen but fallen since the 1953 increment. Governor Petitbon, intervening to break the impasse, admitted the correctness of this argument but favored the wage raise because unemployment had become acute and those who still had jobs were supporting more and more idle relatives. This time, however, he introduced a sliding wage scale which he overoptimistically believed would put an end to strikes for wage increases. If the prices for 12 selected "commodities of prime necessity" rose, wages would automatically and proportionately increase. Yet almost exactly one year later, in August 1956, a general strike occurred in which one of the demands was for higher wages. The strikers now argued that there were 18, not 12, commodities of prime necessity whose prices had risen by 10 percent without any corresponding wage increase. The administration and the employers yielded and the minimum wage was increased by another 5 percent. This victory established as standard procedure biennial if not annual pay raises. The minimum wage was raised 5 percent in 1958, 8 percent in 1961, 6 percent in 1963, 5 percent in 1964, and 10 percent in 1966. At last reports it came to over D.F. 35 an hour for wage earners in the Djibouti zone.

In regard to fringe benefits, the lot of workers in Djibouti became an ever-happier one. To prevent further rises in living costs, the government in 1964 froze the prices for drugs, rents, and certain foods consumed by the native population. Family allowances had been introduced for all but domestic servants and agricultural wage earners in 1955, but they benefited only the 1,000-odd local workers who could produce an officially registered marriage certificate. During the ensuing years this led to a marked growth in the registration of vital statistics and consequently in the number of wage earners who qualified for family allowances. The allowance for each child up to 15 years of age, initially D.F. 500 per month, was raised to D.F. 600 in 1963, and at the same time the marriage allowance was increased from D.F. 750 to 900. In regard to polygamous marriages, the allowances applied only to the wage earner's principal wife and his first six offspring. But these comparatively minor restrictions were among the few limitations to the government's policy of growing benevolence to Djibouti's wage earners.

If Djibouti's wage earners were enjoying steadily improving working and living conditions, the same could not be said of the majority of Djibouti's population. The government offered permanent employment to only about one-fourth of the town's actual wage earners, and largely to skilled workers at that; the rest of the active male population depended for jobs on the volume of Djibouti's trade. In the mid-1950's the rise in unemployment began to alarm the French authorities. By 1954 the decline of Ethiopia's trade and of salt exports had deprived 7 to 8 percent of Djibouti's wage earners of work. Although some of the unemployed had never worked and others were unemployable, they were in the minority, and there were many cases of severe hardship, particularly among the war veterans. Private employers were reportedly taking undue advantage of the overabundant supply of laborers, and French Union Assemblymen were told of instances where unskilled workers were being paid less than the minimum wage or had been arbitrarily dismissed.[51] The main difficulty at this point arose from the fact that the trade depression coincided with the increase in wages and other benefits arising from application of the Overseas Labor Code for those who were actually employed. The result was a rapid growth in the influx of foreigners in search of work, most of whom were unskilled tribesmen from British Somaliland. To their number were added indigenous nomads who had been compelled to leave the hinterland by a prolonged drought.

Various means of remedying this situation were proposed. One was to build a drydock at Djibouti, which among other advantages to the Territory would create more jobs. But the government kept postponing a decision on this matter, and in the meantime unemployment increased. After the first closing of the Suez Canal, late in 1956, the situation worsened again. The newly installed government council received from the French Treasury a subsidy of 90 million Metro. francs with which to combat unemployment. It was decided to use this fund to employ 300 jobless men in Djibouti to undertake road repairs.[52] Such measures, nevertheless, were only palliatives, and again the Territory had to depend on an upturn in the volume of its trade to take up the labor slack. In the meantime the union of British Somaliland with Somalia caused a still greater influx into Djibouti of impoverished and unskilled foreigners looking for remunerative employment. The situation of Djibouti's labor, instead of becoming more stable, was growing more fluid and chaotic.

This aggravation of Djibouti's unemployment problem gradually caused a change in the government's outlook and policy. Although the authorities did not cease trying to improve and regulate working and living conditions for wage earners, they turned progressively to a more positive approach. One tangible evidence of their new viewpoint was the addition of an employment office to the Labor Bureau. By the end of 1964, after about one year's operation, the new agency had found jobs for 300 of its

1,000 or so applicants. At about the same time the Labor Inspector made a special and generally successful effort to organize the port's dockworkers and to associate their representatives more closely with the operations of the Bureau, though he did not succeed in forming a dockworkers' union. Still another constructive step was the proposal to enable the Territory's youth to qualify for top positions in the economy. Private employers were well known to be reluctant to employ graduates of the local technical schools, preferring to hire cheaper unskilled workers whom they could train themselves. This discouraging factor was certainly one reason why the long projected Centre de Formation Préprofessionnelle did not get under way until the political agitation of 1966 forced the government's hand. By then it had become glaringly apparent that Djibouti's chronic unemployment problem could no longer be regarded as wholly economic and that the influx of foreign Somali job seekers had also given it dangerous political overtones.

The effectiveness of strikes is usually taken as a clue to the strength of a country's labor movement, and the causes for which the unions organize workers' demonstrations as an indication of the degree to which they have been politicized. On both counts French Somaliland's labor organizations would receive an above-average rating. From the outset the Territory's organized labor movement was politically oriented, although the civil servants' unions formed in the mid-1930's were almost wholly concerned with the promotion of their members' professional interests. The oldest and most important labor organization during the last prewar decade was the Union des Gens der Mer. This union was formed by Arabs working in the port of Marseille. In Djibouti it operated as a sort of Arab mafia, with tight control not only over the jobs of dockworkers and sailors but also over cargo and passenger space. It effectively prevented the Somalis from obtaining employment on the docks and on ships, which the Arabs wanted to monopolize.

After the Popular Front government was installed in France in 1936, it encouraged the formation of socialist unions in French Somaliland, particularly among functionaries, both European and native. Their example led to the proliferation of groups that could be called unions only in that they brought together workers in the same occupations, such as tailors and cafe waiters. These men listened to radio broadcasts from Paris telling about the 40-hour working week, paid vacations, and sit-down strikes in the French capital, and this prompted them to organize more so-called unions. One unsympathetic correspondent of an important prewar Paris daily wondered why there had not yet been formed in the colony a "Union de Demoiselles Cousues de Bonne Famille Issa" or a "Syndicat de Dames Décousues" of Djibouti's red-light district.[53]

Aside from his ironic and patronizing attitude, this journalist's main criticism of Djibouti's unions is as valid today as it was on the eve of World War II. Essentially it was that the unions had been organized to reinforce and to give a modern form to traditional tribal solidarity. In the 1930's, the long-standing hostility between Issas and Afars was still confined to the hinterland pastures, probably because there were as yet only a few Afars in Djibouti, where they were economically insignificant. The growing competition between Issa and Arab merchants in the capital was extended to the labor scene. According to the same journalistic source, the forming of a union by Somali workers was immediately followed by that of Arab laborers in the same occupation, and vice versa. Automatically the members of one such union became the sworn enemy of the other's members, simply because they belonged to the rival ethnic group. Thus on May Day 1939, the radical Union des Gens de Mer and the rival Somalis' union "clashed in the market area and cut each other to pieces." Because of Djibouti's development as a trading port, ethnic rivalries were rapidly reinforced by economic competition. In the spring of 1939 about 400 Issas had been unemployed for some months because the shipping companies had dismissed them in order to employ the harder-working and sturdier Arabs.

The growing strife between rival unions impelled the administration on the eve of World War II to try to exert some control over the labor movement. Because of the radical and monopolistic goals of the Union des Gens de Mer and even more because of the danger of unions' being organized along radical lines, the governor tried to bring all the organized laborers into a single body that would be under the control of a European official authorized to arbitrate labor conflicts. With the advent of World War II, however, and the resultant economic problems in Djibouti, all questions concerning labor organization were relegated to the background.

The Free French who controlled France's postwar government were committed to the promotion of labor unions in their overseas dependencies, so not surprisingly workers' organizations revived rapidly in the Territory. Perhaps because of the small number of wage earners and their concentration in Djibouti, the local administration managed to control the development of unions there more closely than in other French territories in Africa. By 1948, the number of unions had been reduced to three major ones and these had been federated into a Union Territoriale des Syndicats. Each of the three member unions elected its own officials, who chose representatives to serve as officers of the Union des Syndicats. The Territory's employers were also organized, mainly according to their spheres of economic interest, but the most important one of the four was the Union Syndicale Interprofessionnelle des Entreprises de la Côte Française des Somalis.

Membership in the Union des Syndicats was estimated in 1947 to total 1,200, of which nearly 150 were Europeans.[54] Because of their experience and sophistication, this European minority dominated the Union and oriented it toward affiliation with the socialist French *centrale* of the Force Ouvrière. The European members being mostly French civil servants, the Union's first objectives were improvements in the salaries, bonuses, and other amenities for functionaries. That it was successful in this endeavor was shown by the advantages it won for the civil service in the first post-war years.

This Union has remained the single most important labor organization in the Territory; it is affiliated with the Force Ouvrière, and by extension with the International Confederation of Free Trade Unions. As of 1966 its membership comprised about 20 percent of Djibouti's 10,386 wage earners, including some 650 Europeans.[55] Of its 15 member unions, nine are composed of 1,550 African workers, mainly in the petroleum and building enterprises and in the administration.[56] The closeness of its ties with the government is indicated by the location of its headquarters alongside those of the territorial Inspectorate of Labor. Its officials are consulted by the administration on labor questions, and upon occasion it has been the spokesman for its members' demands for improved pay and working conditions. But because of its government sponsorship and conservative orientation, this Union has played only a minor role in the labor agitation that has increasingly affected the Territory's economic and political life. In any case, the instability of Djibouti's labor force and the large size of its foreign component make it difficult for any union organized on interracial lines and on a territorial basis to be effective.

The relationship between the growing influx of alien Somalis and the unemployment problem in Djibouti had naturally not escaped the attention of the local administration, but many years passed before any remedial action was taken. Members of the French Union Assembly were informed on November 18, 1954, that 80 percent of the personnel employed by private companies in Djibouti and 50 percent of the railroad staff were foreigners. A year and a half later, that Assembly was asked to give its opinion of a proposal drafted by the Minister of Overseas France to empower the government of French Somaliland to control the immigration of foreigners into the Territory and to set a limit on the number of aliens each company would be allowed to employ. At that time it was estimated that Djibouti had 15,000 foreign residents, the great majority of whom were from British Somaliland and Somalia.[57] Of the 6,500 persons permanently employed in the city in 1956, about 2,000 were aliens.[58]

The Minister's proposal was also submitted to the representative council, which rejected it as "inopportune" in January 1957. Later, however, its members, as well as the government council, accepted a suggestion from the chamber of commerce establishing in general terms the proportion of foreigners to French citizens that should be employed by any given concern. Big business was well represented at the time in the council, and private employers strongly opposed any measure that would limit the existing reservoir of cheap labor or restrict their freedom to employ aliens, whom they considered far more efficient than the Issas and Afars. In 1960, however, the administration returned to the charge, for the imminent unification of British Somaliland and Somalia made it almost inevitable that Somali irredentism would be preached by the Republic's nationals, who made up such a large proportion of the Territory's labor force. On March 14, 1960, the local government, without asking the chamber's advice, sent a circular to all Djibouti employers requiring them to file a declaration concerning the number of foreigners in their employ and to notify the Labor Bureau of any future changes in their personnel.

The Djibouti chamber of commerce reacted promptly and strongly to this move, and in a resolution its officers claimed that application of the new ruling would be "catastrophic."[59] They accepted the principle of giving job preference to French citizens, but only if the Labor Bureau could offer them properly qualified candidates. The chamber then proceeded to conduct its own inquiry into the current status of alien wage earners in Djibouti, and learned that the older and larger the enterprise, the more closely it conformed to the official directives in regard to the proportional employment of citizens and foreigners. Such firms had had the time to train their own staff, and in any case were so important that their operations could not escape close official scrutiny, as did the smaller ones. In short, the chamber maintained that it was unjust to ask employers to dismiss experienced and reliable employees just because they were foreigners, it was unwise to impose such restrictions on the labor market just at the time when the government was trying to encourage foreign investments, and finally it would create an unfortunate precedent if the authorities yielded to political pressure on an issue that was essentially an economic one.

Once more the government temporized, but the political turn taken by the strike of December 1962 hardened its attitude. In 1963 it enforced the measure requiring employers to file declarations concerning the nationality of their employees, and also introduced identity cards which must be presented by all job applicants.

The first two postwar strikes that affected the Territory were conducted by Ethiopian railroad workers at Diré Daoua, and none of the Territory's laborers was involved in them. The 1947 strike paralyzed the Ethiopian section of the railroad for two months beginning in March; the second strike started in August 1949, and though it lasted only a few days it was followed by a lockout. Although both strikes allegedly had some political motivation and although 20 Frenchmen belonging to the railroad staff were wounded in the 1949 strike, the issue at stake was ownership of the railroad and it had no direct relationship to French Somaliland's internal political or economic situation.

In the early 1950's the Issa politician Mahmoud Harbi gave the local labor movement a new orientation when he assumed leadership of the Somali workers. Under his direction a strike was launched at Djibouti on August 17, 1953, without the formulation of any precise demands by the strikers. The servants in European households were persuaded not to report for work that day, the automobiles of high officials were attacked by the strikers, and the Labor Inspector was hit on the head by a stone. The fact that no Arabs were manhandled during the few days the strike lasted led some observers to conclude that Harbi had organized it in collaboration with his new-found allies in Aden and South Arabia.[60] Radical French sympathizers, on the other hand, argued that a hundred workers had been arrested at Djibouti simply because they had asked for a strict application of the Overseas Labor Code in the Territory.[61]

The government's severity proved to be a deterrent to labor agitation, for nearly three years elapsed before Djibouti's population staged another demonstration, and it was apparently related to the depressed economic situation. Some hundreds of unemployed Somalis, after parading in front of the governor's residence, went to the native marketplace, where they caused some damage to houses and cars. The police made three arrests and in the ensuing violence one person was killed and 20 were wounded. This was the unhappy ending to a demonstration believed to have been initially launched to persuade a senatorial mission then visiting Djibouti to approve the drydock project that would create jobs for the unemployed.[62]

The next strike, which occurred two months later, was more widespread and lasted longer than its predecessors. It began without warning on July 27, 1956, as a result of the refusal by the Société des Petroles to provide free hospitalization to a sick worker.[63] It soon spread throughout the private sector, affecting all but trading firms. The strikers stiffened their demands, the administration and the employers yielded, and yet the strike continued until August 20, when the terms offered were finally accepted. The pointless prolongation of this strike indicated the inability of the labor leaders to control the workers, who apparently resented the use by the government of Senegalese troops as strikebreakers for the unloading of ships.

Beginning in late 1962, strikes began to take a more distinctively political turn, and one that was increasingly related to events in neighboring Somalia. Somali dockworkers struck for four days in December, and when the Afar vice-president of the government council, Ali Aref, appealed to them to return to work they answered with insults.[64] Once again the troops replaced the strikers and the government arrested their ringleaders. The 27 among them who were found to have entered the Territory illegally were expelled. Six months later the governor forbade the laborers to hold their traditional May Day parade "lest the troubles in nearby Somalia spread to French Somaliland."[65] Nevertheless, 200 defied the governor's edict and paraded; they were dispersed by the police, this time without violence. The governor, in commenting on the demonstration, noted that two of the most representative unions had not participated. "The militants of the opposition who were among the most active organizers of the parade ordered it to take place without daring to put their decision to a vote by union members. All the public and private sectors functioned normally."

The pattern of French Somaliland's labor agitation and the government's reaction to it had by then been set. Strikes and labor demonstrations, though increasing in number and in political motivation, were still relatively few compared with those in many African countries. Generally speaking, the government has met labor's demands for improved working conditions and pay, but has not given in to the political demands that have accompanied and sometimes motivated them. Thus, in September 1966, the strike by Somali dockworkers for higher pay was acceded to, but not the demand that followed for the resignation of the Ali Aref government. Yet when Ali Aref returned to power after the referendum of March 1967, he showed that the Somalis were not the only ethnic group intent on politicizing the labor movement. Not only did he replace the Somali dockworkers by Afars, but he began withdrawing identity cards from the Somali wage earners.[66]

The sharp decline in the port's activity after the closing of the Suez Canal in June 1967 caused considerable unemployment among the dockworkers, and their political activities have been, probably temporarily, relegated to the background. Some of them have been deported and others have been transferred to the hinterland to work on road-building. It is anticipated that the Afars will permanently and to a large degree replace the Somalis. This is indicated by the building in Djibouti of special housing facilities for Afar laborers who have come from Obock and Tadjoura and brought their families with them. Whether or not they will become as efficient a labor force for the port as were the Somalis remains to be seen, but in all likelihood the Afars will be more docile politically.

NOTES

Chapter One

1. The writers are indebted for the basic material in this section to the writings of E. Aubert de la Rue, E. Chedeville, H. Deschamps, M. Emerit, L. Heudebert, H. Labrousse, A. Lippmann, Père Luc, H. Marcus, A. Martineau, L. Minne, L. Pagne, E. de Poncins, G. Poydenot, D. de Rivoyre, C. E. Rochet d'Héricourt, I. de Salma, P. Soleillet, S. Touval, and B. Uzel. Also helpful was the series of articles entitled "La Naissance de la Côte Française des Somalis," in *Le Réveil de Djibouti*, May 14–July 9, 1966.

2. Deschamps, Decary, and Menard, p. 45.

3. See his *Secrets de la Mer Rouge, La Croisière du Hachich, Vers les Terres Hostiles d'Ethiopie,* etc.

4. Jouin, pp. 142–62.

5. See his *Guerriers et Sorciers en Somalie.*

6. *Ibid.,* p. 179.

7. See Lippmann, p. 26, and Dives, "Chez les Afars et les Issas."

8. Goum, p. 11.

9. Orsini, *Francia contro Italia in Africa.*

10. See Hess, p. 173, and Askew.

11. See the eye-witness account by H. Deschamps, governor of French Somaliland at that period, in Deschamps, Decary, and Menard, pp. 48 *et seq.*

12. See Jouin, "Les Troupes Somalies pendant les Deux Guerres Mondiales."

13. Drysdale, *The Somali Dispute,* p. 60.

14. Moyse-Bartlett, p. 571.

15. See *Le Monde,* July 12, 1946, for relevant extracts from the account published in *The London Gazette,* which was based on reports of the East Africa campaign by Generals W. Platt and A. G. Cunningham.

16. Monfreid, *Le Radeau de la Méduse,* p. 161.

17. Moyse-Bartlett, p. 475.

18. See *Le Figaro,* Dec. 13, 1945.

19. See *Bulletin d'Information,* Ministère des Colonies, Paris, July 16, 1945.

Chapter Two

1. Syad, "Djibouti, Terre sans Dieu et sans Espoir."

2. Muller, "Les Populations de la Côte Française des Somalis."

3. *Le Réveil de Djibouti,* May 16, 1963.

4. Chedeville, "Quelques Faits de l'Organisation Sociale des Afar."

5. See two articles entitled "Mariage à Tadjoura," *Le Réveil de Djibouti,* Jan. 14, 21, 1967.

6. *Africa,* April 1966.

7. As related to Captain R. Muller.

8. See Duchenet, *Histoires Somalies.*

9. Lippmann, p. 91.

10. Doudoub, pp. 9 *et seq.*

11. *Ibid.,* p. 12.

12. *Ibid.,* pp. 8–18.

13. *Ibid.,* pp. 18–20.

14. Chauvel, "Les Jeunes qui Tiennent la Rue."
15. Mallet, "Djibouti: Problèmes Ethniques et Politiques."
16. *Le Réveil de Djibouti,* Mar. 11, 1967.
17. Muller, "Les Populations de la Côte Française des Somalis."

Chapter Three

1. *Le Réveil de Djibouti,* Mar. 30, 1946.
2. Report by R. Dronne, National Assembly debates, July 24, 1950.
3. Luchaire, "Le Conseil Représentatif de la Côte des Somalis."
4. *Marchés Coloniaux,* Sept. 22, 1956.
5. See articles on the history of Obock, *Le Réveil de Djibouti,* September and October, 1963; also Potier, "La Circonscription Administrative d'Obock."
6. *Marchés Coloniaux,* Dec. 20, 1947.
7. *Ibid.,* Apr. 24, 1948.
8. P. Decraene, reporting in *Le Monde,* Apr. 21, 1964.
9. *Le Réveil de Djibouti,* Dec. 8, 1964.
10. Castagno, pp. 108–13.
11. See National Assembly debates, Nov. 6, 1959, Oct. 25, 1960, Oct. 25, 1961.
12. Chauvel, "Djibouti: La France n'est pas Seule."
13. Lippmann, p. 11.
14. See Duchenet, *Histoires Somalies.*
15. Deschamps *et al.,* p. 32.
16. See D'Esme, *A Travers l'Empire de Menelik,* pp. 215–16.
17. Muller, "Les Populations de la Côte Française des Somalis."
18. See comments by the president of the higher court of appeal and the district attorney in *Le Réveil de Djibouti,* Oct. 9, 1965.
19. See M. Antonini's report to the French Union Assembly, Mar. 28, 1957.
20. *Tropiques,* May 1955.
21. *Marchés Coloniaux,* Nov. 19, 1949.
22. *Le Réveil de Djibouti,* Oct. 9, 1965.
23. French Union Assembly report, July 7, 1955; Prax, "La Milice de la Côte Française des Somalis."
24. See Hassan Gouled's speech to the Conseil de la République, Dec. 13, 1956.
25. "Les Forces Armées," *Tropiques,* No. 373, May 1955.
26. Jouin, "Les Troupes Somalies pendant les Deux Guerres Mondiales."
27. La Documentation Française, *La Côte Française des Somalis,* No. 1321.
28. See report by M. de Gouyon to the French Union Assembly, July 7, 1955.
29. *Marchés Tropicaux,* June 5, 1965.
30. See debates, July 22, 1950.
31. Habib-Deloncle, "Menaces sur Djibouti?"
32. *Le Réveil de Djibouti,* Dec. 25, 1964, and Dec. 31, 1966.
33. *Le Monde,* August 28, 29, 1966.
34. See despatches by Eric Pace in the *New York Times,* Mar. 21, 1967, *et seq.*

Chapter Four

1. See National Assembly debates, session of July 22, 1950.
2. Doudoub, p. 26.
3. *Ibid.,* p. 24.
4. *Climats,* Sept. 5, 1949.
5. *Marchés Coloniaux,* Nov. 19, 1949.
6. *Ibid.,* Nov. 5, 1949.
7. *Ibid.,* Sept. 30, 1950.
8. Doudoub, p. 27.
9. *Ibid.,* p. 29.
10. See debates, session of June 13, 1956.

11. Gouled, "La Côte des Somalis, la France, et les Autres."
12. A.F.P. dispatch from Djibouti, Aug. 15–16, 1958.
13. *Ibid.*
14. See Hassan Gouled's letter to the editor, *Le Monde,* Aug. 16, 1958.
15. Gouled, "La Côte des Somalis, la France et les Autres."
16. A.F.P. dispatch from Djibouti, Sept. 19, 1958.
17. I. M. Lewis, "Modern Political Movements in Somaliland."
18. *Ibid.*   19. Doudoub, p. 30.
20. Touval, p. 128; see also Syad, p. 17.
21. National Assembly debates, July 18, 1960.
22. Speech to the territorial assembly, quoted in *Marchés Tropicaux,* Nov. 5, 1960.
23. Touval, p. 129.
24. *Marchés Tropicaux,* June 11, 1960.
25. *Le Monde,* Aug. 5, 1960.
26. *Marchés Tropicaux,* Dec. 31, 1960; *Africa,* No. 13, June 23, 1961.
27. *Ibid.,* Feb. 25, 1961.
28. *Ibid.,* Apr. 1, 1961.
29. *Le Monde,* Apr. 9–10, 1961.
30. See National Assembly debates, June 25, July 23, 1963.
31. For the text of the Arta declaration, see *Le Réveil de Djibouti,* Sept. 21, 1963.
32. For a detailed account of the results of this election by circumscription, see *Le Réveil de Djibouti,* Nov. 23, 1963.
33. This correspondence was printed in the June 22, 1963, issue of *Le Réveil de Djibouti.*
34. *Revue des Deux Mondes,* Feb. 1, 1967.
35. Chauvel, "Djibouti: La France n'est pas Seule."
36. The description here of the events of August 25–26 is based upon accounts carried in *Le Monde,* the *New York Times,* and *Le Réveil de Djibouti.*
37. *Afrique Nouvelle,* Oct. 5, 1966.   38. *Le Monde,* Sept. 18, 1966.
39. Radio Djibouti broadcast, Oct. 17, 1966.   40. *Le Monde,* Oct. 29, 1966.
41. *La Croix,* Apr. 7, 1967.
42. See *Le Monde Diplomatique,* March 1967; *Jeune Afrique,* Feb. 19, 1967; *Marchés Tropicaux,* Feb. 25, 1967.
43. *New York Times,* Mar. 19, 1967.   44. *Ibid.*
45. *Le Réveil de Djibouti,* Mar. 25, 1967.   46. *Le Monde,* Mar. 21, 1967.
47. *Ibid.,* Apr. 22, 1967.   48. *Le Réveil de Djibouti,* June 3, 1967.

Chapter Five

1. Decraene, "La Crise Ouverte à Djibouti."
2. *Le Monde,* Sept. 8, 1967.
3. See Marcus, "The Foreign Policy of the Emperor Menelik."
4. *Bulletin d'Information,* Ministère des Colonies, Sept. 17, 1945.
5. *Climats,* Aug. 13, 1947, June 23, 1948, Apr. 29 and Dec. 3–9, 1953.
6. See, *inter alia, Marchés Coloniaux,* Sept. 13, 1947.
7. See National Assembly debates, Feb. 9 and Mar. 30, 1954; Conseil de la République debates, Feb. 25, 1954; French Union Assembly debates, Feb. 26, 1954.
8. National Assembly debates of Dec. 16, 1959.
9. I. M. Lewis, *Peoples of the Horn of Africa,* p. 157.
10. Mallet, "Djibouti."
11. See R. K. P. and E. S. Pankhurst.
12. The best published account of its organization and history is to be found in *Jeune Afrique,* Sept. 10, 1966. Additional data were published in *Le Figaro,* Mar. 17, 1967; *New York Times,* Apr. 27, 1967; and *Le Monde Diplomatique,* June 1967.

13. *New York Times,* Mar. 15, 1967.
14. *Ibid.,* Aug. 24, 1967.
15. See *Christian Science Monitor,* Apr. 15, 1967.
16. *Ethiopian Herald,* Aug. 28, 1966.
17. Doresse, "Les Récents Accords Franco-Ethiopiens."
18. *Ethiopian Herald,* Aug. 29, 1966.   19. *Addis-Soir,* Sept. 23, 1966.
20. *Le Réveil de Djibouti,* Sept. 24, 1966.   21. *Le Monde,* Oct. 12, 1966.
22. *Ibid.,* Apr. 7, 1967.   23. Darcy, "L'Avenir de Djibouti."
24. I. M. Lewis, "Pan-Africanism and Pan-Somalism."
25. Touval, p. 84.
26. Lamy, "Le Destin des Somalis."
27. *Marchés Tropicaux,* June 18, 1960.
28. Castagno, "The Development of Political Parties in the Somali Republic," p. 552.
29. Radio Mogadiscio, Apr. 18, 1964.   30. *Le Réveil de Djibouti,* Sept. 18, 1965.
31. Radio Mogadiscio, June 2, 1966.   32. *Ibid.,* July 5, 1966.
33. *Ibid.,* Aug. 25, 1966.
34. In an interview with a correspondent of the Agence France Presse, reported in *Somali News,* Sept. 9, 1966.
35. Radio Mogadiscio, Mar. 13, 1967.
36. See various issues of *Le Populaire* and *La Croix* during March 1967.
37. Bayne, p. 14.
38. *New York Times,* Mar. 8, 1967.
39. *Le Réveil de Djibouti,* Aug. 5, 1967.
40. Bernier, "Naissance d'un Nationalisme Arabe à Aden."
41. *Le Monde Diplomatique,* November 1966.
42. National Assembly session of July 5, 1956.
43. Castagno, "Conflicts in the Horn of Africa."
44. Agence France Presse dispatch from Cairo, Mar. 10, 1967.
45. *Christian Science Monitor,* Mar. 18, 1967.

Chapter Six

1. See articles by R. Lamy and R. Muller.
2. *Le Réveil de Djibouti,* Dec. 31, 1966.
3. Jourdain and Dupont, p. 130.
4. *Guide Annuaire de la Côte Française des Somalis,* p. 104.
5. *Le Réveil de Djibouti,* Oct. 8, 1966.
6. See Lacour, series of six articles.
7. *Le Réveil de Djibouti,* Sept, 23, 1967.
8. See Conseil de la République debates, Dec. 13, 1956.
9. *Le Réveil de Djibouti,* Sept. 23, 1967.
10. French Union Assembly debates, Mar. 27, 1952.
11. See Muller.
12. National Assembly debates, Oct. 25, 1960, and Apr. 27, 1961.
13. Interview with Hassan Gouled, *Le Réveil de Djibouti,* July 25, 1964.
14. *Le Réveil de Djibouti,* Oct. 8, 1966.
15. Ferry, "Esquisse d'une Etude Ethnique du Lycée de Djibouti en 1963–1964."
16. See Muller; Deschamps *et al.,* p. 30; and I. M. Lewis, *Peoples of the Horn of Africa,* p. 128.
17. See the report of the Antonini mission, French Union Assembly debates, Mar. 28, 1957.
18. *Le Réveil de Djibouti,* May 30, 1964.   19. Chauleur, "Referendum à Djibouti."
20. *Le Monde,* Sept. 23, 1966.   21. *Le Figaro,* Sept. 25–26, 1966.

22. Ferry, "Esquisse d'une Etude Ethnique."

23. A.F.P. despatch from Djibouti, Oct. 4, 1966.

24. *Le Monde,* Sept. 21, 1966.

25. *Mousset,* "Referendum à Djibouti."

26. *Le Réveil de Djibouti,* May 22, 1965; Oct. 15, 1966.

27. Speech to the territorial assembly, May 15, 1963.

28. *Le Réveil de Djibouti,* Oct. 29, 1966.

29. In 1966 a daily newspaper, *Addis-Soir,* replaced the monthly *L'Ethiopie d'Aujourd'hui,* founded by A. Gingold-Duprey in 1952.

30. See Doresse, "Les Récents Accords Franco-Ethiopiens."

31. See *La Croix,* Mar. 1, 1967.

32. *Le Réveil de Djibouti,* May 14, 1966.

33. La Documentation Française, "La Côte Française des Somalis," No. 2774.

34. Europe–France–Outre-Mer, *L'Afrique d'Expression Française,* No. 423, 1965.

35. Ali Aref's speech to the territorial assembly, *Le Réveil de Djibouti,* Dec. 15, 1962.

36. *Le Réveil de Djibouti,* Dec. 12, 1964.

37. La Documentation Française, "La Côte Française des Somalis," No. 2774.

38. Darmendrail, "La Réussite d'une Expérience à l'Echelle Africaine."

39. "Djibouti, le Quartier du Stade."

40. General Billotte's speech to the territorial assembly, *Le Réveil de Djibouti,* May 14, 1966.

41. D'Esme, "La Côte Française des Somalis."

42. Fouquet, p. 51.

43. Report of the Antonini mission, French Union Assembly debates, Mar. 28, 1957.

44. *Le Réveil de Djibouti,* Nov. 10, 1960.

45. Darmendrail, "Le Réussite d'une Expérience à l'Echelle Africaine."

46. See articles in *Le Réveil de Djibouti,* Feb. 2, 1963, and May 29, 1965; *Pount,* January 1967; *L'Afrique et l'Asie,* No. III, 1966; and *Croissance des Jeunes Nations,* November 1966.

Chapter Seven

1. *Marchés Tropicaux,* Dec. 25, 1965.

2. See Grolée.

3. See Ali Aref's speech to the territorial assembly, quoted in *Le Réveil de Djibouti,* Dec. 15, 1962.

4. La Documentation Française, "La Côte Française des Somalis," No. 2774.

5. *Ibid.*   6. *Le Réveil de Djibouti,* July 28, 1964.

7. *Ibid.,* Aug. 5, 1967.   8. *Marchés Tropicaux,* Dec. 25, 1965.

9. General Billotte's speech to the territorial assembly, quoted in *Le Réveil de Djibouti,* May 14, 1966.

10. Muller, "Les Populations de la Côte Française des Somalis."

11. *Le Réveil de Djibouti,* Aug. 26, 1967.   12. *Ibid.,* Jan. 6, 1963.

13. *Marchés Tropicaux,* Feb. 18, 1967.   14. *Le Réveil de Djibouti,* Aug. 8, 1964.

15. French Union Assembly debates, Aug. 2, 1955.

16. La Documentation Française, "La Côte Française des Somalis," No. 2774.

17. *Marchés Tropicaux,* Dec. 25, 1965.

18. *Marchés Coloniaux,* Sept. 13, 1947.

19. French Union Assembly debates, Feb. 28, 1956.

20. Pasques, "Une Immense Réserve de Sel"; see also *Le Réveil de Djibouti,* June 13, 1964.

Chapter Eight

1. La Documentation Française, "La Côte Française des Somalis," No. 2774.

2. *Le Réveil de Djibouti,* Sept. 16, 1967.

3. Governor Tirant's speech to the territorial assembly, Dec. 8, 1964.
4. *Marchés Coloniaux*, Aug. 18, 1956.   5. *Ibid.*, Feb. 14, 1948.
6. *Ibid.*, Apr. 23, 1955.   7. *Ibid.*, May 28, 1955.
8. I. M. Lewis, *The Modern History of Somaliland*, p. 136.
9. For detailed data on French Somaliland's budgets, see *Marchés Coloniaux*, Dec. 20, 1947; Feb. 14 and May 15, 1948; Dec. 17, 1949; Jan. 10 and Dec. 26, 1953; June 19, 1954; Apr. 23 and Aug. 27, 1955; Aug. 18, 1956; Jan. 5, 1957; and *Marchés Tropicaux*, Dec. 14, 1957, Jan. 4, 1958; Mar. 10, 1962, Apr. 13 and June 8, 1963; Apr. 25 and Dec. 26, 1964; Jan. 22, 1966; Mar. 4, 1967.
10. Deschamps, Decary, and Menard, p. 62.
11. Lippmann, p. 91.
12. La Documentation Française, "La Côte Française des Somalis," No. 2774.
13. Lamy, *op.cit.*
14. Deschamps, Decary, and Menard, p. 58.
15. *Marchés Coloniaux*, Aug. 2, 1947.
16. See Tavernier, "La Rayonnement de Djibouti."
17. Borlée, "La Côte Française des Somalis."
18. *Marchés Coloniaux*, Oct. 4, 1947.
19. La Documentation Française, "La Côte Française des Somalis," No. 2774.
20. *Le Réveil de Djibouti*, Apr. 25, 1964.
21. *Ibid.*, Feb. 11, 1967.
22. *New York Times*, Mar. 26, 1967.
23. La Documentation Française, "La Côte Française des Somalis," No. 1321.
24. *L'Afrique d'Expression Française*, Europe–France–Outre-Mer, No. 423, 1965.
25. *Le Réveil de Djibouti*, May 14, 1966.
26. See Marchat, "Nuages sur Djibouti."
27. *Marchés Tropicaux*, Apr. 1, 1967.
28. French Union Assembly debates, Feb. 28, 1956.
29. See Martineau, p. 586.
30. Pottier, "Le Chemin de Fer Franco-Ethiopien de Djibouti à Addis Abéba."
31. *Marchés Coloniaux*, June 10, 1950.
32. Robequain, p. 515.
33. *Marchés Coloniaux*, Mar. 12, 1955.
34. See speech by P. Boiteau, French Union Assembly debates, Feb. 26, 1954.
35. National Assembly debates, Dec. 16, 1959.
36. *Marchés Tropicaux*, Dec. 25, 1965.   37. *Le Réveil de Djibouti*, Nov. 21, 1964.
38. *Ibid.*, May 14, 1966.   39. See *Afrique Nouvelle*, Sept. 22, 1965.
40. *Le Monde Diplomatique*, November 1964.
41. Marchat, "Nuages sur Djibouti."
42. *Marchés Coloniaux*, Oct. 18, 1947.
43. *Le Réveil de Djibouti*, Sept. 25, 1965.
44. French Union Assembly debates, July 24, 1956.
45. La Documentation Française, "La Côte Française des Somalis," No. 2774.
46. *Le Réveil de Djibouti*, Nov. 26, 1966.
47. Tholomier, "La Main-d'Oeuvre des Travaux Publics en Côte Française des Somalis."
48. Muller, "Les Populations de la Côte Française des Somalis."
49. Tholomier, "La Main-d'Oeuvre des Travaux Publics en Côte Française des Somalis."
50. *Le Réveil de Djibouti*, Nov. 28, 1964.
51. French Union Assembly debates, Feb. 28, 1956.
52. *Marchés Tropicaux*, Dec. 28, 1957.   53. *Le Journal*, Feb. 23, 1939.
54. *Marchés Coloniaux*, July 26, 1947.   55. Labor Digest No. 106, 1966.
56. For a list of most of these unions and the number of their members, see *Guide Annuaire de la Côte Française des Somalis*, 1959, p. 154.

57. French Union Assembly debates, July 24, 1956.

58. La Documentation Française, "La Côte Française des Somalis," No. 2774.

59. Chamber of commerce of Djibouti, minutes, Sept. 1, 1960 (mimeographed).

60. *Marchés Coloniaux,* Sept. 8, 1953.

61. P. Boiteau speaking in the French Union Assembly, Feb. 26, 1954.

62. Conseil de la République debates, July 24, 1956.

63. A.F.P. dispatch from Djibouti, Aug. 7, 1956.

64. *Marchés Tropicaux,* Dec. 29, 1962.

65. A.F.P. dispatch from Djibouti, May 7, 1963.

66. *Le Monde,* April 27, 1967.

BIBLIOGRAPHY

A.B., "La Grande Somalie," *Chroniques de la Communauté,* May 1960.

Aden Bourale, "Dans Ce Pays la Réalité est-elle un Elément Secondaire?," *Le Réveil de Djibouti,* May 30, 1964.

"L'Affaire de Djibouti," *Revue des Deux Mondes,* Feb. 1, 1967.

"L'Agriculture en Côte Française des Somalis," *Le Réveil de Djibouti,* July 16, 25, 1964.

"Air-Djibouti: Une Compagnie en Plein Essor," *Le Réveil de Djibouti,* Jan. 7, 1967.

Albospeyre, M., "La Côte Française des Somalis: Problèmes Economiques et Politiques," C.H.E.A.M., Mémoire No. 2873, Dec. 9, 1957.

―――― "Les Danakil du Cercle de Tadjoura," *Cahiers de l'Afrique et l'Asie,* No. 5, 1959.

Aloys, Père, *Capucins Missionaires en Afrique Orientale,* Toulouse, 1931.

"Amélioration de l'Habitat à Djibouti," *La Revue Française de l'Elite Européenne,* December 1965.

Askew, W. C., "The Secret Agreement between France and Italy on Ethiopia, January 1935," *Journal of Modern History,* XXV, 1953.

"L'Association pour la Protection de la Jeunesse en Côte Française des Somalis," *Le Réveil de Djibouti,* Nov. 10, 1960; Apr. 28, May 5, 1962; Mar. 21, 28, 1963.

Aubert de la Rue, E., *La Somalie Française,* Paris, 1939.

Bayne, E. A., "Somalia and the United States. Part I: The Somali Predicament," American Universities Field Service report, April 1967.

Bernier, T., "Naissance d'un Nationalisme Arabe à Aden," *L'Afrique et l'Asie,* No. 44, 1958.

Borlée, M., "La Côte Française des Somalis," *Bulletin de la Société Royale Belge de Géographie,* Année 48, 1924.

Bovet, L., "Les Relations Economiques de Djibouti avec l'Ethiopie," *Etudes d'Outre-Mer,* January 1954.

Castagno, A. A., "Conflicts in the Horn of Africa," *Orbis,* July 1960.

―――― "French Somaliland," in H. Kitchen, ed., *The Educated African,* New York, 1962, pp. 108–13.

―――― "The Development of Political Parties in the Somali Republic," in *Political Parties and Integration in Tropical Africa,* Berkeley, Calif., 1964.

Chailley, M., "Chez les Danakil," C.H.E.A.M., Mémoire No. 3167, 1951.

——— "L'Habitation à la Côte Française des Somalis," C.H.E.A.M., Mémoire No. 3169, 1952.

——— "Fables du Pays Danakil," C.H.E.A.M., Mémoire No. 3777, no date.

Chauffard, E., Hugues Le Roux, C. Mondon-Vidailhet, and R. Maumer, *Les Populations de la Côte des Somalis et des Régions Voisines,* Paris, 1908.

Chauleur, P., "Referendum à Djibouti," *Etudes,* December 1966.

Chauvel, J.-F., "Les Jeunes Afars à leur Tour se Manifestent," *Le Figaro,* Sept. 24–25, 1966.

——— "Les Jeunes qui Tiennent la Rue," *Le Figaro,* Sept. 24–25, 1966.

——— "La Fraction Somalienne Assurée de l'Appui de Mogadiscio," *Le Figaro,* Sept. 21, 1966.

——— "Djibouti: La France n'est pas Seule," *La Revue de Paris,* October 1966.

——— "Menace sur la Corne d'Afrique," *Le Figaro,* Mar. 17, 1967.

Chedeville, E., "Quelques Faits de l'Organisation Sociale des Afar," *Africa,* XXXVI, No. 2, April 1966.

Conover, H. F., compiler, *Official Publications of Somaliland, 1941–1949, A Guide,* Washington, D.C. (Library of Congress), 1960, pp. 34–35.

"La Côte Française des Somalis," special issue of *Marchés Tropicaux,* Dec. 25, 1965.

"Côte Française des Somalis" (mimeographed), *Bulletin de la Chambre de Commerce,* Djibouti, March 1959.

"Crise Politique après le Referendum en C.F.S.," *Afrique Nouvelle,* Apr. 5, 1967.

Darcy, R., "L'Avenir de Djibouti," *Tour d'Horizon,* No. 79, October 1966.

Darmendrail, J.-M., "La Réussite d'une Expérience à l'Echelle Africaine," *La Revue Française de l'Elite Européenne,* December 1965.

Dashan, T., "L'Anatomie d'une Tromperie," *Remarques Africaines,* No. 289, May 4, 1967.

Decraene, P., "La Crise Ouverte à Djibouti," *Le Monde Diplomatique,* November 1966.

——— "La Côte Française des Somalis avant le Referendum," *Le Monde Diplomatique,* March 1967.

——— "Côte des Somalis: Lendemains Incertains," *Le Mois en Afrique,* April 1967.

Deschamps, H., R. Decary, and A. Menard, *Côte des Somalis–Réunion–Inde,* Paris, 1948.

"Les Différends Territoriaux avec la Côte Française des Somalis, l'Ethiopie, et le Kenya," *L'Afrique Actuelle,* No. 6, March 1966.

Dives, E., "L'Affaire Achinoff," *Tropiques,* March 1962.

——— "Chez les Afars et les Issas," C.H.E.A.M., Mémoire No. 2861, April 1963.

"Djibouti," special number of *La Revue Française de l'Elite Européenne,* December 1965.

"Djibouti, le Quartier du Stade," undated (official pamphlet).

La Documentation Française, *Notes et Etudes Documentaires* (Paris), "Djibouti et le Chemin de Fer Franco-Ethiopien," No. 122, Aug. 25, 1945.

―――― "La Côte Française des Somalis," No. 1321, Apr. 28, 1950.

―――― "Evolution Economique et Sociale de la Côte Française des Somalis," No. 1854, Mar. 27, 1954.

―――― "Traité Franco-Ethiopien Relatif au Chemin de Fer de Djibouti à Addis Abéba," No. 2658, Nov. 12, 1959.

―――― "La Côte Française des Somalis," No. 2774, Apr. 29, 1961.

―――― "Consultation du 19 mars 1967 de la Population de la Côte Française des Somalis: Rapports de la Commission de Controle et de la Commission de Recensement et de Jugement," No. 3593, May 20, 1967.

Doresse, J., "Les Récents Accords Franco-Ethiopiens," *Revue Juridique et Politique,* October–December 1966.

Doudoub, I. A., "Esquisse Ethnique des Divers Groupements Autochtones de Djibouti," Ecole Nationale de la France d'Outre-Mer, Mémoire No. 1110, 1962 (typescript).

Douteau, H. P., "Le Port de Commerce de Djibouti 1965," *La Revue Française de l'Elite Européenne,* December 1965.

―――― "1965: Le Port de Commerce de Djibouti Fait le Point," *Europe–France– Outre-Mer,* No. 423, 1965.

Drysdale, J., *The Somali Dispute,* London, 1964.

―――― "The Problem of French Somaliland," *Africa Report,* November 1966.

Dubois, H.-P., *Cheminot de Djibouti à Addis Abéba,* Paris, 1959.

Duchenet, E., *Histoires Somalies,* Paris, 1936.

Ducla, B. de, "La Ville de Djibouti Dispose Maintenant d'Eau en Abondance," *Europe–France–Outre-Mer,* No. 423, 1965.

Dusseaulx, R., "Notes sur l'Evolution de la Situation Economique de la Côte Française des Somalis en 1956 et au Début de 1957," June 1957 (mimeographed).

Emerit, M., "Le Premier Projet d'Etablissement Français sur la Côte des Somalis," *Revue Française d'Histoire d'Outre-Mer,* No. 179, 1963.

"Erythrée; Fédération Avortée, Guérilla Réussie," *Jeune Afrique,* Sept. 10, 1967.

d'Esme, J., "La Côte Française des Somalis," *Le Domaine Colonial Français,* Tome 3, Paris, 1930, pp. 85–104.

―――― *A Travers l'Empire de Menelik,* Paris, 1947.

Eugène, J., "Djibouti, Pont-levis de l'Afrique sur le Moyen-Orient," *Forces Aériennes Françaises,* July 1955.

Europe–France–Outre-Mer, *Côte Française des Somalis,* No. 423, April 1965.

―――― *L'Afrique d'Expression Française,* 1965, 1966, 1967.

Ferry, R., "Le Destin des Somalis," C.H.E.A.M., Mémoire No. 3041, 1958.

―――― "La Toxicomanie du Kat à Djibouti," *L'Afrique et l'Asie,* No. 75, 1966.

———— "Esquisse d'une Etude Ethnique du Lycée de Djibouti en 1963–1964," *Pount,* October 1966.

Fouquet, G., *Mer Rouge,* Paris, 1946.

Gallo, M., *L'Affaire d'Ethiopie,* Paris, 1967.

Gandillon, P., "La Houille d'Or," Paris Colonial Exposition, 1931 (pamphlet).

Gaulle, Gen. Charles de, *Mémoires de Guerre, l'Appel 1940–1942,* Paris, 1954.

Gingold-Duprey, A., *De l'Invasion à la Libération de l'Ethiopie,* Paris, 1947.

Gouled, Hassan, "La Côte des Somalis, la France et les Autres," *Union Française et Parlement,* No. 25, July 1957.

Goum, Alli, *Djibouti, Création Française, Bastion de l'Empire,* Paris, 1939.

Grolée, J., "Les Ressources en Eau de la Côte Française des Somalis," *Industries et Travaux d'Outre-Mer,* July 1962.

Guedel, J., "Incidences Médico-Sociales de la Consommation du Kat en C.F.S.," *Pount,* January 1967.

Guide Annuaire de la Côte Française des Somalis, Djibouti, 1959.

Habib-Deloncle, M., "Menaces sur Djibouti?," *Union Française et Parlement,* No. 73, May 1956.

Hess, R. L., *Italian Colonialism in Somalia,* Chicago, 1966.

Institut National de la Statistique et des Etudes Economiques, *Recensement de la Population de la Côte Française des Somalis (Population Non Originaire), 1956,* Paris, 1957.

"L'Islamisme à la Côte Française des Somalis" (anonymous typescript, undated).

Jacob, A., "Somalis Tourmentés et Courtisés," *Le Monde,* Dec. 27, 28, 29, 1963.

Jouin, Y., "Les Troupes Somalies pendant les Deux Guerres Mondiales," *Revue Historique de l'Armée,* No. 4, November 1963.

Jourdain, H., and C. Dupont, *D'Obock à Djibouti,* Paris, 1933.

Jouve, J., "Le Musée de Djibouti," *Pount,* October 1966.

Kalfan, A., "Au Lendemain du Referendum de Djibouti," *Remarques Africaines,* No. 291, June 1, 1967.

Kammerer, M., *La Mer Rouge, l'Abyssinie et l'Arabie depuis l'Antiquité,* Cairo, 1929.

"Labor Conditions in French Somaliland," *Labor Digest* (U.S. Department of Labor), No. 106, 1966.

Labrousse, H., "La Côte Française des Somalis," *Tropiques,* March 1953.

———— "La Pénétration des Français en Mer Rouge," *Le Réveil de Djibouti,* Mar. 10, 17, 31, Apr. 14, 21, 1962.

Lacour, G. de, "L'Enseignement en Côte Française des Somalis," *Le Réveil de Djibouti,* Sept. 30, Oct. 7, 14, 21, 28, Nov. 11, 1961.

Lamy, R. (R. Ferry), "Le Destin des Somalis," *Cahiers de l'Afrique et l'Asie,* No. 5, 1959.

Le Brun-Keris, G., "Djibouti, Terre Nécessaire et Menacée," *La Vie Intellectuelle,* October 1956.

Lena, A., "Un 'Oui' qui est un Sursis, un 'Non' avec du Sang," *Jeune Afrique,* Apr. 2, 1967.

Leroi-Gourhan, A., and J. Poirier, "La Somalie Française," in *Ethnologie de l'Union Française* (Paris, 1953), I, 422–40.

Lewis, H. S., "The Origins of the Galla and Somali," *Journal of African History*, VII, No. 1, 1966.

Lewis, I. M., *Peoples of the Horn of Africa: Somali, Afar and Saho*, London, 1955.

—— "Modern Political Movements in Somaliland," *Africa*, July, October 1958.

—— *A Pastoral Democracy*, London, 1961.

—— "Pan-Africanism and Pan-Somalism," *Journal of Modern African Studies*, Nos. 1, 2, 1963.

—— *The Modern History of Somaliland: From Nation to State*, London, 1965.

—— "Prospects in the Horn," *Africa Report*, April 1967.

—— "Recent Developments in the Somali Dispute," *African Affairs*, April 1967.

Lippmann, A., *Guerriers et Sorciers en Somalie*, Paris, 1953.

Luc, Père, "De Gabodu-ti à Djibouti, ou l'Origine d'un Nom," *Le Réveil de Djibouti*, Oct. 9, 1965.

Lucas, M., "Renseignements Ethnographiques et Linguistiques," *Bulletin de la Société des Africanistes*, V, 1935.

Luchaire, F., "Le Conseil Représentatif de la Côte des Somalis," *Recueil Penant*, November 1950.

Mallet, R., "Djibouti: Problèmes Ethniques et Politiques," *Revue de Défense Nationale*, December 1966.

Marchal, O., "Djibouti: Pour un Oui, Pour un Non," *Format Spécial*, Apr. 6, 1967.

Marchat, P., "Nuages sur Djibouti," *Revue Militaire Générale*, Dec. 10, 1966.

—— "L'Ethiopie Millénaire à la Veille du Referendum," *Revue de Défense Nationale*, March 1967.

Marcus, H. G., "The Foreign Policy of the Emperor Menelik, 1896–1898: A Rejoinder," *Journal of African History*, VII, No. 1, 1966.

—— "A Danzig Solution?," *Africa Report*, April 1967.

Martineau, A., "La Côte des Somalis," in G. Hanotaux and A. Martineau, *Histoire des Colonies Françaises*, Paris, 1931, IV, 577–89.

Menier, M. A., "Le Retour de la Mission Marchand," *Revue Historique de l'Armée*, No. 4, November 1963.

Menil, P., "La Côte Française des Somalis Reste Politiquement Stable mais est Revendiquée par le Gouvernement de Mogadiscio," *Le Monde*, Aug. 24, 1960.

Ministère de la France d'Outre-Mer, *La Côte Française des Somalis*, Paris, 1950.

Minne, L., "Ainsi Naquit Djibouti," *Le Réveil de Djibouti*, Oct. 10, Nov. 21, 1959; July 12, 1960; Mar. 20, 27, Apr. 3, 10, 1965.

Monfreid, Henri de, *Secrets de la Mer Rouge*, Paris, 1932.

—— *Vers les Terres Hostiles d'Ethiopie*, Paris, 1933.

———— *Le Radeau de la Méduse,* Paris, 1958.

Monmarson, R., *Chez les Clients de la Mer Rouge,* Paris, 1948.

Monsterleet, R., "Djibouti, un Condominium 'de Fait,' " *L'Afrique Actuelle,* November–December 1966.

Mousset, P., "Referendum à Djibouti," *La Revue des Deux Mondes,* Apr. 15, 1967.

Moyse-Bartlett, H., *The King's Rifles,* Aldershot, 1956.

Muller, R., "Les Populations de la Côte Française des Somalis," *Cahiers de l'Afrique et l'Asie,* No. 5, 1959.

"La Naissance de la Côte Française des Somalis," *Le Réveil de Djibouti,* issues from May 4 to July 9, 1966.

"Le Nouveau Régime du Chemin de Fer Franco-Ethiopien," *L'Economie,* Feb. 4, 1960.

Oberle, Ph., "L'Habitat des Bergers Issas," *Le Réveil de Djibouti,* Dec. 31, 1966.

———— "Mariage à Tadjoura," *Le Réveil de Djibouti,* Jan. 14, 1967.

Orsini, Paolo d'Agostino, *Francia contro Italia in Africa,* Milan, 1939.

Pankhurst, R. K. P., "Colonialism in the Gulf of Tajurah—an Historical Perspective," *Ethiopian Herald,* June 7, 8, 1966.

Pankhurst, R. K. P., and E. S. Pankhurst, *Ethiopia and Eritrea 1941–1952,* London, 1953.

Pasques, G., "Une Immense Réserve de Sel: le Lac Assal en Côte Française des Somalis," *Industries et Travaux d'Outre-Mer,* August 1959.

Poinsot, J.-P., *Djibouti et la Côte Française des Somalis,* Paris, 1964.

Potier, M., "La Circonscription Administrative d'Obock," C.H.E.A.M., Mémoire No. 4100, 1966.

Pottier, R., "Le Chemin de Fer Franco-Ethiopien de Djibouti à Addis-Abéba," *Encyclopédie Mensuelle d'Outre-Mer,* Document No. 26, March 1954.

Prax, Capt., "La Milice de la Côte Française des Somalis," *Tropiques,* March 1954.

"Que se Passe-t-il à Djibouti?," *Ordre,* July 12, 1946.

Robequain, C., *Madagascar et les Terres Dispersées de l'Union Française,* Paris, 1958.

Roussel, J.-P., "Djibouti et l'Ethiopie," *Sciences Politiques,* April 1939.

Salata, F., *Il Nodo di Gibuti,* Milan, 1939.

Sampaio, M., "Au-delà du Referendum," *Jeune Afrique,* Mar. 26, 1967.

———— "L'Indépendance dans Cinq Ans," *Jeune Afrique,* Feb. 19, 1967.

Schneyder, P., "Le Dossier Djibouti," *Communautés et Continents,* No. 4, October–December 1966.

Siriex, P. H., "Djibouti et ses Problèmes," *France–Outre-Mer,* March, June 1956.

Somalia, Ministry of Somali Affairs, "French Somaliland in True Perspective," Mogadiscio, 1966.

Sordet, M., "Resorber l'Opposition Héréditaire," *Jeune Afrique,* Apr. 9, 1967.

Syad, W. J. F., "Djibouti, Terre sans Dieu et sans Espoir," C.H.E.A.M. (thesis, typescript), 1959.

Tavernier, M. P., "Le Rayonnement de Djibouti," C.H.E.A.M., Mémoire No. 2919, Jan. 7, 1958.

Thillard, J., *Le Domaine et la Propriété Foncière à la Côte Française des Somalis,* Angoulême, 1925.

Tholomier, R., "La Main-d'Oeuvre des Travaux Publics en Côte Française des Somalis," *Industries et Travaux d'Outre-Mer,* No. 15, February 1955.

Toscano, M., "Francia ed Italia di Fronte al Problema di Gibuti," *Rivista di Studi Politici Internazionali,* Florence, January–June 1939.

Touval, Saadia, *Somali Nationalism,* Cambridge (Harvard Univ. Press), 1963.

Tropiques, Côte Française des Somalis, special issue, May 1955.

Uzel, B., "La Colonie d'Obock et le Gouverneur Lagarde, Artisan de l'Amitié Franco-Ethiopienne," E.N.F.O.M. Mémoire, 1951 (typescript).

Vermont, M. R., "La Corne de l'Afrique, *Afrique Contemporaine,* No. 30, March–April 1967.

Verrier, P., "Réforme Monétaire et Réforme Fiscale à la Côte Française des Somalis," *Bulletin de l'Association pour l'Etude des Problèmes de l'Union Française,* No. 55, July 1952 (mimeographed).

PERIODICALS AND NEWSPAPERS OF THE AREA

Addis-Soir (Addis Ababa)
Ethiopian Herald (Addis Ababa)
Le Réveil de Djibouti (Djibouti)
New Times and Ethiopia News (Addis Ababa)
Pount (Djibouti)
Somali News (Mogadiscio)

DEBATES OF FRENCH PARLIAMENTARY BODIES

National Assembly
Conseil de la République
French Union Assembly

INDEX

Abdoulkader Moussa Ali, 83, 98, 153
Abyssinia, x, 4f
Aden, xii, 5, 12–19 *passim*, 31, 37, 65, 130–32, 158, 177, 181, 183, 194–204 *passim*, 216, 224. *See also* Great Britain; South Arabia
Administration: Africanization of, 44, 48, 50f, 69, 144; French officials, xi–xii, 10, 17–21 *passim*, 34, 38, 44–51 *passim*, 63, 68, 70, 72, 76, 79, 82, 87, 88–89, 95, 97, 100, 107, 152, 155, 156, 164f, 182. *See also* Civil service
Afars: characteristics and social structure, 4, 23, 24–26, 29, 36, 51–53, 156, 168–69, 215; relations with government, xi, 6f, 10–11, 24, 25–26, 40, 42, 51, 54, 71, 73, 80–86 *passim*, 108, 120, 127, 174–75, 226; relations with Issas and other Somalis, 5, 10f, 24, 37, 47, 51–53, 71, 79, 81, 85, 92, 94, 97ff, 132, 221, 225
Africanization, *see under* Administration
Agriculture, 9, 29, 32, 47, 48, 67, 167–72 *passim*, 174, 188–90 *passim*, 214
Aid, French, xii, 69, 71, 85, 89ff, 100, 117, 141–45 *passim*, 161, 163, 182f, 185–90 *passim*, 205, 208–9, 212, 219. *See also* Common Market; F.I.D.E.S.
Airfields and air transport, 57, 188, 193, 196, 210, 211–12
Animal husbandry, *see* Herding
Arab community, 5, 9, 20, 31–34, 36–42 *passim*, 53, 61, 63–66 *passim*, 72f, 79, 89, 95, 127, 133–35 *passim*, 139, 152–54 *passim*, 161, 169f, 175, 196, 215–16, 220f, 224. *See also* South Arabia; Yemen
Arab League, *see* Middle East countries
Aref, Ali (Ali Aref Bourhan), 25, 50, 76–88 *passim*, 90–100 *passim*, 133, 190, 225
Arms traffic, 9, 13, 31, 130
Army, role of, xi–xii, 7–15 *passim*, 20–21, 34, 38, 44ff, 54–60, 63, 87, 90, 95–98 *passim*, 105, 125, 127, 183, 187f, 206, 215, 225
Autonomy, 75f, 78, 91f, 190

Banking, 34, 106, 180, 195–99 *passim*. *See also* Currency; Exchange control
Bouraleh, Egué, 83, 91, 101
Bourhan, Ali Aref, *see* Aref, Ali
Bourhan, Hamed, 84, 110, 111
Bourhan, Omar Mohammed, 83
Budgets, territorial, 39, 49, 50–51, 56, 99, 145, 169, 179, 181, 183–86, 211

Caravans, 5, 9ff, 46, 48, 178
Chamber of commerce, 38f, 62, 145, 181, 198, 223
Cheicko (Mohamed Ahmed Issa), 86f, 90f, 94, 101, 152
China, Communist, role in East Africa, 73f, 102, 113, 123
Chirdon, Hussein Ali, 84, 100
Civil service, xi–xii, 14, 21, 31, 34, 44f, 48–51, 184–88 *passim*, 214–22 *passim*. *See also* Administration
Climate, *see* Physical environment; Rainfall
Commercial interests: Arab, 89, 130, 134, 161, 196–97, 221; French, xi, 6, 14f, 61, 89, 176–78 *passim*, 180, 183, 195–97 *passim*, 214, 223; Indian, 196–97, 215. *See also* Investments; Trade
Committee for the Liberation of Djibouti, 84–85, 110, 114, 124
Common Market, European, 151, 161, 166, 188
Concessions, land, 39, 44, 169, 178
Cooperatives, 170f, 176
Cost of living, 48, 180f, 198, 217f
Coubèche, Saïd Ali, 42, 62–68 *passim*, 181
Crime, 51–53, 55, 64, 88, 150, 162. *See also* Law and courts; Riots
Currency, 48, 78, 100, 130, 180–83 *passim*, 190, 193, 195, 217. *See also* Banking; Exchange control

Danakil, *see* Afars
Defense, *see* Army; *Gendarmerie*; Militia
De Gaulle, Gen. Charles, xii, 16, 20, 21n, 45, 49, 51, 59, 68ff, 75, 76, 86–92 *passim*, 102,

115f, 123, 125–27 *passim*, 133f, 187, 210

Deportations, 30, 35, 37, 60, 89, 94–99 *passim*, 104, 117, 127–29 *passim*, 154, 216, 225f

Deschamps, Gov. Hubert, xii–xiii, 17, 152

Dini, Ahmed, 74ff, 82ff, 86, 94, 190

Djama Ali, 62ff

Djibouti: blockade (1940–42), 17–20; development, 8ff, 30, 160–62, 166, 180f; population, 30f, 35, 45. *See also* Port of Djibouti

Duties, export and import, 39, 180–84 *passim*, 193

Education: expenditures for, 142–46 *passim*, 184–89 *passim*; higher, 69, 78, 133, 144–54; Koranic, 139, 146–48 *passim*; mission, 140–43 *passim*, 147–49 *passim*; nomad, 33, 146–48; primary, 141–44 *passim*, 147–49 *passim*, 153, 163; secondary, 95, 141, 143–44, 148f, 153f; technical, 141–48 *passim*, 155, 163, 220. *See also* Youth

Egypt, role in Red Sea area, x, 7, 72, 103, 109, 122, 131–35 *passim*, 158. *See also* Middle East countries; Suez Canal

Elections, 33, 61, 66ff, 72ff, 79–82 *passim*, 86, 92, 97f, 100, 131

Electorate, 35–45 *passim*, 53, 58–59, 61–67 *passim*, 71f, 79–82 *passim*, 85–86, 92, 94–95, 96, 98, 100, 127, 150

Electric power, 22, 179, 188

Eritrea, 3, 12f, 15, 102, 106, 109, 111–14, 133, 177, 192, 194, 199, 201, 208

Etat civil (registration of vital statistics), 41 53, 99–100, 218

Ethiopia: foreign trade, xi, 8, 12f, 104, 130, 176–78 *passim*, 180–82 *passim*, 186, 191–92, 194–202 *passim*, 206f, 219; Italian occupation, *see* Italy; relations with France and Territory, 3, 8, 11, 14, 15–16, 37, 60f, 70f, 75, 77, 82, 84, 90, 98, 103–18, 124, 126, 156, 158, 163, 181f, 201, 204f, 208–10; relations with Somalia, xi, xii, 110, 116–23 *passim*, 128f. *See also* Eritrea

European community, 8–21 *passim*, 34–37 *passim*, 40, 43, 47ff, 51, 61f, 81, 87, 95, 131, 140, 188, 190, 214, 217, 222

Exchange control, 192, 197. *See also* Banking; Currency

Exports, 175–78 *passim*, 180–83 *passim*, 190–96 *passim*, 200, 219. *See also* Ethiopia, foreign trade; Trade, transit

F.I.D.E.S., 143, 145, 167, 171, 176, 187–89 *passim*, 200, 211, 213

Fishing, 34, 46, 175–76, 189, 213f

Food supply, 22, 24, 48, 159, 162, 170–76 *passim*, 184, 189f, 192f. *See also* Agriculture; Djibouti, blockade

Forestry, 46, 168, 211, 213

Franco-African Community, 69f, 75, 78

Free French, 16–19 *passim*, 21, 57, 69, 105, 192, 207, 221

Gadaboursis, 31, 41, 43, 62f, 84, 153

Gaddito, Orbisso, 83, 90

Gendarmerie, 34, 47, 54f, 87, 89, 215

Germany, role in East Africa, 7, 13

Gouled, Hassan, 49, 56, 64–70 *passim*, 73–84 *passim*, 88, 92ff, 100, 108, 148, 178, 188

Goumané, Ahmed, 68, 70, 72f

Gourat, Barkhat, 73, 81ff, 90

Government council, 66–92 *passim*, 99f, 124, 148, 204, 217, 219, 223

Great Britain, role in Red Sea area, x, xi, 5–21 *passim*, 69, 102, 105, 112, 118–23 *passim*, 130–32, 196, 207

Greater Somalia movement, *see* Pan-Somalism

Greek community, 34, 140, 197, 214

Haile Selassie, 11, 15f, 18, 25, 77, 90, 103–18 *passim*, 128, 210

Handicrafts, 46, 47–48, 142, 150, 156, 168

Harbi, Mahmoud, 62, 64–79 *passim*, 84, 123, 131f, 151, 224

Health, *see* Medical services

Herding, 5, 9f, 23–28 *passim*, 46–47, 52–53, 105, 121, 167–75 *passim*, 188f, 213f

Hides, production and trade, 174, 190–94 *passim*

Housing, 50, 159–62 *passim*, 188, 217, 226

Hunting, 46, 159, 173

Idriss, Moussa Ahmed, 79ff, 86–97 *passim*, 151

Immigrants, 29–37 *passim*, 55, 79, 81, 87, 92, 95, 108, 117, 120, 148, 154, 213, 215, 219, 222f. *See also* Arab community; Somalis

Imports, 48, 171, 179–84 *passim*, 190–93 *passim*, 196, 200. *See also* Ethiopia; Trade, transit

Independence, 37, 51, 59, 70–79 *passim*, 84–104 *passim*, 110f, 115–17 *passim*, 125–35 *passim*, 152, 154, 187, 190

Indian community, 34, 153, 196f, 215

Industry, 176, 178–80 *passim*, 195

Investments, private, 161, 175, 180–84 *passim*, 189, 209, 223. *See also* Commercial interests

Irredentism, Somali, *see* Pan-Somalism

Islam, 5, 10, 23, 26, 32–33, 46, 53–54, 65–66, 114, 118, 122, 128, 132, 134f, 139–40, 163, 175. *See also* Middle East countries; Nasser; Pan-Somalism; Somali Republic; South Arabia; Yemen

Issa, Mohamed Ahmed, *see* Cheicko

Issacks, 28–33 *passim*, 43, 70–73 *passim*, 153

Issas: characteristics and social structure, 4–5,

23–31 *passim*, 36, 51–53, 62, 156, 214f;
relations with Afars, *see under* Afars; relations with government, 7f, 10–11, 24, 28,
42, 51, 54, 76, 98, 119f; relations with immigrant communities, 29, 62–65, 108
Italy, role in East Africa, x, 6f, 11–18, 45,
56f, 104–14 *passim*, 118–21 *passim*, 177,
182, 192, 194, 206f

Jewish community, 33, 215
Justice, *see* Law and courts

Khat, 29, 32, 89, 151, 153, 159, 163–65, 215

Labor: legislation, 184, 214–19 *passim*, 224;
supply, 22, 29f, 32, 133, 172, 203, 205,
213–19 *passim*, 223; unions, 14, 30, 39,
65, 80, 102–3, 216–18, 220–22, 224f. *See
also* Strikes; Unemployment; Wages
Lagarde, Gov. L., 7–11 *passim*, 46, 56, 104,
107, 199
Land tenure, 29, 168–69, 173. *See also*
Concessions
Languages, 23ff, 134, 143, 147, 156, 158
Law and courts: customary, 27–28, 52–53,
54, 139; French, 10, 38, 43, 53ff, 62, 78,
82, 87f, 91ff, 96, 100–101, 169, 181, 183f,
193, 196; Koranic, 53–54, 139f, 150. *See
also Loi-cadre*
Liban, Hassan, 72, 91
Liberation Front of the Somali Coast
(F.L.C.S.), 84f, 110, 123–29 *passim*
Literacy, 97, 150, 153, 157. *See also*
Education
Living standards, 154f, 172, 215
Loi-cadre (June 23, 1956), 43ff, 49f, 66, 69,
77, 83, 141, 143, 150f, 169, 184, 188

Martine, Jean, 42, 61ff, 65
Medical services, 9, 20, 47, 140, 158–60,
163–64, 171, 174, 184, 188f, 217, 225
Middle East countries, x, xi, 65, 72, 102f,
109, 113–18 *passim*, 122, 130–32, 158. *See
also* Egypt; South Arabia; Yemen
Militia, 31, 34, 51, 54, 55–56, 60, 215
Minerals, 47, 178, 179. *See also* Salt production and trade
Missions, Catholic, 47, 140–41, 147–49
passim, 162, 171

Nasser, Gamal Abdel, 34, 77, 103, 109, 132–
34 *passim. See also* Egypt
Nationalism, territorial, xii, 49, 74, 77, 115,
150. *See also* Independence
Nomads, 8–9, 10, 30, 38, 46f, 54ff, 105–8
passim, 121f, 139, 145–50 *passim*, 159f,
162, 167–75 *passim*, 183, 189f, 205f, 213f,
219. *See also* Afars; Issas; Somalis
Notables (*okal*), 25–29 *passim*, 42, 45, 52,
54, 68, 70, 99

Obock, 6, 7–8, 12, 20, 31–36 *passim*, 44, 46,
56, 67, 80, 95f, 140–46 *passim*, 162f, 167,
195, 211f, 226
Obsieh Boeuh, 82, 84
Organization of African Unity, 83ff, 103f,
110, 115, 117, 122–29 *passim*

Pan-Africanism, 103, 122
Pan-Arabism, xi, 140
Pan-Somalism, xi, 37, 45, 49, 58, 69, 74–84
passim, 103, 108f, 114, 118–23 *passim*,
129–33 *passim. See also* Somali Republic
Physical environment, ix, 3–4, 8, 23, 47, 160,
211. *See also* Water Supply
Planning, economic, 187–89 *passim*, 204. *See
also* F.I.D.E.S.
Police, *see Gendarmerie*; Militia
Political parties, 30, 49, 62, 66–75 *passim*,
79–86 *passim*, 90–100 *passim*, 119, 127–29
passim, 151
Population, 8, 24, 30–36 *passim*, 40, 44–47
passim, 67, 95, 172
Port of Djibouti, xii, 9, 12, 14, 19–22 *passim*, 30, 44, 57f, 65, 85, 97, 99, 100, 104–9
passim, 118, 131, 180–95 *passim*, 199–204,
209, 216, 220, 225. *See also* Suez Canal
Press, 19, 151, 155, 157
Protestants, 140, 155
Public works, *see* Port of Djibouti; Railroads;
Roads

Radio, *see* Telecommunications
Railroads: construction, 6–10 *passim*, 30, 35,
104f, 115, 191, 199, 204–6, 210, 213; control and operation, xi, 10–15 *passim*, 18ff,
22, 47, 57, 75, 82, 85, 105–9 *passim*, 117f,
161, 181–87 *passim*, 191–201 *passim*, 206–
11, 224
Rainfall, 3–4, 160, 167, 173, 189, 211
Referendum: of March 1967, xii, 31, 35, 37,
59, 60, 89–98 *passim*, 104, 116f, 126–29
passim, 133–35 *passim*, 150, 152, 165, 175,
190, 198, 204, 225; of September 1958, 45,
59, 62, 69–73 *passim*, 86, 91, 109, 127
Religions, *see* Greek community; Islam; Missions; Protestants
Representative council, 38–43, 62–67 *passim*,
106, 183f, 208, 211. *See also* Territorial
assembly
Revenues, territorial, *see* Aid; Budgets; Common Market; Duties; F.I.D.E.S.; Taxation
Riots, 34f, 40, 59, 63, 71, 87, 88–96 *passim*,
100, 104, 115, 125–27 *passim*, 131, 135,
152, 154f, 165, 185, 198, 204, 224
Roads, 46, 56, 107, 188, 210–11, 219,
226

Saget, Gov. L., 88ff, 95, 97, 127, 155, 165,
168
Sahatdjian, Albert, 86, 90, 93–94

Salt production and trade, 5, 20, 46, 161, 169, 176–78, 190f, 194f, 202, 214, 219

Shell (nacre), production and trade, 34, 175, 194, 196

Shipping, *see* Port of Djibouti; Suez Canal

Slave trade, 5, 9, 24, 31, 130

Social welfare, 59, 140, 153, 162–63, 188, 217–19 *passim. see also* Housing; Medical services; Missions

Somaliland, former British, 3, 17, 30, 45f, 62, 69ff, 75, 95, 108f, 118–22 *passim,* 126, 129, 153f, 180, 196, 219, 223

Somali Republic: relations with Ethiopia, *see under* Ethiopia; relations with Territory, x, xi, 37, 60, 70ff, 79, 85, 90, 95, 99, 103, 110, 119, 123–29, 132–35, 158, 198, 223. *See also* Pan-Somalism

Somalis, 4, 14, 17, 27–40 *passim,* 57, 60, 62, 73, 82, 120f, 126, 129, 131, 135, 150–56 *passim,* 215f, 220, 222, 224–26 *passim. See also* Deportations; Gadaboursis; Issacks; Issas

South Arabia, xi, 37, 102, 130–32, 139, 212n, 215, 224. *See also* Aden; Arab community; Great Britain; Yemen

Soviet Union, role in Red Sea area, x, 102, 114f, 119, 123, 133

Strikes, 65, 80, 88, 97, 106, 131, 194, 198, 203, 207, 217f, 220, 224–25. *See also* Labor, unions

Subsidies, *see* Aid; Common Market

Suez Canal, x, xi, xii, 6, 37, 100, 109, 118, 130–32 *passim,* 151, 188–93 *passim,* 198, 203f, 219, 225. *See also* Egypt

Sultanate: of Aoussa, 11, 25, 105, 108, 111; of Gobaad, 4, 7, 10f, 24–25, 46f, 171; of Rahayto, 4, 24–25, 46, 108; of Tadjoura, 4–10 *passim,* 24–26, 46, 52, 74. *See also* Tadjoura

Tadjoura, 5, 8f, 26, 31, 34, 36, 44, 46–47, 67, 80, 95f, 140, 143, 146, 153, 167, 179, 200, 211f, 226. *See also under* Sultanate

Tariffs, 39, 130, 180–84 *passim,* 193

Taxation, 9, 25, 39, 44, 164, 172f, 180–86 *passim,* 193f, 197, 203

Telecommunications, 19, 44, 49, 100, 151, 157–58, 188

Territorial assembly, 49, 66–86 *passim,* 90, 99, 102, 111, 124, 164, 169, 184. *See also* Representative council

Tirant, Gov. R., 51f, 87f, 146, 155, 160, 164

Trade, foreign, *see* Ethiopia, foreign trade; Exports; Imports

Trade, local, xi, xii, 5f, 31–34 *passim;* 46, 170, 175, 180f, 190, 193, 195–99, 214, 221

Trade, transit, 9, 130, 174, 181–86 *passim,* 190–95 *passim,* 199–202, 204. *See also* Port of Djibouti; Railroads

Transportation, *see* Airfields; Caravans; Port of Djibouti; Railroads; Roads

Tribalism, *see* Afars; Gadaboursis; Issacks; Issas; Somalis

Unemployment, 74, 86, 152, 177, 189f, 213f, 218–22 *passim;* 224f. *See also* Labor

United Nations, 84f, 94, 103–12 *passim,* 117, 119f, 124–31 *passim*

United States, role in Red Sea area, x, 102, 105, 109, 114f, 119, 132, 208

Vichy regime, 16–21 *passim,* 48f, 57, 105

Wages, 48, 50, 88, 203, 216–25 *passim. See also* Labor

Water supply, 9f, 24, 160, 166–74 *passim,* 188–90, 195

Women, position of, 26, 29, 66, 80, 140, 145, 149–50, 165, 173, 218

Yemen, 31f, 65, 103, 130, 158, 171, 212, 215–16. *See also* Arab community; South Arabia

Youth, 34, 52, 79, 86, 88, 95–96, 103, 111, 135, 151–57 *passim,* 162–64 *passim. See also* Education

DATE DUE

5-8-70			
FEB 22 1972			
JUN 14 1973			
GAYLORD			PRINTED IN U.S.A.